Supporting lifelong language learning
Theoretical and practical approaches

D0415737

Centre for Information
on Language Teaching and Research

The Centre for Information on Language Teaching and Research provides a complete range of services for language professionals in every stage and sector of education, and in business, in support of its brief to promote Britain's foreign language capability.

CILT is a registered charity, supported by Central Government grants. CILT is based in Covent Garden, London, and its services are delivered through a national collaborative network of regional Comenius Centres in England, the National Comenius Centre of Wales, Scottish CILT and Northern Ireland CILT.

CILT Publications are available through all good booksellers or directly from:

Central Books, 99 Wallis Rd,
London E9 5LN.
Tel: 020 8986 4854. Fax: 020 8533 5821.

The Open
University

Those wishing to obtain information about courses and teaching opportunities should contact the Regional Centre of The Open Univeristy in their area; or the Central Enquiry Service, The Open University, PO Box 200, Walton Hall, Milton Keynes MK7 6AA. Tel: 01908 653 231 or visit The Open University web page: www.open.ac.uk/

supporting

lifelong

language

learning

theoretical and practical
approaches

edited by
Lore Arthur and Stella Hurd

CILT
Centre for Information
on Language Teaching and Research

The Open
University

The views expressed in this publication are the authors' and do not necessarily represent those of CILT or The Open University.

Every effort has been made to trace copyright holders and to obtain their permission to reproduce copyright material. If any proper acknowledgement has not been made, or permission not received, we would invite the copyright holder to inform us.

Acknowledgements:

The editors are grateful for the comments they received on draft manuscripts from:

Graham Bishop, Dorothy Calderwood, Marie-Noëlle Lamy, Margaret Nicholson, Duncan Sidwell and the External Assessor Dr Rob Rix, Trinity and All Saints, University of Leeds, on behalf of The Open University; and Edith Esch and Alan Moys on behalf of CILT.

First published in 2001 by CILT in association with The Open University.

Cover photography © 2000, Barbara Ludman/iwitness.org.uk

ISBN 1 902031 45 8
2004 2003 2002 2001 / 10 9 8 7 6 5 4 3 2 1

Printed in Great Britain by The Cromwell Press.

CILT Publications are available from: **Central Books,** 99 Wallis Rd, London E9 5LN. Tel: 020 8986 4854. Fax: 020 8533 5821. Book trade representation (UK and Ireland): **Broadcast Book Services,** 2nd Floor, 248 Lavender Hill, London, SW11 1JL. Tel: 020 7924 5615. Fax: 020 7924 2165.

Contents

Foreword

Writing the foreword to this book gives me the opportunity to pay tribute to the long-standing commitment of its editors, Lore Arthur and Stella Hurd, to the support and encouragement of adult language learning. In 1992 I wrote an introduction to their previous publication, *The adult language learner*, which while in print, was for many years required reading for teachers working in the field. This new title, *Supporting lifelong language learning* reflects the shifts in focus and emerging priorities of the last decade. Whereas *The adult language learner* provided a practical manual on how to teach, *Supporting lifelong language learning* concentrates on broadening the perspectives and understandings of teachers, focusing both on the processes involved in successful learning and also on the changing political, cultural and technological context which characterises the opening of the 21st Century.

While many of the features of the current scene were anticipated in *The adult language learner* in 1992, the picture remains a tantalising mix of exciting prospect and uncertain reality. Perhaps the most exciting prospect of all is the spin-off from the information technology revolution which is still unfolding around us. The combination of ever cheaper global communication, the personal computer, the Internet and satellite television represents a potent resource for the would-be language learner, both at home and increasingly (if all too slowly in many instances) in the classroom.

In terms of public policy, we are in the midst of a major reform of the organisation and funding of post-school education, with the establishment of a national Learning and Skills Council arising from the government's imaginative proposals in the 1999 White Paper, *Learning to succeed.* On the plus side, this initiative brings with it the prospect of a coherent and fully professionalised lifelong learning provision, in a field which has suffered for too long from fragmentation and under-investment. At the same time, government is still seemingly locked into the often unsustainable demarcation between 'vocational' and other courses when it comes to funding. In *The adult language learner* I warned that this was 'likely to threaten the heterogeneity and richness of the adult languages class as many of us have known it', and, alas, that fear has all too often been realised.

Adult learners remain, however, resilient and determined, and their commitment to language learning is undimmed. In spite of the ambivalence of government and the hostility of sections of the press towards European issues in recent years, public attitudes to the importance of capability in languages have become steadily more positive. Organisations as diverse as The Open University, NIACE, CILT and the BBC have played a central part in responding to and reinforcing this momentum. The Nuffield Languages Inquiry has further raised the profile of languages and set a challenging policy agenda for government.

The prospect for lifelong language learning remains therefore a stimulating one, and in this context I commend the range and ambition of this new publication and the authoritative insights its contributors give, as we reach for the prize of a truly plurilingual society.

Alan Moys
Secretary, Nuffield Languages Inquiry

Introduction

LORE ARTHUR AND STELLA HURD

All of us learn all the time. Often we are not aware of it. We learn at home or at work, informally from friends, partners and colleagues or more formally by taking part in organised forms of learning, whether it be for pleasure or for vocational purposes. We learn from reading or viewing, from doing something different, from listening or simply observing others. Learning, therefore, is not restricted to a particular group of people or to particular times. Rapid globalisation means that many more people travel, often to other countries, or work in multilingual settings; they are likely to receive or seek new information available on the Internet or take part in different kinds of international networks and generally conduct their affairs in a multicultural environment. Increasingly, all of us have to learn new skills and be flexible over how we organise our personal and working lives.

Many language tutors have no problem adapting to this new kind of environment. They work all sorts of hours, often in more than one institution, and remain responsive to the needs of individual learners, many of whom face similar challenges. H.H.Stern wrote in 1983 (:515) that:

> ... language teachers – probably more than other professionals – find that they are constantly bombarded from all sides with a surfeit of information, prescriptions, directions, advice, suggestions, innovations, research results, and what purports to be scientific evidence. ... It is difficult to find one's way through this maze.

This kind of statement, although written some time ago, is relevant even now and is likely to be so for many years to come.

What are the aims of the book?

This book seeks to identify some of the changes which have taken place in recent years. **Supporting** learning implies guiding learners throughout all stages of their learning experiences within the context of an educational institution. It means

1

accepting learners as individuals by recognising that they have a variety of reasons for wanting to learn the language, different life experiences and expectations together with different needs, abilities, learning styles and learning strategies, all of which affect the learning situation.

From a tutor's point of view it seems important, therefore, to understand the nature of language learning and second language acquisition in order to relate the personal and practical insights gained from teaching to the theoretical principles accepted in the wider professional field. This enriched knowledge enables tutors to design courses and plan lessons to professional standards; to use materials effectively, including those offered by computer technology; to evaluate teaching methods and approaches employed; to give effective feedback to learners; design assessment tasks and mark these according to criteria agreed within the institution and accepted within the professional world of language teachers.

There are other factors to be considered: educational institutions, particularly those which are dependent on public sector funding, are increasingly required to demonstrate **value for money**. For example, they have to submit records of student attendance on courses which, in many instances, are characterised by quantifiable pre-determined learning outcomes, continuous assessment and end-of-course examination. These are usually linked to quality assurance processes which seek to demonstrate good teaching practices and learner satisfaction. Tutors, irrespective of the kind of institution in which they work, are expected to be **professionally competent** and to take part in some form of continuing professional development – just as many other people in different areas of work take part in further training and staff development.

The term **lifelong** can be used in different ways. It has been widely used in adult education circles for many decades but has more recently been promoted in various educational policies on a worldwide basis. Learning, it is argued, does not cease once initial education has finished but is an on-going process right throughout life. However, a shift of emphasis has taken place away from what was at one time understood to mean lifelong education or teacher-centred approaches, to **lifelong learning** or **learner-centred approaches**. The term implies that learners are self-directed and autonomous and hence responsible for their learning. It is the role of the tutor together with the institution to **promote and support** that learning in the most effective way possible.

Teaching another language is a surprisingly sophisticated process. There is a great diversity of learning needs and there are many different types of language courses. The courses you are involved with may be in adult, further or higher education, in distance education, or part of a languages degree. Levels of language may range from complete beginners to advanced level or you may be teaching on specialists courses. Your students may be young or old, have English as a first or second language, be learning for pleasure or for vocational purposes. You may see them several times a week, once a week, rarely or never at all as can happen in distance learning. All, however, will need your support and expertise.

Your aim will be to motivate your students and to maintain that motivation throughout the course. It will help you, therefore, to enhance your understanding of:

- learners' needs and expectations;
- learner differences and strategies;
- the nature of second language acquisition;
- teaching for effective intercultural communication;
- how to evaluate different approaches to teaching;
- how to plan lessons effectively;
- how to develop skills in listening, speaking, reading and writing;
- how to exploit computer technology effectively;
- how to analyse and respond to errors;
- how to check that learning has been achieved
- how to develop your understanding of theoretical approaches and relate these to your own professional practice.

The focus in this book, therefore, is not only on practical aspects of the process of teaching but also on the underlying principles which inform good practice. **Part One** of this book examines many theoretical issues in relation to understanding language learning and learners by accepting that both language tutors and language learners are involved in similar processes. The chapters in **Part Two** are concerned with teaching methods and approaches, including lesson planning, skills development and the use of resources. The impact of computer technologies on language learning is examined in **Part Three,** while **Part Four** looks at the role of feedback and assessment and **Part Five** considers the professional contexts of language tutors as lifelong learners themselves.

How to use this book

The book is not intended to be read from cover the cover but used as an ongoing support for all those involved in language teaching. It can therefore be studied in whatever sequence or depth seems appropriate. It aims to cater for both tutors new to adult learning who may be looking for guidance on learning and teaching methods and ways to acquire professional accreditation, and for experienced tutors wishing to update their knowledge and gain more theoretical depth. For example, you may be a relatively inexperienced teacher and feel you will benefit most from reading about more practical aspects in chapters 2 and 4 before looking at the other chapters.

You may be particularly keen to find out about telelearning and other aspects of on-line tuition which are discussed in Part 3. Alternatively, you may be a very experienced tutor and be looking for the more theoretical aspects, or wish to take advantage of the extensive lists of references at the end of each chapter. Whatever your particular needs and interests, we hope that the book will have something to offer you, and that it will help you to develop or improve current practice. You will be able to measure your own success as a tutor by observing your learners and the extent to which they are able to communicate confidently and competently with a native speaker of the target language, ultimately without your intervention. Furthermore, by consolidating your professional knowledge and understanding, you will be able to recognise and appreciate successful learning wherever and whenever it takes place.

PART 1

UNDERSTANDING LANGUAGE LEARNING AND LEARNERS

It is generally accepted that adult language learners have varying and complex reasons for wanting to learn another language and that learning takes place in many different ways, in and outside formal education. Learners may be supported by tutors who themselves may work in a variety of institutions each of which has its own cultures and competing sets of demands. Contemporary theoretical approaches to language learning can be equally complex and, at times, confusing. The following four chapters in this Part, therefore, aim to clarify some of the key concepts and issues appropriate to the professional discourse of foreign/second language teaching and the learning environment.

The opening chapter looks at the professional context of language tutors, their personal development and motivation. It examines the institutional context in which many work and looks at shared common concerns. Chapter 2 focuses on the foreign/second language we teach, which may or may not be the tutor's mother tongue. It refers to the evolving nature of language, the study of languages, and their relation to the world-wide domination of English, and ends by looking at aspects of the culture and intercultural communication in language teaching. Chapter 3 examines critically some of the key concepts in and proponents of the theories of second language learning and language acquisition. Questions are raised in relation to a 'natural way' of language learning, of input and output and of how new language is processed in the learner. Chapter 4 concerns itself with the learners of a foreign/second language by looking at questions such as: What do we really know about language learners? What have they in common and what makes them individually different? How do these differences affect learning in groups? What are the implications of such diversity for the foreign/second language tutor?

1

Tutors as lifelong learners

LORE ARTHUR

Most tutors of another language are highly motivated, keen to work with students, interested in trying out different teaching methods and open to suggestions from both students and colleagues. On the whole, tutors love the language they teach and appreciate the culture of the country or countries in which that language is spoken. They thrive on the interaction with learners and the 'buzz' of a good lesson, when learners are responsive to challenges and motivated to improve their language. So what is particular about teaching another language? What keeps language tutors motivated? How did they become language teachers in the first place? This chapter aims to address the questions by considering:

- the professional development of tutors in post-compulsory education;
- the institutional context in which many tutors work;
- the sharing of a common purpose.

Professional development

Studies have shown that people become teachers of foreign languages for a number of different reasons. Nott (1992), for example, examined factors which contribute to the supply and demand of modern language teachers in secondary schools and higher education. He noted disparate, even conflicting factors such as the public perception of teaching as a profession, the attractiveness of other career options, government policies towards modern languages, and the status of modern languages in the curriculum. However, the supply and demand of schoolteachers in Britain as in most countries in the world is state controlled. Most schoolteachers, therefore, follow a regulated and conventional career pattern. By contrast, those teaching in post-school or post-compulsory education, that is those in adult, further, higher education or industry and commerce, come from a wide range of cultural, academic and professional backgrounds. Their professional development has often been patchy and their career structure uncertain. They may have studied the other language at university and have spent time in that particular country and obtained a recognised teaching qualification, which allows them to teach in schools or further education colleges.

7

Other tutors, for a variety of reasons, no longer live in their own country, and happen to have become language teachers through personal circumstances. It is likely that they have obtained graduate status in their own countries either in the language they teach or in a different subject altogether. Often those 'native speakers' develop a love for language teaching and obtain professional teaching and academic qualifications later on in their lives. Then there are postgraduates or foreign languages assistants in higher education who teach foreign/second languages although they have relatively little experience, and who rarely receive adequate training. There are, therefore, then many different pathways to becoming a foreign/second language tutor, as the statements below indicate:

> My first language is French. I am from a family of teachers and not only that, both my father and my two brothers studied English at university. My parents tried to see whether they could persuade me to read classics, so apart from English I studied Latin and Greek. Then I went to the United States where I met my husband. And that is how I ended up teaching French in England.

> Well, my mother was Welsh, but my first language is English. We lived in India straight after I was born so we spoke Hindi a lot of the time. I wanted to be a social worker but I decided to travel and to use my languages as a bi-lingual secretary. My French was a lot stronger than my German. So I ended up in Germany where I taught English, which is how I became a teacher of languages. I then went to University to study law, languages and commerce and then obtained a PGTC in French and German – and here I am. (Arthur and Starkey 1999)

Equally diverse is the range of qualifications obtained by those teaching languages outside the school sector. Research in The Open University found that among its tutors for either French, German or Spanish 49.1% had English as their first language, 15.4% were French, 16.6% German and 10.1% Spanish native speakers. Out of all of those 69.8% were formally recognised as secondary teachers in Britain. 7.1% of French, 4.1% of German and 3.0% of Spanish tutors were formally recognised as a teacher in their own countries (Arthur and Starkey 1999). Most work part-time and, as the Interim Report of the Nuffield Languages Inquiry confirmed, usually change jobs frequently. These changes affect the quality of the language learning experience many people have (Nuffield 1998:56–57). It should not come as a surprise bearing in mind that there is as yet no nationally, even internationally, recognised language teacher qualification, which is geared to the specific needs of language tutors and which would give tutors in post-compulsory education the professional recognition they deserve (see also chapter 18).

The providers

Irrespective of the kind of institution in which language learning takes place, post-school or post-compulsory education has its own agenda and its own set of difficulties. Here the supply of language teachers is not prescribed by government policies, as is the case in school education, but rather by the number of students wishing to enrol on a particular course at the beginning of an academic term or year.

At first sight, adults nowadays seem to have a great deal of choice: they can enrol for evening classes organised by adult education centres, further education colleges, universities, even sixth form colleges, or learn independently in open learning centres or via distance learning courses. Some join language-training courses available in industry and commerce. Others pay high fees in private language schools or learn on their own with the help of an increasingly wide range of audio-visual or computer-mediated courses at their disposal. However, the provision for language courses in most regions remains patchy in terms of the range of languages and levels available to students. Furthermore, most institutions require a specific number of enrolments before a class is even allowed to start. It is not surprising that students and language tutors in these institutions have to face considerable uncertainty at the beginning and throughout the academic year.

The main providers of foreign/second languages courses are:

- local education authorities (LEAs) who offer a range of services in either adult education institutes (AEIs) or community centres;
- further education colleges;
- higher education institutions including The Open University;
- some voluntary agencies such as the Workers' Educational Association (WEA),
- private and public sector employers;
- distance learning agencies – including the media.

Public sector institutions which provide language courses, such as universities, further education colleges, sixth form colleges and adult education centres, are restricted by their own funding arrangements and policy requirements. For example, the Higher Education Funding Councils for England (HEFCE) or Scotland (SHEFC) – Wales and Northern Ireland have similar arrangements – are responsible for allocating public funds for teaching and research in universities. Further education and sixth form colleges, which were at one time under the control of a local education authority, are autonomous institutions financed through the respective Further Education Funding Councils. The provision of adult education, on the other hand, is the responsibility of a local education authority.

In order to understand the changes that have taken place in recent years though, it is necessary to refer back to the 1944 Education Act. The Act made local authorities responsible for the provision of adult education, which was at that time regarded as activity-oriented learning for pleasure or leisure. This dilemma between what is functional and goal-oriented and what is a leisure-time pursuit has bedevilled foreign language learning for many years. The 1992 Higher and Further Education Act, however, effectively removed leisure-time education from government subsidy in favour of goal-oriented learning, that is, learning for certification, accreditation and vocationalism (see chapter 16). The1992 Act ensures that all language courses should lead to an accredited qualification such as a vocational one or a General Certificate of Secondary Education (GCSE). More significantly, Schedule 2 of the Further and Higher Education Act (1992) sets out clearly what type of adult education course will receive state funds and under what conditions. Thus the government sees fit to fund, above all, courses with a vocational orientation and those which lead to end-of-course assessment. Not covered by the Act, and therefore not funded from state controlled resources, are courses which fall outside Schedule 2 work, that is those which offer leisure-time activities and liberal education or education for its own sake. These are either partly or wholly funded by the local education authorities.

In the years following the 1992 Act, numerous adult education centres were closed or taken over by further education colleges or merged with, for example, the respective local authority's youth and leisure services. It is not surprising therefore that across Britain the provision of foreign languages courses in this particular sector of education is very patchy indeed. Further education colleges, on the other hand, were able to increase their adult education population to over 51%. Many further education colleges and universities have adult education departments which offer courses in foreign/second languages, though the type of classes offered may vary.

Change, it seems, is a key characteristic of our contemporary world. Following the publication of the 1999 White Paper *Learning to Succeed,* the Department for Education and Employment (DfEE), is in the process of establishing a national Learning and Skills Council which, together with local Skills Councils, will deliver all post-16 education and training (excluding higher education) in England from April 2001 onwards. The intention is that these Councils will work closely with all other agencies providing lifelong learning activities which will include: working in partnerships with local education authorities, arrangements for adult and community learning, and providing information, advice and guidance to adults. All these developments will, in due course, impact on adults learning foreign/second languages, their tutors and the type of courses available to them.

The provision of modern languages in universities is equally complex. In the main, specialist undergraduate or postgraduate teaching takes place in a Department or School of Languages. The term 'specialist' refers to full-time or part-time undergraduate study in one or more languages. In specialist undergraduate departments of, for example, French, German or Russian, substantial changes have taken place over recent years. Whereas 40 years ago almost all higher education courses were characterised by predominantly post-A level intake, by the study of literature, translation into and out of the target language, academic essay writing and 'conversation classes', the picture is now more complex: more languages are offered at lower levels, particularly at beginners level or *ab initio*. In terms of pedagogy, there is now less emphasis on translation, especially in the early stages of an undergraduate degree. However, the study of the literature and related cultural studies of the target country or countries is still an important component in many undergraduate courses, particularly in the older more established universities. This can be a source of tension for some lecturers, particularly for those who are keen to develop research in their own subject and do not see their career evolving only around language teaching.

In other universities, particularly the newer ones, there are no specialist or 'pure' language degrees. Here language study is always linked to other disciplines (see Wakeley et al. 1995). The term 'non-specialist' is often also used in connection with

Institution Wide Language Programmes (IWLPs), which are offered in most universities to all undergraduates, irrespective of their subject of study. Students of engineering, for example, or history of art, can opt for a language module within an IWLP programme and therefore gain credits needed for the completion of their degree. IWLP programmes usually offer modular courses in a wide range of languages and at a variety of levels. Here again, each institution has its own arrangements. In some universities there are also self-access centres or language centres, which provide material for independent study and which are open to all students of that university and perhaps adults from the local community. In these self-access centres learners can, if they wish, make use of technology for language learning and are helped in their efforts to learn languages by a variety of learner support systems. The main purpose is to help learners become more independent and able to exploit foreign languages outside the institution, especially through the mass media (Esch 1994).

Language learning via The Open University offers yet another model of provision. With over 200,000 students The Open University represents 21% of all part-time higher education students in the UK. It is therefore one of the world's largest distance teaching universities and offers courses in French, German and Spanish to about 6,000 adults every year. In The Open University the term 'open' means that potential students do not need to have obtained qualifications which satisfy the entry requirements of conventional universities. The term 'open' in education can be cloaked in many different mantles. In distance learning, it usually refers to students' individual freedom to choose what they learn, how they learn, and where they learn, whether and when they have their learning assessed. Within the constraints of undergraduate provision in higher education, however, the curriculum remains 'closed', which means that for most students the pace, start and finishing times as well as modes of assessment are fixed and hence outside the student's control. It is important therefore to understand the culture and mission of the institution in which teaching takes place, the kind of options students have and the barriers they experience.

Sharing similar concerns

The complexity of provision, however, applies to all educational institutions, irrespective of their specific funding and policy frameworks. Each organisation, even each building, has its own culture, ethos and atmosphere with different facilities and different kinds of support to its students. Some teaching rooms are well equipped while others, particularly those in adult education, have few resources and facilities conducive to language learning. On the other hand, if the institution has a strong commitment to the teaching of foreign/ second languages, then it is likely that it will support these policies by effective marketing and publicity to attract students, and by offering the appropriate facilities and resources. It is worth noting that institutions are obliged by the various funding councils to provide policy statements with clear information about service priorities, which should reflect widespread consultation and collaboration. This means that an institution has responsibilities not only towards its students but also towards its full-time and part-time teaching staff, just as part-time or full-time teachers can claim certain rights of the providing institution. These are usually stated in various mission statements and quality assurance documents available on request. There is then a complex relationship between the learner, the tutor and the organisations, with all three partners creating the learning environment in which teaching takes place as the diagram indicates:

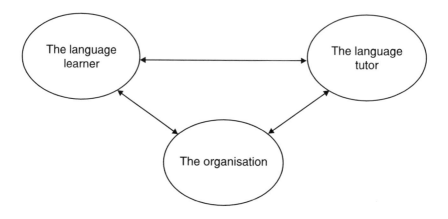

Figure 1: The learning environment

Language learners start with a wide range of abilities, linguistic levels of competence, and expectations of the tutor and the organisation (see chapter 4). Equally, tutors have different levels of teaching experience, competence and commitment to language teaching. Both tutors and students motivate each other – just as the organisation can help to create a climate conducive to learning.

Most educational institutions in either adult/further or higher education even those in private language schools or industry and commerce, depend on a large number of part-time hourly paid tutors who have no fixed contract or guarantees of employment. In practice, this means that before the beginning of an academic year many tutors do not know if they have a class to teach by the time the course is scheduled to start. Most, particularly those teaching less popular languages or courses at advanced levels, may face days and weeks of uncertainty until they know that they will have a viable number of students for the coming academic year. Nevertheless, language tutors, it seems, are able to adapt to a variety of learning situations and are, by necessity, flexible, creative, open-minded and responsive to a multitude of different needs and requirements. They may teach large or small groups or even one-to-one. Alternatively, they may support learners in self-access centres or distance education. Each mode offers different challenges.

Irrespective of the type of course, all tutors of a second/foreign language share a number of concerns, such as motivating students and understanding how students learn another language in the most effective way. In addition, many tutors, particularly those teaching minority languages, frequently have to devise their own syllabuses, create their own teaching materials and devise their own assessment schemes. In many respects then tutors are more than classroom 'teachers', they are also facilitators of learning. This is quite an important distinction: after all, students can learn another language without a tutor, but tutors cannot teach without learners.

Tutors involved with independent study in self-access or language learning centres have different priorities. The learner may need help with the selection of material and the prioritising of objectives; he or she needs to have a regular sense of achievement if independent study is to be rewarding and motivation to be maintained. The design and selection of teaching material appropriate for independent study, as opposed to classroom teaching material, is therefore central to working in a self-access centre.

For tutors in a distance learning university such as The Open University, neither option on its own is an appropriate one. Here tutors do not control the curriculum or the teaching content nor are they entirely free to organise their lessons around students' needs and wishes. Tutors in distance learning have to accept a different role – one which both supports and facilitates learning, in the knowledge that the initial teaching and learning has taken place in advance of the tutorial and is therefore outside the tutor's control. It is the set of course materials, however, which provide the formal teaching input in that sense, but tutors have to mediate between the teaching material and the learners, e.g. help with clarification, provide opportunities for further practice, consolidation and extension and the development of transferable learning strategies. The most difficult aspect for tutors is to develop language learning in response to the needs of the learners and to learning objectives stipulated in the course materials which, without glossing over problems, genuinely allows each student to progress (Murphy 1998). This shift of role is indeed one of the key elements for tutors involved in distance learning. It can be illustrated in the following way:

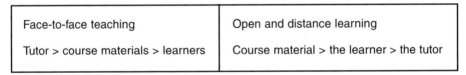

Face-to-face teaching	Open and distance learning
Tutor > course materials > learners	Course material > the learner > the tutor

Figure 2

Learning theories which have influenced much of education in recent years focus on learner-centred notions of experiential learning and reflective practice. The challenge of these theories, whether it be for distance education or for face-to-face teaching, is that they must enable learners to bring into the course the experiences they have had, before and during the course of study, and must stimulate them to engage with these and the course concepts through critical reflection (SOL 1995). Adult learning theories, according to Knowles (1984) in particular, argue that learners have accumulated experiences which can be a rich source for learning and that adults become ready to learn when they experience the need to know something. The same applies to language tutors. They too have a rich resource of personal and professional experiences and their desire to find out more about language teaching is usually prompted by a need to extend their professional knowledge. Experiences and the need to want to know something are linked to learning by doing and reflecting so that new learning can be achieved. Probably the best known 'learning from experience' theory is linked to Kolb's (1984) Learning Cycle which states that learning requires: concrete experience, reflective observation, abstract conceptualisation (see chapter 17 for further details).

But what does this mean in practical terms? It means that both learners and tutors share this process of lifelong learning; they think or reflect about what they have learnt and try to adapt what they have known before to the new learning.

Irrespective of the institutional context and philosophy in which tutors and learners find themselves, all language tutors are increasingly expected to be highly professional in all activities they undertake. What, then, are the characteristics of these good teachers? Some possible defining qualities may be:

- they are excellent linguists and have an expert knowledge of the subject area;
- they can communicate their subject clearly;
- they use a variety of teaching techniques which promote learner interaction;
- they can adapt their teaching to unanticipated problems learners may experience;
- they can help learners to develop confidence;
- they have developed an empathy with learners' difficulties in learning;
- they have developed a learner-centred approach to teaching;
- they have a learning theory to inform their teaching;
- they constantly reflect on all aspects of their own teaching and learning.

(Adapted from Gibbs 1999:5)

All these characteristics are important. However, it is worth remembering that tutors develop these over a period of time. It is the process of reflection on teaching which enables tutors to become skilled and professional. All language tutors are 'experts' in their own way with their own strengths and weaknesses. They have a common bond in their desire to help language learners develop their maximum potential.

References

Arthur L and H Starkey, *Intercultural communication and identities*, Research in progress (The Open University, 1999)

Department for Education and Employment, White Paper *Learning to succeed,* (DfEE, 1998)

Esch E (ed), *Self-access and the adult language learner* (CILT, 1994)

Gibbs G, *How students learn. Teaching in Higher Education* (The Open University, 1999)

Knowles M and Associates, *Andragogy in action* (Houston: Gulf Publishing, 1984)

Kolb D A, *Experiential learning* (New Jersey: Prentice Hall,1984)

Murphy L, in *Supporting language learning. A handbook for associate lecturers* (The Open University, 1998)

Nott D, 'Modern language teachers: supply and demands' in *Language Learning Journal,* 6 (September 1999)

Nuffield Languages Inquiry, *Where are we going with languages*? (The Nuffield Foundation, 1998)

Nuffield Languages Inquiry, *Languages: the next generation. The final report and recommendations of the Nuffield Inquiry* (The Nuffield Foundation, 2000)

2

Language, languages and cultural awareness

LORE ARTHUR

Why does language provide such a fascinating object of study? Perhaps because of its unique role in capturing the breadth of human thought and endeavour. We look around us, and we are awed by the variety of several thousands of languages and dialects. Expressing a multiplicity of world views, literatures and ways of life. We look back at the thoughts of our predecessors, and we can only see as far as language lets us see. We look forward in time, and find we can plan only through language. (Crystal, 1987:1)

As language tutors we are likely to have a great affinity for the language or languages we teach, and considerable knowledge of the cultures and countries in which the language is spoken. Yet we may not always fully understand the subtleties or complexities of our first language nor the range of communication skills offered in the language of teaching. This chapter, therefore, aims to address:

- issues in language awareness;
- the study of language in linguistics;
- language varieties and the role of English;
- intercultural communications and their implications for teaching.

Issues in language awareness

Many language tutors, in common with many other people, love and admire the use of language in poetry, literary texts, word games and any other medium which emphasises words and thoughts expressed through language. However, people also readily and often vociferously complain about what they consider to be 'poor language' or 'bad style' in a highly subjective manner. Issues of language can therefore be contentious, just as attitudes towards and perceptions of language are, it seems, complex and elusive. Yet they are part and parcel of every person's life and belief system. People identify themselves – and are identified by others – through language and the way they use language. Language can also be used as an instrument of power designed to include some and exclude others. The way language tutors use language

16

when giving instructions or when explaining, for example, grammar items, has implications for the individual's learning process. When communicating with learners of the other language, tutors often use a 'simpler form' of that language with learners at lower levels, and a more 'advanced' form with learners at higher levels. They may employ other forms of language such as body language – eyes, facial expressions, hands and arms – depending on their own personality and cultural background.

What then is language? Not surprisingly there aren't any easy answers. Even linguists struggle with definitions. Some think of language in terms of an instrument that is used to convey intentions and meaning. Others perceive language the way it is used in social interactions involving shared knowledge and assumption between speakers. Language is a social construct which, in the words of Fairclough (1998) *'is important enough to merit the attention of all citizens'*. So what do we mean by language?

Whichever way one views language, it is important to realise that there is no finite entity called 'language'. Instead, the word 'language' embraces a multitude of different concepts and connotations. These change, adapt or even disappear as part of an evolving process. Language tutors need to understand that the language they teach is highly complex, and constantly evolving, which makes the learning of that language exciting, challenging and frustrating at the same time – precisely because it is an ongoing, never-ending process. This realisation is important for the following reasons:

- Some students may think that another language can be mastered in its entirety with little time and effort.

- Some language teachers have a narrow concept of language: they see it structured around grammar only and teach accordingly. They tend not to consider the many different aspects of language needed for effective communication in a variety of different cultural, social and historical contexts.

The study of language in linguistics

In the context of academic studies the concept of language crosses many disciplines, that is, not only pure and applied linguistics but also biology, philosophy, anthropology, sociology, psychology, education, among others. Language and ethnicity, for example, looks at the relationship between language use and ethnic background; language and identity refers to the role of language in providing the speaker with individuality and group membership, while language and ideology examines language as a political weapon (Trask 1999). The study of neurolinguistics is still in the early stages of development. In due course, it may shed light on how we learn, use and remember language, thereby solving that riddle of whether or not there is such a thing as innate language with a universal grammar system (see chapter 3).

For language teaching purposes it helps to distinguish between the structure of language and language as a means of communication. Jacob Grimm (1785–1863), for example, who is best known for his fairy tales, investigated the structure of languages, and in particular the relationship between Indo-European languages and the consonants these languages share. The rules which govern these sound shifts became known as 'Grimm's law'. To this day, Grimm is considered to be the forefather of modern linguistics. Equally influential was Ferdinand de Saussure (1857–1911) who taught Sanskrit, Gothic and Old High German, first at the University of Paris and subsequently in Geneva, and who became widely known with the posthumous publication in 1915 of his *Course in General Linguistics.* Central to Saussure's theory is his distinction between *langue* and *parole.* What Saussure called *parole* or the 'executive side of language' denotes actual utterances and *langue* refers to the shared set of structural properties underlying language usage. This distinction is still relevant nowadays. Linguists and language teachers consider both the message (content) and the means (communication) in their perception of language. Both these notions have influenced what is commonly known as the 'communicative approach' (see chapter 6).

Embedded in the concept 'communicative' is the understanding that language does not only consist of grammar and vocabulary, but also of a multitude of different components, contexts and cultures as well as individual needs and responses, which lead us to examine what language consists of and what functions and purposes it serves. Communicative language competence can be considered as comprising:

- The sociolinguistic component – relating to social contexts and situations in which communication takes place, and conventions such as rules of politeness, rules governing age and gender differences or personal relationships, the use of formal and informal language, and all forms of intercultural communication. The academic field of sociolinguistics relates the social use of language to linguistic forms, social settings, differences in themes and topics and the contexts in which communication takes place. For example: *Shut that door, for heaven's sake! Would you mind very much shutting the door?*

- The linguistic component – for example, grammatical structure of words (morphology), the grammatical structure of sentences (syntax), the study of sound systems (phonology), the study of articulatory and acoustic phenomena (phonetics), the extent and precision of vocabulary (lexicology). For example, these two sentences – *Fred is off his head* and *Fred is office head*! – could not be more different to a native speaker in the spoken form. A non-native speaker, on the other hand, might not be able to hear the difference in stress and intonation and therefore completely misunderstand the meaning.

- The pragmatic component – consisting of knowledge about the other country or countries and the skills needed to use the language. Scholars involved in this area of study regard language as an area of action; they are interested in spoken and written utterances, 'speech acts', and the performance or function of these speech acts within communication. The study of meaning and semantics is a particularly complex area of language study. Pragmatics looks at functional purposes needed to express utterances such as *Two pounds of butter, please.*

Language varieties and the role of English

There are other ways of looking at language itself, or at individual languages or language varieties and the elements they may share or may not share with others. What, for example, is a language as opposed to a dialect? Both convey not only geographical information but also social information about their speakers. Conceptually, dialects refer to a distinct grammar and vocabulary range and possible pronunciation, and a regional accent refers only to pronunciation. Other problems of definition occur where dialects are spoken throughout an area. For example, speakers of northern Germany cannot understand those in eastern Switzerland although both speak a form of the same language. In Japan, there are major dialect differences, the southern dialects of the Ryukyu Islands being markedly different from the standard language based on the Tokyo dialect. Arabic is spoken by over 150 million people as the first language. However, Classical Arabic is the language of the Koran, and the sacred language of Islam, and thus known to Muslims worldwide (see Crystal 1994). In Europe, there are almost 50 languages spoken by its inhabitants. Minority languages, state-supported or not, have been spoken as indigenous languages for thousands of years and form an integral part of Europe's cultural and linguistic heritage. Several languages, for example, are spoken in Spain, all of which give rise to pronounced regional consciousness, a sense of separate identity and a feeling of belonging. Other EU member countries have rich cultural and linguistic traditions. For example, in the United Kingdom there are over 500, 000 Welsh speakers and about 142, 000 people who claim to have knowledge of Irish in Northern Ireland, just as there are 67, 000 speakers of Gaelic (European Bureau for Lesser Used Languages 1998). London, has been described as the most multilingual capital of the world, with representations of between 250 and 300 languages. Not surprisingly, its citizens come from many different former colonies, but there are numerous other languages spoken which come from all parts of the world including continental Europe.

It is as a consequence of socio-economically or politically determined processes of immigration, that the traditional patterns of language variation across Europe and elsewhere have been considerably extended over the past two or three decades. Nowadays about a third of the population under 35 in urban Europe has an ethnic minority background. All of these factors have implications for language tutors who can, and should, no longer assume that they will be teaching monolingual and monocultural students. Paradoxically, as the English language expands as an international and intranational language and while it is the language of the Internet, 90 per cent of the world's languages will either be extinct or doomed to extinction by the end of the next century. A language – or rather its last remaining speaker – dies every two weeks. Graddol (Nuffield 1998) considers that this language loss is closely associated with a loss of cultural diversity, together with a loss of small communities and their specialised knowledge and social practices.

Much to the dismay of those teaching and promoting the use foreign/second languages, however, the onslaught of the English language world-wide seems unstoppable by virtue of the political and economic progress made by English-speaking nations in the past 200 years, and it is likely to consolidate its position across the world. It is estimated that 470 million people have English as a mother tongue and a further 1.5 billion use it as a second or third language (Crystal, 1997). English has official status in over 60 countries. These figures are estimated to be on the conservative side. Already 75 per cent of the world's mail and 70 per cent of electronic mail sent on the Internet is written in English. The world's stock markets, international banks, and most transnational companies conduct their affairs in English.

In the United Kingdom, therefore, it is not entirely surprising that the ability to speak another language has rarely achieved its deserved educational or social status as the *Final Report of the Nuffield Inquiry Languages: the next generation* (2000) confirms. The Report states (:14):

> *English alone is not enough. In the face of such widespread acceptance and use of English the UK's complacent view of its limited capability in other languages is understandable. It is also dangerous. In a world where bilingualism and pluralingualism are common place, monolingualism implies inflexibility, insensitivity and arrogance. Much that is essential in our society, its health and its interests – including effective choice in policy, realisation of citizenship, effective overseas links and openness to the inventions of other cultures – will not be achieved in one language alone.*

Intercultural communication and implications for teaching

Most of us think of language as a means of communication with two or more people, or even with oneself, in a social context and social interaction. The word communication derives from the Latin equivalent of 'common' (*communis*) which denotes an interaction between a sender and a receiver who exchange thoughts, ideas, experiences and impressions in specific locations at a given moment in time. There is an assumption that they have something in common.

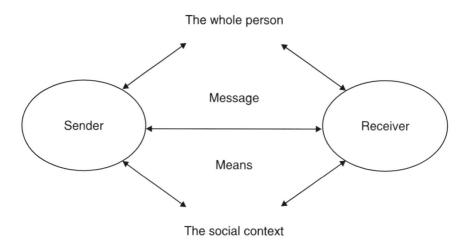

Figure 3

Communication, therefore, is fundamental to all human relations. It is a broad concept. It not only involves senders and receivers who negotiate messages (content) in a specific manner (means) but also emotions, attitudes and personal or social relationships.

Both senders and receivers adhere to accepted and culturally determined conventions about, for example, how to address each other, when and how to interrupt, how to maintain the dialogue or seek clarification. Much more important, however, are the disturbances and deviations that impede communication and which often lead to insecurities and tensions. All of us know from everyday experiences that even when both senders and receivers of messages communicate in their first language, such miscommunications occur regularly and in almost all kinds of social settings. Effective communication skills in any language are complex and require verbal dexterity, sensitivity, understanding, intuition and empathy.

Culture-specific ways of speaking can also provoke misunderstanding and even prejudice. The French tend to make requests using the future tense, imperatives and *il faut,* thereby conveying the impression of authoritarianism, impatience and assertiveness. Germans, it seems, use fewer **downgraders** (please, sort of, I guess) than their English-speaking colleagues. Instead, Germans use more **upgraders** (absolutely, I am sure, you must understand) which to English ears makes them sound assertive if not aggressive (Clyne 1994). Native speakers of English do not really care about the state of health when they ask others *How are you?* Not all non-natives recognise that this question is part of a greeting routine, which by nature has no meaning (Saville-Troike 1989). There are language routines in social behaviour which have to be learnt by non-native speakers. These include greetings, leave taking, jokes, complements and other formulaic language. Language tutors know from everyday experiences just how culturally sensitive they have to be when in contact with speakers of other languages and cultures. The use of first names and informal address widely accepted in English-speaking countries and classroom settings can cause confusion and be considered too familiar to many students from different cultural backgrounds.

Other factors influence cross-cultural understanding. Non-verbal language such as posture and movement, stretching hands, bowing, facial expressions, gaze and eye movement, gestures and proximity such as intimate distance, personal distance, and public distance, as well as verbal communication, all of which have a particular role to play in the teaching of second/ foreign language. Many students from different cultural backgrounds find the informal teaching style and the emphasis on group interaction so prevalent in this country disconcerting. Many expect a more formal teaching style and need time to settle down.

The academic discourse, both in written and spoken form may also vary. Clyne (1995), in his discussion on communication patterns, describes how in many countries across the world essay-writing is far less important than in English-speaking countries where it is a major part of assessment across the curriculum. In many continental countries and those of East and South East Asia, **content** is paramount in expository discourse rather than the structure of the **argument**. English-speaking students, on the other hand, are encouraged when writing to use advance organisers to make the text more predictable – and digressions are often misunderstood. All these factors influence ways of teaching and learning. In many institutions language tutors will have learners from different countries who have been brought up in different cultural traditions and who suddenly find themselves in an English-speaking teaching environment where learners, for example, are asked to take part in role plays or other group activities and where the tutor is not presented as the figure of authority. It is not surprising that in such instances cross-cultural communication difficulties are likely to occur.

What do we mean by 'culture'?

Within continental intellectual tradition, the notion of culture is linked to the creative aesthetic achievements and individual performance; in the Anglo-American world, on the other hand, the concept is understood in a far more pluralistic sense. The issue of culture can be a source of confusion to many language tutors, particularly those who are not English native speakers, as the following statements indicate:

> The British have no awareness of culture!
>
> Language teaching helps me to stay in touch with my own culture.

However, there are other tensions:

> I teach German but I am Austrian. Austrian culture means a million different things to me. I could not begin to describe it.
>
> I am a teacher of French. I teach French culture yet I am Swiss. I feel more comfortable teaching French culture than Swiss culture. You can become self-conscious about your own culture. (Arthur 1995: 12).

It is not difficult to see how complex and subtle notions of culture can be, and the difficulties these can present to language tutors whose attitudes and feelings about the other country or countries will vary, depending on whether or not they are teaching their first language or on the personal experiences they had of that country.

Paradigms of intercultural communication pose a multitude of questions, yet offer few, answers. Their interpretation rests on one's own understanding and perception of a given context and situations. Cultural understanding is therefore not readily transferable from one country to another or from one speech community to another, particularly if language barriers intervene. It involves notions of **culture, language** and **thought** in an interdependent relationship, all of which have occupied scholars for centuries. In linguistics, concepts of culture usually involve knowledge, ideas and artefacts. As such culture may be observable (a behaviourist definition) or related to organised and shared interpretation, that is, how individuals make sense of their environment. Goodenough's definition of culture (in Hymes 1964) is widely stated in this context:

A society's culture consists of whatever it is one has to know or believe in order to operate in a manner acceptable to its members. Culture is not a natural phenomenon; it does not consist of things, people's behaviour or emotion. It is the form of things that people have in their minds, their models of perceiving, relating and otherwise interpreting them.

Others see culture as a process of interpreting symbols and meaning, and the interrelationship between meaning, experience and reality (a symbolic definition). In this instance, culture is a dynamic process, ongoing, giving rise to symbols which may be viewed historically. Interwoven with concepts of culture are those of cultural identity and stereotyping. All involve a sense of belonging to a particular group of people set apart from those who do not belong to the same group and who seem to be different.

Implications for teaching

The term 'culture' is a flexible and often confusing term. For example, in his *Notes Towards the Definition of Culture* T.S.Eliot said that he had to remind himself that culture:

> *... includes all the characteristic activities and interests of a people: Derby Day, Henley Regatta, Cowes, the twelfth of August, a cup final, the dog races, the pin table, the dart board, Wensleydale cheese, boiled cabbage cut into sections, beetroot in vinegar, nineteenth century Gothic churches and the music of Elgar.*

T.S. Eliot, it needs pointing out, was not an Englishman but an American who belonged to a certain period in time (1888–1965) and moved in particular social circles. This citation then poses dilemmas: not everybody in England will share the same sentiments and not everybody will understand the references to, for example, Cowes or Derby Day. Even foreigners who have lived in England for some time will find it hard to catch the essence of Eliot's sense of English culture unless, of course, they have lived in England for some time and shared the same social values. Notions of culture and a common understanding remain to the outsider, it seems, idiosyncratic, ephemeral and difficult to grasp. They relate, above all, to the individual's sense of identification and of belonging to particular groups of people.

How would language tutors working with a similar text, taken from a foreign language source, deal with all the implications embedded in such texts? They would have to ask themselves:

- What are learners likely to know on the basis of their own experience and knowledge before they study the text?

- What is it that I want learners to understand and know about the country after they have studied the text in relation to the syllabus?

- Does the text contain socio-cultural information which learners may or may not fully comprehend – for example, historical content or political background knowledge?

- What is complex and in need of explanation – idiomatic expressions, metaphors, cultural references, graphs or illustrations?

- What do I as a tutor, have to know about the text and its content or the author in order to use if effectively?

The teaching of cultural aspects arises quite naturally in teaching situations. For example, current affairs lends itself to further exploration for the sake of mutual understanding in most cases. Tutors and students alike discuss topics of interest as they arise out of the materials or given circumstances. Cultural aspects are good motivators and often lead to reflection and hence better understanding, not only about the 'other' culture but also about one's own .

Indeed, what used to be known as *Landeskunde* in German, *civilisation* in French or *area* or *cultural background studies* in English plays an increasingly important role in an integrated language teaching curriculum. By using authentic materials from the target country in the classroom or in distance learning and by encouraging learners to draw on their own knowledge and experience, tutors usually encourage the making of comparisons between both countries. It is generally accepted that language learners should not only study language and the cultural context, but that, in the words of Stern (1983) they should be made aware of the interaction between language and culture (*Language IN culture, culture IN language*).

The emphasis on authenticity, real life contexts and native speakers of the target language, text books and other media is intended to convey not only factual knowledge about the target country or countries, – though even factual knowledge needs to be embedded in some kind of historical or sociocultural background if the learner is to make any sense of it at all – but also how people in different countries collectively and individually perceive and understand matters in relation to themselves and the rest of the world. The cultural dimension, then, involves knowledge about the target country or countries on the one hand and, on the other, reflection and deep-level understanding about values and belief systems other than one's own. Byram and Risager (1999) refer to three related aspects:

- *First of all, there is the aspect of cultures in general, irrespective of the link with the specific language, of communicative competence which enables a foreign-speaker of a language to understand the ways in which language can be used in a specific sociocultural context and can refer to cultural knowledge and pre-suppositions of specific groups of native-speakers.*

- *Second, there is the ability of a foreign speaker to reflect upon his or her own culture, how it appears to outsiders, and how a relationship can be established between it and the culture of others in order to facilitate communication, despite different cultural perspectives.*

- *Third, there is the ability of the teacher of foreign languages to mediate between learners' cultures, to stimulate learners' interest in other cultures.*

Learning about another culture encourages comparative reflection in relation to one's own culture. Learners, therefore, often gain knowledge and understanding not only about other ways of perceiving and doing things, but also why they themselves behave in a certain manner or why institutions have evolved in a particular way and the meaning attached to these. These processes of reflection lead to enhanced understanding and the construction of new, mutually shared knowledge.

The amount of time and proportion allocated to developing cultural knowledge and understanding will vary within the period of learning. Learners and course syllabuses as well as assessment criteria have their own agenda which may determine the space, pace and depth which can realistically be allocated to any one of them. However, one of the main components of successful language learning rests in the ability of both students and tutors to maintain their motivation throughout a course of study. The cultural element in language teaching is enjoyable and stimulating, particularly if it occurs in response to students' interests or current affairs. Tutors and students need to develop deep and cumulative levels of understanding, both consciously and subconsciously, which at the same time help consolidate and extend a range of language skills.

References

Arthur L, 'Understanding culture: a research-in-action project' in *Languages Forum,* 1, 4 (Institute of Education, London, 1995)

Byram M and K Risager, *Language teachers, politics and cultures* (Multilingual Matters, 1999)

Crystal D, *The Cambridge encyclopaedia of language* (Cambridge University Press, 1987)

Crystal D, *An encyclopaedic dictionary of language and languages* (Penguin Books, 1994)

Clyne M, *Intercultural communication at work. Cultural values in discourse* (Cambridge University Press, 1994)

Clyne M, *The German language in a changing Europe* (Cambridge University Press, 1995)

European Bureau for Lesser Used Languages, *A mini guide to lesser used languages in the European Union* (Dublin: European Bureau for Lesser Used Languages, 1998)

Fairclough N, *Language and power* (Longman, 1998)

Nuffield Languages Inquiry, *Where are we going with languages?* (Nuffield Foundation, 1998)

Saville-Troike M, *The ethnography of communication* (Basil Blackwell, 1989)

Trask R L, *Key concepts on language and linguistics* (Routledge, 1999)

3

Language learning and second language acquisition

JOHN KLAPPER

Spanish nursery children playing word games, British students following lectures at a Spanish university and French adults listening to a teacher explaining the Spanish subjunctive are all engaged in the same basic enterprise. There are, however, clear differences between these settings for learning Spanish. When we talk about language learning, it is important to distinguish the learning of an additional language, which may be a second or foreign language and which we shall call 'L2', from the learning of the mother tongue, or first language or 'L1' (e.g. the Spanish children above). The learning of second language, L2, is known in professional circles as second language acquisition (SLA). It is a term which denotes both conscious, instructed language learning (our French adult learners) and sub-conscious naturalistic language acquisition (the British students in Spain). SLA does not normally differentiate between second and **foreign** language acquisition, even though the process may differ in some respects in these two settings.

Theories of SLA explore such key issues as:

- the nature of L1 and L2 acquisition;
- the role of L2 learners' errors;
- linguistic 'input' and 'output'
- the cognitive processes involved in acquisition;
- the effectiveness of instructed language acquisition.

This chapter will consider all these issues but will focus on instructed learning and seek to show the relevance of pedagogical theory to classroom practice. SLA is also significantly affected by such **individual** learner differences as age, aptitude, personality, cognitive style, learning strategies and motivation – these are considered in the following chapter.

Learner errors and interlanguage

Imagine asking one of your students to tell you how they spent their summer holidays. The chances are their reply, whether written or spoken, will include errors of tense,

26

vocabulary, agreement, word endings, etc. Some of these errors will be repeated a number of times; some aspects of language may be used incorrectly only once, while others may be used correctly, then incorrectly and then correctly again. It is easy for tutors to criticise such language use, especially one-off errors, for falling short of target language norms, and traditionally teachers have considered most errors to be the result of a lack of care or attention on the learner's part.

However, all language tutors will be aware that learners frequently produce incorrect forms when they know the correct ones, and it is the tutor's task to distinguish **errors**, the result of deficient knowledge, from such **mistakes** which are merely occasional slips or lapses (see also chapter 13). Many of the errors which learners make do not resemble either L2 or L1 forms, and it has therefore been suggested that they must be part of an internal learner system (Corder 1967). Subsequent study has confirmed that some learners' errors are indeed regular and systematic. This new kind of language used by learners is often referred to as **interlanguage** (Selinker, 1972). Interlanguage refers to an autonomous language system which is dependent on its own rules. The system changes constantly as learners progress in the language: for example, leaners apply a new rule in one context and then gradually learn to apply it in another.

A significant feature of interlanguage, however, is its variability (Tarone, 1988). At any stage of their development learners sometimes use one form and sometimes another; this may involve one correct and one incorrect form, or two incorrect forms may alternate – probably the greatest source of tutor despair! Yet the choice of these forms is not entirely arbitrary: after some initial free variation, which may be a necessary stage in acquiring grammatical structures, learners start to use variable forms systematically, gradually improving these forms until they are correct. This systematic variability applies to the development of particular grammatical structures: for example, they may have mastered the French imperfect tense but their use of 'de' and 'à' following adjectives may still vary freely. However, it is also well known that many learners never progress to target-language use in certain grammatical structures (Ellis 1997). Most tutors can detect in their learners the beginnings of 'fossilisation', which indicates that learners do not seem to make further progress in the learning of L2. This happens particularly in advanced learners: for example, final year undergraduates still produce basic errors in sentence structure or verb endings – despite many years of tuition, or some older learners, who have been attending advanced classes for years, still make basic errors and have a poor pronunciation. In such cases tutors need to give serious consideration to how to maintain students' motivation. If, for example, a student's pronunciation does not seem to improve, then the tutor may want to concentrate on other aspects such as stress and intonation rather than try to improve the pronunciation.

The 'natural' route

A major concern of early interlanguage research was to establish whether L2 learners developed in consistent ways and whether there was a 'natural' or universal route of development. The work was encouraged by L1 acquisition research (Brown, 1973) which suggested that toddlers and young children learning their mother tongue follow a predictable route in acquiring various structures. A considerable number of studies followed, and these did, indeed, show that those learning a second language follow a broadly similar sequence to those learning the first language, passing through distinct, if general stages which are common to both naturalistic and instructed learning (Ellis 1985). However, this apparent universality of language development does not preclude variations within general stages. Thus learners, possibly under the influence of their particular first language or of their approach to learning, may well omit a minor step within a stage or add an extra step. For example, in the early stages learners may say 'Do you not like this apples?' or 'He buy oranges' while, in due course, learners will use complex structures with relative clauses such as 'Do you know the man who works at the hospital?'

The important point of all this research, as far as the language tutor is concerned, is to recognise that acquisition of a particular grammatical structure is incremental, that learners do not move suddenly from no knowledge to perfect mastery of the structure, but rather progress gradually **towards** native-like proficiency. In these transitional stages the learner is formulating working models or hypotheses about the grammar of L2. Insights from interlanguage research thus underline the systematic nature of L2 acquisition and suggest that L2 learning is, to a large extent, universal, controlled by internal cognitive processes independent of both the way in which L2 is learned (instructed or naturalistic) and the background or personality of the individual learner. This does not mean, however, that the natural sequence renders instruction redundant or that interlanguage is impervious to outside influences. This is a question we shall return to in due course.

Input and output

All theories of SLA agree that in order to learn the language, the learner must be exposed to the second language, or L2 'input', either in natural settings or in formal teaching situations. Where they differ is on the function of this L2 input. Perhaps the most (in)famous view of this is Krashen's (1985) 'input hypothesis'. Krashen, unlike others, makes a distinction between **second language learning**, that is the formal processes of language learning, for example, **the conscious** learning of rules and vocabularly, and **second language acquisition**, that is, the natural, informal learning which involves mostly **subsconscious** processes. For Krashen the crucial factor is **meaningful input:** for language to be successfully acquired, as opposed to unsuccessfully learnt, the target-language input must be novel, it must be relevant to learners' interests, must contain structures that are a little beyond their current level of competence and must be understood by them. Krashen introduces the concept of **monitor users.** Monitor users, he argues, edit their second language output when it does not interfere with communication. In this context he speaks of **overusers** and **underusers** of monitoring systems. *'Overusers typically have a hesitant, overcareful style of speaking, thanks to their overconcern with correctness and constant rule searching'* (Krashen 1985). The monitor underuser, on the other hand, does not seem to use the conscious grammar at all. Typical underusers judge grammaticality by intuition or 'feel', that is, they use their subconsciously acquired system, rather than a conscious grammar.

However, Krashen's theories have come under attack on a number of fronts and are now viewed with suspicion. Most theorists and researchers recognise the interplay between both processes which take place in language learning. In other words, most learners learn both formally and informally, consciously and subconsciously as their progress in the language. Furthermore, it appears that the communicative approach to language teaching (see chapter 5) is still inadequate: it presupposes massive exposure to L2 and plentiful opportunities for interaction – and even then the end of the language learning outcome is defective.

These terms, input and output, belong to the **computer model of SLA:**

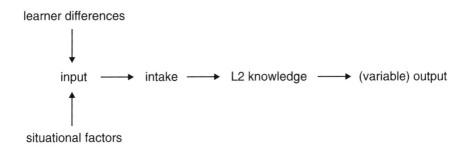

Figure 1: (Adapted from Ellis, 1985: 276)

According to this, conceptualisation of the language learning process is dependent on both the individual and the situation in which learning takes place. However, most language learners are unable to cope with all of the input, and only those bits which are attended to enter the short-term memory as **intake** (see also chapter 4). The learner's innate language-processing capacity also stores some of the intake in long-term memory as L2 knowledge which can be either implicit or explicit. Implicit knowledge equates with learners having no conscious awareness of what the rules consist of; explicit knowledge is knowledge **about** the language which students have reflected on and can use to plan production. These two types of L2 knowledge are then used either in speaking or writing as output, in which both correct and incorrect L2 forms can freely alternate.

Universal Grammar and SLA

Before refining this model, we need to consider the use some SLA researchers have made of Chomsky's ideas on language acquisition. For Chomsky language learning is unique to human beings and language learning is an independent mental faculty separate from the general cognitive processes involved in intellectual development. His complex theories revolve around the notion of a **universal grammar** (UG). By this he means that there are linguistic principles which are thought to regulate the 'parameters', or distinctive forms, of any particular language. Language acquisition, according to Chomsky, is a process of hypothesis-testing in which the learner uses his/her language acquisition device (LAD) to match the grammar of L1 against the principles of UG. The LAD is said to be triggered by linguistic input. It is this innate device that is responsible for mother tongue acquisition. This is offered as an answer to the so-called **logical problem of language acquisition**, the fact that the input children receive is too impoverished to act as a model for the language they are able to produce, i.e. that children are able to create utterances they have never heard before. However, all UG researchers reject the notion that the learning of L2 rules can normally be transformed into native speaker competence: learners may be able to use the knowledge they gain from the grammar book and apply it with gradually increasing speed, but this knowledge cannot be compared with the native speaker's knowledge which derives from instinctive awareness of the relevant parameter setting (Towell & Hawkins, 1994). UG is a theory of language, not specifically of SLA, and the picture it presents of the SLA process is far from clear. Given its narrow focus on competence and formal grammatical properties, rather than on performance and functional applications of language, tutors are likely to find its application to SLA falls seriously short of what they are looking for, i.e. insights into how to develop the ability to use language for the purpose of communication.

Cognitive approaches to SLA

By contrast, SLA researchers working in the cognitive tradition believe linguistic input is broadly comparable to all the other kinds of information the human mind processes, and language learning is therefore not to be distinguished from other facets of cognition. Furthermore, in rejecting the approaches to SLA based on L1, they point to crucial differences between L1 and L2 learners. They argue that L2 learners:

- can already communicate effectively and do not usually **need** to learn L2 in the same way they need L1;
- have different (and variable) motivations for learning L2;
- can use L1 strategically or as a resource to get at and to express meaning;
- are more highly developed cognitively and have greater problem-solving abilities than L1 learners;
- are subject to the influence of a range of affective factors.

Cognitive theory sees SLA as the learning of a complex skill, one in which a range of sub-skills must be practised in **controlled processing** until they can be integrated into automatic or fluent performance. This movement from controlled to automatic processes also involves the movement of knowledge from short- to long-term memory. When speaking freely and focusing on meaning, L2 learners employ automatic language skills, but when they focus attention on their speech, controlled processes come into operation and performance is affected – in the same way that such automatic skills as typing are likely to slow down when too much attention is paid to them (McLaughlin, 1987). This is why test situations result in more accurate production, as the material demands the application of controlled processes.

Apart from developing automatic procedures, the learner also needs to organise and structure the information acquired. This involves restructuring the cognitive representations which have already been internalised. Restructuring has been offered as an explanation for the non-linear development of L2, for backsliding or loss of accuracy with aspects of language that seemed to have been mastered (Lightbown, 1985b). Although practice generally automates sub-skills and leads to improved performance, the reorganisation of internal representations of knowledge can lead to a (temporary) reduction in performance. What seemed to be well established, now seems unstable – for example, the very common overuse of the French subjunctive shortly after learners have first been introduced to it. This restructuring accounts for the U-shaped behaviour of interlanguage referred to earlier.

Cognitive approaches distinguish **declarative** from **procedural** knowledge. The former is knowledge **of** facts, memorised rules and bits of language; the latter is the knowledge **how** to process language and apply rules with speed and accuracy. Procedural knowledge '*accounts for how learners accumulate and automatize rules and how they restructure their internal representations to match the target language*' (McLaughlin, 1987). **Automatisation** of language equates with the ability to produce correct grammatical forms when the focus is on the message one is seeking to convey and no attention is available to focus on form. This automatisation, however, can only occur as a result of considerable practice in language use. Through practice, linguistic knowledge is reorganised and stored as a '*network of routines, fixed or semi-fixed expressions which can be activated at speed, thereby equipping the learner to handle the communicative stress typical of much real-time communication*' (Batstone, 1994). To give a practical example, learners might learn grammatical rules which they initially apply conscientiously (the rule that French direct object pronouns precede indirect object pronouns). After ample practice the rule begins to sound right and the learner abandons the conscious application of the formal rule and applies it automatically.

In the initial phase, a language structure is met and understood as an unanalysed whole tied to a particular context. Through use the learner becomes aware of its distinctive features and of the regularity in the way it is used; this helps to discriminate it from other structures and to form a basic concept. A tentative rule is then formed and applied in varied practice activities linked to feedback or correction. At this stage there may be some minor restructuring as the provisional rule is extended or revised in the light of evidence about exceptions. Sometimes the readjustment of rules may not occur for a long time after the structure is first met as refinements of or exceptions to the rule may not be met until later. Increasingly, however, it is applied with accuracy and speed. Sequences deriving from controlled processing now become automatic and are stored as units in long-term memory, which makes them readily available and requires little of the learner's attention. With greater fluency and automaticity the learner's attention can be released to focus on higher levels of processing, that is the development and integration of more complex skills.

Form-focused instruction

This relatively new area of SLA research is the one most closely linked to tutors' everyday practice. The term refers to any attempt to *'draw the learners' attention to language form either implicitly or explicitly'* (Spada, 1997), and encompasses teaching grammar rules and providing learners with feedback on errors. It focuses on:

- the differences made by second language instruction;
- whether particular types of instruction are more effective than others;
- whether form-focused instruction benefits some learners more than others;
- whether certain aspects of language are more susceptible to instruction than others.

The following brief discussion will concentrate on the first two of these.

If, as has been suggested, all learners have an in-built language syllabus which dictates how and at what stage they acquire aspects of grammar, can instruction (either face to face or via the course material in the distance learning context) do anything to change their interlanguage system? Is form-focused teaching or instruction not redundant? Several early studies (see Ellis, 1985) showed that, in fact, instruction has no effect on the sequence of second language acquisition, as revealed in naturalistic language use. Only when learners had to focus on form (for example, in test-like situations) and were tested for short-term retention did formal instruction show any significant benefits. This applied regardless of whether learners were adults or children and of whether instruction was in a foreign- or second-language setting. Furthermore, as we have seen, Krashen and others promoted the view that grammatical rules and correction could actually impede **natural** L2 development.

More recent work, however, suggests that the benefits of instruction are not just evident in careful language use but also in free communication. Yet it seems that some structures (utterances) are affected permanently, while others are not. Apart from such factors as the type of instruction and the particular structure involved, a key variable here is whether learners subsequently hear and use the L2 structure in free communication (Ellis, 1997). What all studies of instructed SLA show is that instruction helps learners to progress more quickly and that they are more likely eventually to achieve higher levels of L2 proficiency than those who did not learn the language in formal teaching situations (Long, 1983, and Ellis, 1989). The explanation for this seems to be that instruction has a delayed effect: it may be unable to intervene in the natural process of L2 development, but it can make learners aware of aspects of language structure they might otherwise ignore in input and can 'prepare' them by providing a **hook** on which to hang a new structure when they are developmentally ready to acquire it (Lightbown, 1985a). In other words, instruction works indirectly. It adds to learners' declarative knowledge. Although learners at first may not be able to process a given structure, the teaching of that structure helps to make it more **marked**, or salient, with the result that learners become sensitised to that structure in input and then, once they reach the appropriate stage in their development, begin the process of proceduralising that structure (Ellis, 1990: 168–169) and move through the stage more quickly. In the long term, it is this speeding-up of the learning process which, it is hypothesised, prevents the fossilisation of grammatical structures so evident in many naturalistic adult learners.

With regard to the most effective type of instruction, research is still relatively underdeveloped and hence the picture is rather less clear. As we have seen, many SLA theories consider input to be crucial to the development of learner interlanguage since it provides positive evidence about L2. However, work on classroom processes and procedures (see Spada, 1997: 75) has found that a focus on form within meaning-based instruction, especially one which aims at consciousness-raising, i.e. making learners aware of particular grammatical features in the input, produces greater benefits than using either form- or meaning-focused work on its own.

Conclusion

SLA research is still, relatively speaking, in its infancy and its findings are as yet not clear enough, nor do they command sufficiently broad agreement to allow one to prescribe in any detail how language tutors should go about their business. Maybe indeed this should never be expected, for the SLA researcher's agenda is rarely that of the classroom teacher, and

> [...] teaching is an art as well as a science [...]. There can be no 'one best method', however much research evidence supports it, which applies at all times and in all situations, with every type of learner. Instead, teachers 'read' and interpret the changing dynamics of the learning context from moment to moment, and take what seem to them to be appropriate contingent actions, in the light of largely implicit, proceduralized pedagogic knowledge'. (Mitchell & Myles, 1998)

Nevertheless, language acquisition theories can provide an account of language learning which allows tutors to interpret their own classroom experiences and to establish for themselves a methodological framework which facilitates better informed pedagogical decisions. Such a framework would need to take note of both the cognitive view of SLA, which sees interlanguage developing as a result of the learner's capacity for using declarative knowledge to promote procedural knowledge, and the nativist or linguistic view, which considers interlanguage to be the product of UG, of an independent linguistic faculty. It may well be that both views of SLA are valid, with some elements of SLA resulting from innate linguistic processing and others from the application of general cognitive abilities, although it is probably true to say that it is the cognitive view which corresponds most closely to L2 tutors' experience of the pedagogical process.

The framework would also need to address the following findings of SLA research:

- error is an inevitable and essential part of language learning and variability a central feature of interlanguage;
- L2 grammatical competence develops gradually, following a largely invariable route or sequence which is not susceptible to direct intervention by instruction;
- there are differences in the precise **order** in which learners develop grammatical structures;
- some language 'parameters' need re-setting and require closer attention than others;
- automatic processing of language with a focus on meaning can develop out of controlled processing where the focus is exclusively on form;
- all learners are prone to regression;
- language acquisition often involves a 'U'-shaped development, that is restructuring phases when performance is liable to be especially variable;
- although instruction does not enable learners to acquire grammatical structures **directly**, it helps them to progress more quickly and ultimately to attain greater proficiency.

Translated into the teaching context this means learners need plentiful exposure to L2 and maximum opportunities to engage in meaning-focused communication. At the same time tutors need to ensure via form-focused learning phases, which regularly revisit grammatical structures, that learners' declarative knowledge is gradually brought to the stage where they can use it to develop procedural knowledge. Such 'recycling' of grammar, the frequent revising and development of, in particular, those aspects of L2 which are poorly represented in face-to-face teaching or through the course material together with naturalistic input, means that, no matter what the developmental level of individual learners, all will be ready sooner or later to benefit from various modes of instruction. For all its imperfections and past abuses, the communicative approach is better equipped than other methods to meet these requirements.

References

Brown R, *A first language: the early stages* (Cambridge, MA: Harvard University Press, 1973)

Batstone R, 'Product and process: grammar in the second language classroom' in Bygate M, A Tonkyn and E Williams (eds), *Grammar and the language teacher:* 224–236 (Prentice Hall, 1994)

Corder S P, 'The significance of learners' errors' in *International Review of Applied Linguistics*, 5: 161–169 (1967)

Ellis R, *Understanding second language acquisition* (Oxford University Press, 1985)

Ellis R, 'Are classroom and naturalistic acquisition the same? A study of the classroom acquisition of German word order rules' in *Studies in Second Language Acquisition*, 11: 305–328 (1989)

Ellis R, *Instructed second language acquisition* (Blackwell, 1990)

Ellis R, *Second language acquisition research and language teaching* (Oxford University Press, 1997)

Krashen S D, *Second language acquisition and second language learning* (Pergamon Institute of English, 1981)

Krashen S D, *The input hypothesis: issues and implications* (Longman, 1985)

Lightbown P, 'Can acquisition be altered by instruction?' in Hyltenstam K and M Pienemann (eds), *Modelling and assessing second language acquisition:* 101–112 (Multilingual Matters, 1985a)

Lightbown P, 'Great expectations: second-language acquisition research and classroom teaching' in *Applied Linguistics*, 6: 173–189 (1985b)

Long M, 'Does second language instruction make a difference? A review of the research' in *TESOL Quarterly*, 17: 359–382 (1983)

McLaughlin B, *Theories of second language learning* (Edward Arnold, 1987)

Mitchell R and F Myles, *Second language learning theories* (Arnold, 1998)

Selinker L, 'Interlanguage' in *International Review of Applied Linguistics*, 10: 209–231 (1972)

Spada N, 'Form-focused instruction and second language acquisition: a review of classroom and laboratory research' in *Language Teaching*, 30: 73–87 (1997)

Tarone E (1988), *Variation in interlanguage* (Edward Arnold, 1988)

Towell R and R Hawkins (1994), *Approaches to second language acquisition* (Multilingual Matters, 1994)

4

Understanding language learners

LORE ARTHUR

Tutors of foreign/second languages know that learning another language is by no means a straightforward matter. On the one hand, it can be exhilarating to have a meaningful conversation with a native speaker of that language; on the other, it can be a frustrating and difficult experience. After all, there are hundreds of different words to remember and complex rules to apply. Rather like those attempting to 'keep fit' in group situations, learners feel exposed and vulnerable when confronted with others who seem to speak the language so much better than they can. Then there is an expectation among learners that they should aspire to the linguistic competence of their first language or that of a native speaker of the other language – a near impossible task! But what do we really know about language learners?

To begin with, learners, just like tutors, enter the learning situation with a whole range of different life experiences, attitudes and expectations, most of which are moulded by personal circumstances. In addition, they have complex and varied needs, abilities and personalities.

This chapter, therefore, aims to look at :

- learner motivation;
- individual differences;
- the age factor;
- learning styles;
- learning in groups.

Motivation to learn

Most of us accept that those about to embark on a higher education specialist language degree will have different expectations, motivations and concerns compared with those who want to learn a language for leisure purposes in an adult education centre. Both types of enrolment, however, require a conscious decision and, in many instances, considerable effort, not to mention money. Furthermore, learners have choices; they accept that learning another language means they will have less time and perhaps money available to pursue other activities and competing interests. It is not surprising, therefore, that language advisors, writers of course materials, policy makers and tutors have a keen interest in finding out why people do or do not participate in language learning activities.

Most theories of motivation to learn fall into two broad categories: **extrinsic** and **intrinsic** motivation. Extrinsic motivation refers to external incentives or objectives such as passing an examination or finding a job where knowledge of another language is needed, while intrinsic motivation is less easily defined. It relates to aspects such as gaining confidence in one's ability, or wanting to do something worthwhile for its own sake rather than for external reward. Gardner and Lambert's (1972) influential study on motivation and attitude of language learners distinguishes between **instrumental** and **integrative** motivation. The orientation is said to be instrumental in form if the purpose of the language study reflects the more utilitarian value of linguistic achievement, such as getting ahead in one's occupation. On the other hand, successful learners, it is argued, must be psychologically prepared to adopt various aspects of behaviour, which characterise members of the other linguistic-cultural group. The orientation is integrative if learners wish to learn more about other cultural communities because they are as interested in the other culture as in their own (Gardner and Lambert 1972). Various researchers, including Gardner (1985), link motivation to effort and the desire to achieve a goal as well as attitude towards the subject of learning. Others link motivation to the affect, that is the emotional side of language learning or previous learning experiences.

Research undertaken in the London region of The Open University with students of a French course with a notional entry level of just post GCSE notes that 50% of those questioned about their reasons for wanting to study French gave intellectual stimulation (intrinsic motivation) and cultural interests (integrative motivation) as the main reason. Social reasons also rated highly with 39.6% while instrumental motivation with 20.8% achieved the lowest rating. The Open University report concludes: students are not essentially aiming at career development as a result of studying the course, though their enhanced skills may lead to this. Those whose explicit expectation of the course is to prepare themselves for living in France or being able to communicate at a more sophisticated linguistic level are seen to develop a more general interest in the intellectual aspects of their learning, often overtaking initial instrumental and/or integrative motivation (Schrafnagl, Fage, 1998:33). By contrast, research undertaken by J. Coleman (in Wakely et.al., 1995:1–16) with specialist language students in higher education into motivation showed that in almost all studies, around 80% of respondents stated that they studied the language for future career purposes (instrumental, extrinsic motivation) though respondents also stated that they learned the language simply because they liked it and were keen to travel abroad. There may be other reasons for wanting to study another language. A study with adults undertaken in the years 1990 and 1997 indicates that motivation to learn another language may be linked to good learning experiences at school. When asked if those questioned had enjoyed learning the language at school, over 90% answered 'yes'. Childhood experiences and exposure to other languages clearly matter too. Over 20% had heard foreign languages spoken at home. Close to 50% had visited a foreign country and about 20% had lived in a non-English speaking country as a child. Also striking is the fact that a significant number of learners, around 30%, study another language because they have friends or relatives who speak the language at home (Arthur and Beaton 2000).

Other external factors can influence motivation to study. A change of personal circumstances such as sudden unemployment, bereavement, a break-up of a personal relationship or the onset of retirement can stimulate the desire to start something new. Motivation, according to Skehan (1989), can have other sources. One such source might be an interest in the learning activity itself, referred to as the intrinsic hypothesis. Alternatively, motivation will be influenced and maintained if the learner experiences success in learning, the resultative hypothesis.

> *Those learners who do well experience reward and are encouraged to try harder: learners who do not do well are discouraged by a lack of success, and, as a result, lack of persistence. Motivation would be a consequence rather than a cause of success.* (Skehan, 1989)

Tutors will need to harness that motivation and to build on it, particularly in the early stages of learning, and to ensure that learners want to continue to learn by creating a sense of success and achievement at every given opportunity.

Individual differences

To most foreign/second language tutors the reality will look more complex. There are too many other factors which have a bearing on successful language learning. All of these have led to a plethora of research into Second Language Acquisition (SLA), particularly over the last two or three decades (see chapter 3). Not surprisingly, the question of 'nature' or 'nurture' has bedevilled the professional discourse of linguists here as much as in other areas of education. The question is: are there learners who are born with a talent for language learning, or is it simply a matter of the right kind of teaching? However, for the time being there are no conclusive answers, that is, until the science of neurolinguistics provides further insights into the functioning of the brain. Clearly most learners can achieve a good level of linguistic competence with the appropriate support in a learning environment which suits their individual needs. Nevertheless, a number of persistent questions remain. Why are some learners simply better linguists than others? To what extent is excellence linked to having a good memory, intelligence and personality?

Intelligence has a bearing on how we learn a second language, but to a limited extent. Intelligence is the term used in connection with the use of a whole range of academic skills, that is, the underlying ability to learn rather than what we actually know. Ellis (1985) cites research which distinguishes a) the cognitive/ academic language ability and b) basic interpersonal communication skills, which are required for oral fluency and the social aspects of language learning. It seems that in some people basic interpersonal communication skills are developed 'naturally'. Such people are simply good communicators and thrive on personal interaction, irrespective of their cognitive or academic ability. However, both academic ability and communication skills are needed for the successful learning of another language. Ellis concludes that while intelligence may influence the acquisition of some skills associated with second language learning, such as those needed for formal study, it is much less likely to influence the acquisition of oral fluency skills. We have all come across learners who seem to learn almost 'intuitively' through listening rather than cognitively through using their brain – rather like a guitarist who is able to play music brilliantly yet cannot read music, or the car driver who does not understand the intricacies of the engine but drives with considerable confidence. It seems that a positive attitude may be more effective than intellectual ability, at least to some extent.

Attitude, however, is linked to a sense of 'being good' at something and cannot easily be dissociated from other factors such as the social environment, motivation and what might be described as particular **aptitude** for language learning, a concept which is not easy to define. During the 1960s much research centred on aptitude testing. Most of these tests focus on those characteristics which are regarded as specific to language learning. For example, the ability to pay attention to and discriminate speech sounds, i.e. the 'phonetic coding ability', or the ability to relate sounds to symbols or grammatical sensitivity. Critics of such tests maintain that success in language learning cannot be dissociated from social aspects such as class, age and prior learning experience. In this kind of discussion, terms such as 'remembering', 'forgetting', 'skill', 'inhibition' and 'risk taking' are inevitably influenced by the theoretical approaches of cognitive psychology and psycholinguistics. Some theories consider categories such as conceptual and verbal learning, for example, the ability to gather information, ideas, to think in abstract terms. Other studies concern themselves with skills acquisition such as the articulation of sounds or the linking of sounds to patterns. Perhaps noteworthy is the assumption that having a 'good memory' is thought to be an important factor in relation to success. Speaking spontaneously in the second language requires considerable skill. Such speakers need to be able to draw on chunks of language, almost instantly, from somewhere in their memory bank and then produce that language in a comprehensible manner, all within a matter of seconds – rather like a pianist who can play complex tunes without having to analyse the positioning of the finger which accompanies each note. These are momentous achievements. Speaking the language, therefore, requires the thorough practising of a skill. Various aspects of the task must be practised and integrated into some kind of fluent performance over which the learner has control (McLaughlin, 1987).

Learners frequently complain about having a 'bad memory'. In many people's mind **memory** seems a crucial factor in gaining a sense of confidence. Tutors, on the other hand, tend to overestimate the ability learners have to remember vast quantities of new vocabulary and structures at any one time. Psychological accounts in cognitive psychology of exactly what these memories consist of and how they relate to each other differ somewhat, even after more than 30 years of research. However, there seems a fair agreement that there is some kind of short-term **working memory**, which works in parallel with **long-term memory**, into which what you hear or see is put for a short period – perhaps 10 to 30 seconds. It is then either processed in a way which transfers it to a potentially permanent long-term memory, or dumped and forgotten. In language learning terms, the learner selects and hence acquires new words or structures both consciously and subconsciously. However, producing new language requires more than simple retrieval of words from either short-term or long term memories. The learner actively constructs new meaning and seeks to link new words to his or her own previous knowledge and experience. Learners often want to be creative in the new language, even if they do not have all the words in their memory banks.

During the process of language learning, learners not only become more versatile in the use of the new language, but they also absorb or reinforce information about the culture and society of the country and the language itself. Students, therefore, learn to understand at a deeper level, in addition to gaining knowledge and developing skills. Each learner will do so at his or her own pace and to different levels of competence.

The age factor

As previously indicated, learners differ not only in aptitude and memory but also in age. 'You cannot teach an old dog new tricks' is a widely accepted popular belief. Other sayings suggest 'it's never too late learn', or 'you are as young as you feel'. The question of age in relation to learning is complex and full of contradictions. Much has to do with individual self- perception, attitude, curiosity and willingness to learn. For example, 43.3% of Open University students who took part in a survey investigating learners beliefs about language learning and themselves as language learners demonstrated the commonly held belief that 'ageing has a negative effect on learning' (Hurd 2000).

The effect of age on language learning has been discussed widely in linguistics and language education. Some researchers assume that there is a relationship between the effective acquisition of L2 before and after puberty, though there is little evidence to support this notion. Singleton (1989) offers the following solution:

> *The one interpretation of evidence which does not appear to run into contradictory data is that in naturalistic situations those whose exposure to an L2 begins in childhood in general eventually surpass those whose exposure begins in adulthood, even though the latter usually show some initial advantage over the former.*

The understanding of what is meant by age is equally uncertain. Chronological age is meaningless in itself; like time, we can perceive age in terms of change: no change, no age. Hence, in the words of Cook, age might mean change in the physiology of the brain area, muscles, or auditory equipment involved in speech; older learners may be physically different from younger learners. Or age might mean mental changing relation to short-term memory capacity. Or age might be social development – the forms of interaction typical at particular ages (Cook in Singleton and Lengyel, 1995). Overall, research has shown that there is no reason to assume that the quality of learning deteriorates or even stops with advancing age (Singleton, 1989).

There is, however, some indication that middle-aged or older learners tend to be weaker in the oral/aural domain. In other words, older learners may cope less well with language spoken at natural speed by native speakers: their ability to distinguish sounds may decline in the same way as their ability to pronounce new sounds. On the other hand, middle-aged and older learners want to be more thorough: they tend to like writing and grammar exercises and, above all, they often need to be allowed time to do an exercise well, as most tutors will know from experience. Unfortunately, we often link speed to the notion of intelligence. Speed in learning involves reaction time to perceive the stimulus, transmission time to transmit the message to the brain, and response time to carry out the action. On average, many older learners perceive and assimilate information more slowly than younger people. On the other hand, older learners often draw on their general knowledge of life; they see the connections between one item and another and seek coherence and meaning in their own life situation. They learn best if they feel at ease in the learning situation, if they do not feel pressurised and if they are allowed to follow their own preferred learning style whenever possible.

Preferred styles of learning

In most language classes there are learners who want to be creative in the other language, even with a limited range of vocabulary and grammar. They want to be able to express opinions, tell stories, display knowledge and share ideas. They are the 'risk takers' who do not mind making mistakes. Other students use a more restricted range of expressions, develop fewer ideas, are less adventurous but often produce 'correct', albeit more predictable language. Similarly, some students are more visual than others. They respond to pictures, mind maps, brief bullet points and graphics while others prefer to work with lengthy texts and the written word. While many language learners benefit from visual imagery, others have aural (sound-oriented), kinaesthetic (motion-orientated) or tactile (touch-oriented) learning style preference, and therefore benefit from linking verbal material with sound, motion or touch (Oxford, 1990).

Research into these preferred ways of learning, **learning styles** or **cognitive styles,** refers '*to the manner in which people perceive, conceptualise, organise and recall information. Each person is considered to have a more or less consistent mode of cognitive functioning*' (Ellis, 1985). Cognitive learning theories usually describe individual learning style in terms of opposites: field dependency and field independency; serialist and holist approaches to learning; impulsivity and reflectivity; syllabus-bound and syllabus-free learners; convergent and divergent thinking; data gatherers and rule formers among many others. According to such descriptors, some learners need to see the particular context, the field, in which language occurs, they are considered field-dependent, while the field-independent learner can attach multiple meanings to an item in several different contexts. Similarly the serialist prefers to learn step-by-step in a carefully graded fashion while the holist will want to have an overview of the whole before tackling items step-by-step etc.

Theories around learning or cognitive styles are beset by problems. One of the major difficulties rests in the fact that there are relatively few testing instruments which can reliably measure different cognitive styles. Many of these theories remain in the area of hypothesis and speculation. However, for tutors in the practical classroom context it is important to create a learning environment in which learners feel comfortable and in which as many obstacles or barriers to learning are removed. It helps the tutor, therefore, to know why students want to learn the language, what they as individuals hope to achieve, what they expect of the tutor and how they approach their study.

Tutors who are sensitised to these issues recognise certain characteristics in the learner and may want to build on these. For example:

- A learner who has no particular deep-rooted interest in the language may need challenging from time to time to think more deeply about issues.

- Some students need to understand the objectives and anticipated learning outcomes of a lesson and how these fit into their course of study before they can begin to learn, while others seem to be content to take each step at a time.

- Equally, some students need the tutor less than others; they are less dependent on the learning environment, while others thrive on the social interaction.

While some of these theories are contested and not all are underpinned by valid empirical data, they nevertheless amount to simple common sense that is relevant to all teaching situations. By choosing to consult students, to constantly ask, check, observe, and by engaging with students both individually and collectively within the group, the tutor adopts, perhaps even without knowing, a facilitative, **learner-centred** approach. However, it seems worth noting that:

> ... *language teaching methodologies need to be based on sound principles, and much research remains to be done before we shall be in a position to make claims and wholly confident predictions. In the meantime, we may find that we can achieve a great deal just by consulting with our learners and encouraging them to reflect critically on the learning process. For it seems to be a general rule that human beings perform best when they know what they are doing, why they are meant to be doing it, and by what means they are most likely to do so successfully.* (Little and Singleton in Duda and Riley, 1990)

Learning in groups

Foreign/ second language classes or tutorials are usually highly interactive involving peer or group work and a range of different activities, particularly when compared to the teaching that takes place in most other subject areas. After all, language learners need constantly to practise their verbal skills, which means that learners are encouraged to speak out, to ask questions and express opinions and generally interact with members of the group. While individual differences have a bearing on how students learn effectively, either on their own or with the help of the tutor, there are other factors when learning in a group which can contribute to the individual's sense of achievement. For example, a group of predominantly older learners will function differently from one which is on average younger, though this is not to suggest that older learners learn less effectively than younger ones. Alternatively, some research into personality traits lends support to the view that outgoing, extrovert students are more successful language learners than the more inhibited, introverted. The composition of people with different personalities can affect the group dynamics of a language class to a considerable degree.

We all know from experience that some groups 'gel' better than others. An outsider walking into a foreign language class can sense the classroom atmosphere almost at once. The 'atmosphere' is something intangible and elusive, yet it is easily perceived as being either warm, friendly, informal, relaxed, lively and full of humour as opposed to indifferent, cool, uncooperative or simply dull and lifeless.

> Somehow my beginners students just sat there wanting to be spoon-fed all the time. It was really difficult to get them going. Last week I tried something different: I used icebreakers, followed by a quiz where they had to work in teams. It's surprising what difference these activities have made to the general atmosphere. (Part-time lecturer in Spanish)

The tutor in this example experienced what is common to many groups in the early stages of group development and that is, some learners are reluctant joiners precisely because of the demands a group can make. This can create tension between 'moving towards' and 'pulling away' which, if handled sensitively, is part of the initial integrating process. Thereafter, each group will, in due course, have its own characteristics and dynamic tension. Some merge into cohesive groups where people develop friendships which extend well beyond the teaching situation. This is more likely to happen when classes are held frequently, several times in the course of a month or even week.

At The Open University, on the other hand, where there are relatively few tutorials in the course of a year – indeed, tutors may never have face-to-face contact with some students – the key function of group tutorials is to develop autonomy in the individual learner and to support their independent study, while at the same time practising precisely those skills which are less easy accomplished alone, that is, speaking spontaneously with others in the language of learning. Here it is much less easy to foster lasting group dynamics. Nevertheless, by taking part in pair or small group work learners can, with the support of a skilful tutor, develop the confidence to 'let go', to make mistakes in front of others, to take the initiative and to experiment with new language structures and hence experience a sense of enjoyment and achievement.

Effective group teaching requires interpersonal, organisational and management skills which go beyond the teaching of the language. It means:

- keeping in check the excessively vocal learner and drawing out the quiet one, or not allowing one learner to dominate others;
- building on the strengths of individuals rather than pick on their weaknesses;
- allowing learners to view the tutor as an equal partner in the learning process and hence an integrated member of the group.

Here are some of the steps a tutor may take to strengthen group dynamics:

- making use of activities such as 'ice breakers', role plays and simulations, 'brainstorming' and 'buzz groups';
- planning problem-solving and task based approaches in pair or small group work;
- encouraging students to move around, so that they do not always sit together with the same person;
- setting time aside for free conversation;
- designing group projects to be undertaken outside the classroom;
- organising peer learning;
- setting up self-help groups;
- paying attention to seating arrangements, for example so that the tutor has frequent eye contact with the student who lacks self-confidence or sits next to a particularly vociferous student.
- remembering that outward signs of aggression are often signs of anxiety and stress, or personal problems a person may have which are not related to the learning situation.

These approaches allow most groups, though not all, to develop a cohesiveness and strength which binds differences into a harmonious unit. Jacques (1991) describes how some groups, irrespective of their individual differences, tend to develop their own code of ethics or sets of standards about what is and is not acceptable behaviour. Yet there are no hard and fast rules on how to solve difficult situations. Each one will have its own dynamics and sets of tensions. Most adults are good at handling each others' differences; they often support the tutor. After all, learners are social beings. Most learners are interested in each other as well as in the tutor and are concerned with relationships in a social context which may well extend beyond classroom walls.

References

Arthur L and F Beaton, 'Adult foreign language learners: motivation, attitudes and behaviours' in *Language Learning Journal,* 21: 31–36 (2000)

Duda R and P Riley (eds), *Learning styles* (Nancy: Presses Universitaires de Nancy, 1990)

Ellis R, *Understanding second language acquisition* (Oxford University Press, 1985)

Gardner R, *Social psychology and second language learning: the role of attitudes and motivation* (Edward Arnold, 1985)

Gardner R and W Lambert, *Attitudes and motivation in second language learning* (Massasuchetts: Rowley, Newbury House, 1972)

Hurd S, 'Distance language learners and learner support: beliefs, difficulties and use of strategies' in *Links and Letters,* 7: 61–80 (2000)

Jacques D, *Learning in groups* (Kogan Page, 1991)

McLaughlin B, *Theories of second language learning* (Edward Arnold, 1987)

Oxford R, *Language learning strategies. What every teacher should know* (New York: Newbury House Publishers, 1990)

Schrafnagl J and J Fage, *The good distance learner. An investigation into the background, learning experience and strategies of students in the London region studying L120 'Overture' in 1996* (The Open University Languages, Centre for Modern Languages, 1998)

Singleton D, *Language acquisition: the age factor* (Multilingual Matters, 1989)

Singleton D and Z Lengyel (eds), *The age factor in second language acquisiton* (Multilingual Matters, 1995)

Skehan P, *Individual differences in second language learning* (Edward Arnold, 1989)

PART 2

APPROACHES TO LANGUAGE TEACHING AND LEARNING

There are many adults whose previous experience of learning French, German or, indeed, English consisted largely of rote learning, coping with grammar tables and lists of irregular verbs, together with all the exceptions which make up a series of rules. Learning another language was for many a somewhat arduous task. Lessons were presented by tutors in a very formal manner. Much has changed since then. While language teaching was, at one time, determined by widely accepted tutor-led 'methods', the emphasis nowadays is on differentiated, learner-centred approaches and interactive learning in the context of communicative language teaching.

The task of the tutor is to create a learning environment suited to adult learning and, at the same time, support the requirements made by different educational institutions. The requirements stipulate that courses need to be described in terms of learning outcomes, which affect lesson planning and the use of resources. Chapter 5 looks at the historical development of language teaching methods and approaches, and analyses communicative language teaching in its contemporary setting. The current notion 'eclecticism with principles' is explored fully. Chapter 6 considers practical approaches to course design, lesson planning and the overall planning process, bearing differentiation in mind. The development of discrete and integrated skills such as speaking, listening, reading and writing together with aspects of teaching grammar or vocabulary are discussed in chapter 7. Chapter 8 looks critically at key concepts in relation to learner strategies and autonomy and considers how these fit into the practical context of classroom or tutorial teaching.

5

Approaches to language teaching

JANE WOODIN

This chapter considers some of the key developments in the history of language teaching during the twentieth century, in particular those which led to a shift of emphasis from **tutor-centred methods** to **learner-centred approaches**. These developments were influenced by changing perspectives in general learning theories in psychology, insights gained from research into second language and theories about the functions and purposes of language learning, and, above all, by advances made in educational technology. The intention, however, is not to explore these in detail, but in terms of their relevance to language teaching and learning today.

Grammar and translation: the early beginnings

The evolution of language teaching can be traced as far back as ancient Greece and Rome and the Middle Ages. John Amos Comenius (1592–1670), often referred to as the first modern educator, impressed many writers with his thoughts about language teaching and learning. Towards the end of the last century scholars made a determined effort to introduce modern languages (as opposed to Latin and Greek) into the university curriculum and to reform methods of language teaching. There were various radical and moderate movements which stimulated the debates at the time.

The quest for a good teaching method began as a response to dissatisfaction with the Grammar-Translation approach which originated from the teaching of Latin and ancient Greek and was transferred to the teaching of living languages in the nineteenth century. This approach was not based upon any particular educational or linguistic theory, but was adopted for the teaching of modern languages because this was the way classical languages had been taught. Grammatical accuracy was the ultimate aim and little, if any, emphasis was given to actually speaking the language. A Grammar-Translation method focused largely upon the translation of texts from the mother tongue into the target language and vice-versa. Grammar points were explained in the light of the examples given in the text (Richards & Rodgers, 1986). Translation as a tool for language learning is still used today, particularly with specialist language

49

learners in higher education, most commonly for the study of literary texts. In some cases it may also include other genres, such as journalistic or technical texts.

In the latter half of the nineteenth century increased travel between countries led to methods which incorporated greater focus on speaking. One such example is the Direct Method which required that learning the foreign language should take place 'naturally'. This method became very popular with private language schools (the Berlitz Method, for example, is directly related to the Direct Method) although there were problems associated with such a prescriptive method. References to English or the mother tongue were banished altogether and learners were denied the individual, creative aspect of language learning. Nevertheless, some of these techniques were, at the time, adopted into secondary school language teaching (Richards and Rogers, 1986).

Behaviourism and language teaching methods

Throughout the course of the twentieth century various popular methods emerged: the Oral Method, the Reading Method, the Situational or Structural Method, and so on. The impact of technology on language teaching approaches during the 1960s and early 1970s, such as the reel-to-reel tape recorder and the language laboratory, represented major milestones in the history of language teaching. The so-called audiovisual method, which used pictures of film strips together with sound, and the audiolingual method, based on sound only, were strongly influenced by behaviourist principles.

Behaviourism is one of the major learning theories in psychology. It was developed by Skinner (1957) in relation to first language acquisition and then applied during the 1960s to second language acquisition and the audiolingual and audiovisual methods. According to this theory, language learning is like any other kind of learning in that it involves **habit formation**. Habits are formed when learners respond to stimuli in the environment and subsequently have their responses reinforced so that they are remembered (Ellis, 2000). The **stimulus–response–reinforcement** model influenced foreign language teaching at a time when technology was available for wide-scale use in the classroom and through language laboratories. Using a tape recorder, language tutors could play and replay recordings from a tape, asking learners to repeat what they had heard. 'Drilling' involving particular speech patterns became one of its hallmarks. Learners would listen, repeat and receive positive or negative feedback until satisfactory progress had been made. Often substitutions were made to the drilling, such as a change of subject, to illustrate the change of verb, for example:

> Model: I am about to go shopping
>
> Stimulus: He......
>
> Response: He is about to go shopping
>
> Stimulus: We..... etc.

These kinds of pattern drills were not linked to functional purposes but aimed to practise specific structures or sentences which, though grammatically correct, were usually meaningless to the learner. The tutor played a very central role controlling the stimulus and providing reinforcement. The use of machinery favoured mechanistic responses which fitted perfectly with theories of conditioning. Audiolingual and/or audiovisual language teaching methods placed emphasis on speaking the language which was often presented in specific situations around sequential grammar steps. The use of audio tapes offered the learner a variety of voices instead of just the tutor's in the classroom. In many cases native speakers of the foreign language would be recorded onto the tape. These developments led in turn to integrated multi-media foreign language courses – involving television, audio tapes and text books – such as those pioneered by the BBC in the early 1970s.

Behaviourists approaches to language learning suffered from Chomsky's now famous attack on Skinner and behaviourism (1959) (see chapter 3) and a growing view that language teaching should be based more on the functional ability to communicate rather than on knowledge of structures. However, even today many language tutors still use at least some aspects of behaviourism; some like to use cues to provoke responses or, for example, pattern drills for warming-up chorus work purposes; others seek to reinforce, even reward and 'punish' with comments and feedback from time to time.

Cognitivism

Cognitive theories of learning are concerned with the way in which people learn as individuals – rather than within groups (see chapter 3). Influenced by psycholinguistics, a cognitive approach supports the thesis that learning in general and language learning in particular are internal, mental operations controlled by the individual. Cognitivism has influenced language teaching and learning in a number of ways. Cognitive approaches allow for a two–way learning process; the individual can have an impact on the environment just as the environment can have an impact on the individual. Individual differences in learners are taken into account; the focus is on the learners and helping them to learn in the way that best suits each individual.

The role of the tutor in a cognitive approach is to facilitate learning, as a **guide on the side**. One of the significant contributions of cognitivism has been to place a stronger emphasis upon the need to take into account individual differences in learning needs and styles (see chapter 4). However, the tutor still retains responsibility for ensuring learning takes place, and adapting the teaching to the needs of the learners. According to Chastain (1976):

> *(The role of the tutor is) to organise the material presented in such a manner that what is learned will be meaningful to the learner. To do this he is obliged to consider the student's existing cognitive structure.....His next obligation is to try to couch the material in such a fashion that learners can relate the content to their existing fund of knowledge.*

In the practical world of language teaching many techniques are based on cognitivism such as learning through **problem-solving** and the **discovery** of certain grammatical components or words learners find in texts. Information gap exercises, too, are based on the principles underlying cognitivism, as are many other activities which allow learners to experiment with the new language and thereby sort out many complexities of the language for themselves and according to their own needs.

Humanistic approaches

Language learning approaches which are influenced by humanism have their basis in the belief that language learning is also about developing the learner as a person, taking into account her or his emotional needs. These approaches draw upon counselling theories and can be seen as a reaction against the mechanistic approaches of behaviourism. Humanistic approaches, developed in the 1970s and 1980s, had a considerable impact on adult education in general as well as on EFL (English as a Foreign Language) in particular. For example, the Total Physical Response approach (TPR), developed by Asher (1966), gave learners the choice not to participate until they were ready to do so. Others, such as Suggestopedia (see Lozanov 1978), ensured learners were relaxed through playing baroque music, before any language learning began. Clearly, humanistic approaches to language learning still play an important part in respecting the individual needs of each learner, and also in contributing to the acceptance of the importance of learner's **emotions in the learning process**. It is now widely accepted that if learners are feeling comfortable and relaxed, they will find it easier to learn. This idea was also popularised by Krashen (1982) as the affective filter hypothesis: if learners' affective filter is up (i.e. if they are not relaxed), then they will find it more difficult to learn (see chapter 3).

Language tutors nowadays use a number of activities which are based on humanistic approaches and which are designed to motivate learners, to develop group dynamics and group interaction and generally promote trust by breaking down as many barriers to learning as possible: ice breakers, songs, communicative games and role plays are examples of such activities.

All the developments mentioned above have had some influence upon the shift away from tutor-centred language teaching to student-centred language learning. To sum up:

- Audiolingual and audiovisual methods, though still tutor-centred and grammar-focused, contributed to a greater emphasis on the spoken language and increase in the use of technology.

- Cognitive learning theories have influenced language learning through models of information-processing and through their focus upon individual differences between learners.

- Humanistic learning theories have influenced language learning through their focus upon affective factors involved in learning.

The communicative approach

Other factors shaped current approaches to foreign/second language learning. In the early 1970s, Richterich (1977) and Trim (1980) and others involved in the Council of Europe's Modern Languages Project pioneered a learner-centred approach for all those involved in teaching foreign/second languages on a European-wide basis. Their seminal approach, which broke the mould of all preceding, mainly behaviourist approaches, stunned the language teaching profession at the time. It is a system which credits different levels of learner achievement in relation to what the learner has to do in the target language (e.g. greeting someone, complaining about something, expressing opinions).

A theory of language as communication, however, was first proposed by Hymes (1972) – who used the term **communicative competence** – and later developed by Canale & Swain (1980). It provided a catalyst for new approaches to teaching and learning languages.

The communicative approach to language teaching took as its basic premise the fact that the main purpose of language was communication. According to Hymes, someone who acquires communicative competence has both **knowledge** of and **ability** to use language with respect to:

1. *whether (and to what degree) something is formally possible;*

2. *whether (and to what degree) something is feasible in virtue of the means of implementation available;*

3. *whether (and to what degree) something is appropriate (adequate, happy, successful) in relation to a context in which it is used and evaluated;*

4. *whether (and to what degree) something is in fact done, actually performed, and what its doing entails.* (Hymes, 1972)

Some of the basic beliefs which underpin the communicative approach are:

- language is a system for the expression of meaning;
- the primary function of language centres around interaction and communication;
- the structure of language reflects its functional and communicative uses;
- the primary units of language are not merely its grammatical and structural features but categories of functional and communicative meaning as exemplified in discourse.

Some typical features of a communicative language class are:

- dialogues centred around communicative functions which are not normally memorised;
- contextualisation as a basic premise;
- effective communication;
- emphasis on the **process** of communicating;

- sequencing as determined by any consideration of content, function or meaning which maintains interest;
- language which is created by the individual, often through trial and error;
- fluency and acceptable language as the primary goal: accuracy is judged not in the abstract but in context.

(Adapted from Finocchiaro & Brumfit, 1983)

The communicative approach is far less prescriptive than many of the preceding methods. There is room for translation, focus on structures, drilling, toleration of errors, but all within a basic focus on knowledge and use of language for communication. It influenced language learning and teaching methods initially through the functional-notional approach (Wilkins, 1976) which placed major emphasis upon organising learning in accordance with what people want to accomplish through speech. Examples of functions of language include inviting, persuading and apologising. Notional categories describe larger systems of meanings, such as time, frequency, location. A functional-notional approach attempts to take a more learner-centred approach to language learning, taking the requirements of the learner as the basis for categorising language.

Learners, therefore, need to be actively involved in the classroom in order to practise communication in genuine and meaningful interaction. For example, the tutor cannot encourage learners to communicate if he or she spends most of the time explaining grammar rules to the learners. Similarly, the tutor cannot anticipate exactly what learners will say when communicating with each other. The balance of power is thus shifted, and the tutor must take on a different role from that of the **sage on the stage**, adopting a role more akin to that of **the guide on the side**, a manager of learning, helping learners to communicate in the target language. The communicative approach has therefore contributed significantly to this shift away from the tutor as expert fountain of knowledge.

The communicative approach is currently by far the most widely accepted approach to language teaching and learning, particularly where the aim of language learning relates to communication with native speakers (as opposed to, for example, language learning for academic reading purposes). No one particular way of organising teaching is prescribed; there is scope for the tutor to be inventive and to encourage creativity with the language. The use of authentic materials and activities, often in the form of tasks, is encouraged, in order to ensure that the language class is as relevant as possible to learners.

From the 1970s onwards there is a shift from the method concept to approaches which support learning, as the diagram opposite illustrates:

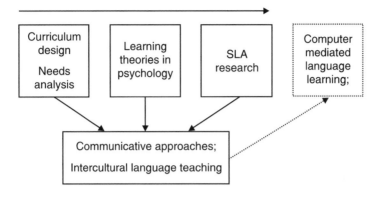

Figure 1

Underlying principles

Within a broadly communicative approach there is plenty of scope for tutors to make their own decisions with regard to teaching and learning. These decisions need to be based on principles; tutors need to be able to justify to themselves, to their learners and to others why certain decisions are taken. One underlying principle for communicative language teaching and learning is the need to balance both **form-based focus** (a focus upon the structure of the language and the way it works) and **meaning-based focus** (a focus on language use in real contexts, and upon the importance of communicating one's message). For example, a learner might say *J'ai arrivé à trois heures (I arrived at three o'clock)*. If the focus of the activity is on form, then the tutor would elicit the grammatically correct form *Je suis arrivé(e) à trois heures*. However, if the focus of the activity is upon meaning, then the tutor might not bother to correct the grammatical error, as it is clear what the learner means.

Many theorists and practitioners have developed underlying principles within the communicative approach. Omaggio Hadley (1993), for example, identifies five guiding principles for organising and planning instruction in a second language which seem particularly helpful:

1. *Opportunities must be provided for students to practise using the target language in a range of contexts likely to be encountered in the target culture.*

2. *Opportunities should be provided for students to practise carrying out a range of functions (tasks) likely to be necessary in dealing with others in the target culture.*

3. *The development of accuracy should be encouraged in proficiency-oriented instruction. As learners learn language, various forms of instruction and evaluative feedback can be useful in facilitating the progression of their skills towards more precise and coherent language use.*

4. *Instruction should be more responsive to the affective as well as the cognitive needs of students, and their different personalities, preferences, and learning styles should be taken into account.*

5. *Cultural understanding must be promoted in various ways so that students are sensitive to other cultures and prepared to live more harmoniously in the target–language community.*

A broadly communicative approach is likely to remain with language teaching and learning for as long as we continue to communicate in different languages across cultures. More recent developments have generally tended to evolve not as alternatives to communicative language teaching, but as alternatives **within** communicative language teaching. For example, models of **intercultural communicative competence** have been developed which still take into account the fundamental need for a communicative approach, but with the incorporation of cultural elements of language learning which are inextricably linked to language and so cannot be ignored (for example, Kramsch, 1993; Byram, 1997.) Intercultural approaches to language learning have become particularly prominent at a point in history when global communication has been moving at a very fast pace, where cultures are interacting at all levels in society and where there are real concerns for a need for respect of cultural difference.

Taking account of developments in communicative language teaching inevitably makes the tutor's task more complex because learners bring experience and beliefs to their learning, and each class will have its own unique balance of learning styles and needs. **Eclecticism with principles** is an approach which will allow for tutors and learners to be involved in the process of ensuring that learning is effective, relevant and appropriate (Richards, 1998, Podromou, 1992). Underlying principles such as those developed by Omaggio (1993) may be particularly useful for tutors starting out in language teaching. Those with a fair amount of experience may wish to look more deeply into the process and incorporate both their own and their learners' experiences and values. In any case, successful approaches to language learning and teaching in today's learner-centred environment require both learners' and tutors' previous experiences to be taken into account, as well as commitment on the part of all involved to engage in the process of improving learning. To this end, it can be useful for tutors to ask themselves questions such as:

- On what principles do I base my approach to teaching and learning?
- How can I ensure that my approach to teaching and learning is relevant and effective?

References

Asher J , 'The total physical response to second language learning' in *Modern Language Journal* 53:133–9 (1966)

Brown H Douglas, *Teaching by principles* (Prentice Hall, 1994)

Byram M, *Teaching and assessing intercultural communicative competence* (Multilingual Matters, 1997)

Canale M and M Swain, 'Theoretical bases of communicative approaches to language teaching and testing' in *Applied Linguistics*, 1 (1): 1–47 (1980)

Chastain K, *Developing second language skills* (New York: Rand McNally, 1976)

Chomsky N, Review of Skinner (1957) in *Language*, 35: 26–58 (1959)

Ellis R, *Second language acquisition,* fourth impression (Oxford University Press, 2000)

Finocchario M and C Brumfit, *The functional–notional approach: from theory to practice* (OUP, 1983)

Hymes D, 'On communicative competence' in Pride J B and J Holmes (eds), *Sociolinguistics:* 269–93 (Penguin, 1972)

Kramsch C, *Context and culture in language teaching* (OUP, 1993)

Krashen S, *Principles and practice in second language acquisition* (Pergamon, 1982)

Lewis M, *The lexical approach* (LTP, 1993)

Lozanov G, *Suggestology and outlines of suggestopody* (New York: Gordon and Breach, 1978)

McLaughlin B, *Theories of second language learning* (Arnold,1987)

Omaggio Hadley A, *Teaching language in context* (Boston: Heinle and Heinle, 1993)

Richards Jack C and T S Rodgers, *Approaches and methods in language teaching* (CUP, 1986)

Richterich R and J Chancerel, *Identifying the needs of adults learning a foreign language* (Pergamon Press on behalf of the Council of Europe, 1977)

Skinner B F, *Verbal behaviour* (New York: Appleton–Century–Crofts, 1957)

Trim J, Developments of a Unit Credit Scheme in Language Learning (Strasbourg: Council of Europe, 1980)

Van Ek J and L G Alexander, *Threshold Level English* (Pergamon, 1980)

Wilkins D A, *Notional syllabuses* (Oxford University Press, 1976)

6

The planning process

JANE WOODIN

All language tutors need to plan classes and design activities within the framework of a syllabus. Many, particularly those teaching minority languages, have to devise their own syllabus and assessment guidelines which are part of a language department's overall curriculum. The planning process, therefore, usually requires consideration of a number of different, sometimes conflicting factors. These include the institutional teaching and learning strategies; the curriculum being followed; the aims of a language course; its intended learning outcomes and assessment requirements.

Planning occurs at all levels of the teaching and learning process, and each level will influence other levels. Planning at institutional level is often reflected in mission statements and overall teaching and learning strategies. These embody the overarching approach into which different programme specifications will need to fit. They cover the general aims and intended learning outcomes of the languages programme. From this, syllabuses for different courses are developed, each fulfilling part of the requirements of the programme specification (see chapter 16). Whatever the constraints upon the planning process, each level will inform and influence other levels of planning; whatever planning occurs before the start of the course will in turn be influenced by the needs, learning styles and expectations of the learners. The aim of this chapter is to look at some of these aspects in more detail. It will cover:

- considerations when planning courses;
- learning outcomes, aims and objectives;
- planning activities for different purposes;
- the use of resources to support language learning.

Considerations when planning a course

Organising teaching is really about designing learning and so is one of the most important activities of a language tutor, irrespective of the kind of institution in which such learning takes place. Teaching, according to D'Andrea (in Fry et al, 1999) involves helping learners to know something they do not already know, and it

58

constitutes a process of change. These intentions are most often implicit or inferred. The conscious planning of teaching and learning makes these intentions explicit and can improve the learning experience.

Planning learning involves far more than simply planning each teaching session; it requires an integrated approach to all aspects of learning. Consultation with all those affected by its outcome, including learners at varying stages of the process, will ensure that planning remains relevant and appropriate in terms of content, process and level. Some considerations are:

- institutional policy/mission statement;
- type of course (e.g. intensive, distance, for specific purposes);
- stated learning outcomes;
- modes of assessment;
- duration of course;
- equal opportunities policies;
- number of study hours a week;
- amount of tutor-learner contact time versus independent study time;
- resources available to tutors and learners;
- involvement of tutors/learners in decision-making process;
- learning and teaching contexts.

At this stage it may be helpful to clarify terms such as the **curriculum** and the **syllabus.** Unfortunately, both are defined in many different ways. Broadly speaking, however, the curriculum refers to a set of principles that govern, or explain, programme areas. With reference to language teaching a curriculum description will include definitions of the various linguistic levels of courses (the meaning of intermediate, advanced, etc), the selection of content and strategies, the evaluation of learner progress in the light of stated learning outcomes, and may also include the link between various language courses and other courses offered within the same institution.

The term syllabus, on the other hand, tends to be used in relation to a particular course or module (which fits into an overall curriculum). A syllabus, or course design, will therefore be more specific and include themes or topics to be covered, language functions and grammatical components, skills to be developed, the sequencing of learning outcomes and modes of assessments. Over the years, the design of a syllabus or language course has differed according to the prevailing school of thought at the time. For example, a structural syllabus generally covers a list of grammatical components which are organised into a perceived order of complexities and importance. The functional-notional syllabus within a communicative approach organises learning in terms of functional needs and is expressed in terms of apologising to someone, greeting someone, expressing opinions etc. In some cases, learners are able to negotiate the syllabus with their tutor in advance of the course. In open and distance learning, however, it is the syllabus design which determines the writing of the course books and the development of other course materials in relation to anticipated learning outcomes.

Learning outcomes, aims and objectives

Most formal learning statements make reference to **intended learning outcomes**, course **aims** and **objectives.** These three terms are often used interchangeably, but they are in fact quite different. Recent years have seen the growing tendency to focus upon learning outcomes; they describe learning in terms of what the learner will actually be able to **do** by the end of the course, shifting the emphasis from what will be taught to what will be learnt. Two outcomes of a practically-oriented language course might therefore be:

By the end of the course the learners will be able to:

- identify the main areas of similarity and difference between the target language culture and the mother tongue culture;
- converse in the target language at near-normal speed on a variety of topics.

Learning outcomes of courses are generally measured through assessment. The two examples given here could be measured through an essay in the target language or mother tongue, and a discussion on a topic chosen by the tutor respectively (see Part 4 on assessment). Learning outcomes can be specified in many terms, some of which are: knowledge and understanding, intellectual/cognitive skills, practical skills, transferable skills/key skills, personal skills and social skills.

Aims are often not measurable in the way that learning outcomes are. They are broad and describe aspects of learning in general terms. Aims are sometimes also concerned with learners' personal development. The aims of the same language course might therefore be to:

- increase awareness of the target language culture;
- develop learners' confidence in speaking spontaneously.

Statements of objectives are generally more specific than aims although the two concepts are often used together. Such statements tend to describe learning from the point of view of the tutor. The objectives of the language course might be:

- to explain the main differences and similarities between the target language culture and the mother tongue culture;
- to provide learners with opportunities for speaking in the target language on a variety of topics.

Learning outcomes place the focus upon the learners, rather than the tutor, and what they will be able to do by the end of the specified time. Most language learning nowadays is undertaken within a broadly communicative framework. Learning aims and outcomes, therefore, are likely to involve some kind of link with being able to use the target language in authentic or 'real life' situations.

What to consider

In almost all cases (possibly with the exception of some conversation classes and some adult education classes), teaching sessions are planned within the structure of a syllabus. Often a scheme of work or study guide will be produced, outlining the course content in terms of a comprehensive timetable, together with materials, activities and assessment dates. A quick glance at the scheme of work can give the tutor an overview of the progression of the learning; it also helps tutors to keep teaching content on track.

It is never easy to plan teaching sessions in detail a long way in advance. It is more than likely that all tutors at some point find themselves asking questions such as:

- What aspects of learning do I consider in the choice of teaching activities?
- Should I focus more on fluency or more on accuracy?
- Should I spend more time helping learners to learn?
- How can I ensure that all learners, even those with difficulties, have a sense of achievement at the end of the lesson?

Not even the most experienced tutor can anticipate all the difficulties or questions that might arise. A rigid plan with no room for change will probably not succeed; a balance between purpose and flexibility is required. Those new to language teaching, according to Arthur (1999), often look for a kind of template, a **model lesson**, where activities are sequenced in an almost mechanical way, according to behaviourist principles, which they can adapt. Communicative language teaching approaches, however, are far more eclectic (see chapter 5); tutors can structure lessons or tutorials in many different ways according to the needs of the learners and individual circumstances. Nevertheless, most would agree that a good lesson or tutorial would normally include most, if not all, of the following elements:

- a sound structure based on careful planning;
- transparent learning outcomes in relation to the syllabus;
- opportunities for each learner to speak the target language;
- some form of group or pair work;
- effective pacing and sequencing of activities;
- links to preceding and subsequent lessons;
- transfer of language learned from the teaching material to different contexts and to the 'real' world.

Further considerations include:

- strategies from early on in the course which will enable the learner to use the language effectively without tutor support;
- the desire for learners to be creative in the target language and to be able to respond to spontaneous utterances;
- the opportunity to ask questions; to 'let go' and make mistakes; to share experiences, skills and knowledge with others.   (Arthur, 1999)

A task-based approach

One such approach to planning classes is a task-based approach. Tasks are particularly useful in a communicative language class, as they can replicate authentic activities, they give a purpose to an activity and they allow for an authentic use of language. Nunan (1989) considers:

> ... the communicative task as a piece of classroom work which involves learners in comprehending, manipulating, producing or interacting in the target language while their attention is principally focused on meaning rather than form. The task should also have a sense of completeness, being able to stand alone as a communicative act in its own right.

A class based upon tasks might have a structure like this, proposed by Willis (1996):

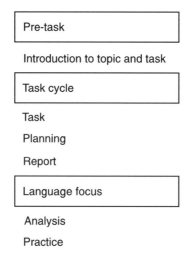

> Pre-task

Introduction to topic and task

> Task cycle

Task

Planning

Report

> Language focus

Analysis

Practice

Figure 1

Skehan (1998), drawing on the work of others, summarises a task as having the following characteristics:

- meaning is primary;
- there is some communication problem to solve;
- there is some sort of relationship to comparable real-world activities;
- task completion has some priority;
- the assessment of the task is in terms of outcome.

> For example, a particular task-based activity might be:
>
> Planning a social outing for about 20 members of a small company.
>
> For a group of adults this is a meaningful task. The task has should be designed in such a way that learners have to find out pieces of information concerning the outing. There are various items of publicity materials in spoken or written form in which such information can be found. Learners therefore have to cope with a range of communication skills; furthermore, the use of authentic materials ensures some sort of relationship with the real world. A time limit is set for the completion of the task and assessment is related to given learning outcomes.

Clearly, task-based classes are communicative in that the learner has to accomplish the task using the target language. The tutor necessarily takes on the role of **guide on the side**, supporting learners by helping them to prepare for the task, do it, analyse the task after completion and focus on the language used during the task. Whether or not a class plan follows rigidly the task-based structure proposed above, it will normally require a balance between meaning- and form-based activities (see chapter 5).

Working with topics

Another common pattern for language classes, particularly at advanced levels, is a topic-based lesson. Depending upon institution, curriculum, syllabus or other factors, a topic-based lesson might be more content-based than task-based. It might also precede a task-based lesson or activity.

Activities revolve around the chosen topic.

> For example, a teaching session based on the topic of smoking might look like this:
>
> 1   Tutor asks who smokes, why they smoke, and the same of those who don't smoke.
>
> 2   Learners discuss in pairs the advantages and disadvantages of smoking and list them.
>
> 3   Learners listen to a collection of recordings of other people talking about smoking and compare their lists with those mentioned on the recording.
>
> 4   In small groups, learners prioritise the statements from both points of view, giving their opinion of the importance of each statement. The tutor then facilitates inter-group discussions, particularly in areas where priorities are different.

The order of these activities could be changed, or completely different activities used. However, the main focus of a topic-based class remains the topic itself, with activities revolving around the main theme. An example of a task which could follow this topic-based class could be an invitation to a radio talk show where students would have to argue in favour or against smoking in public places. Some members of the group would play the role of judges and need to decide by the end of the programme whether to allow smoking in certain public places.

Meaning and form-based activities

Activities which focus upon meaning are communicative in nature and include, for example, finding out train times, arranging to go out with someone, discussing the pros and cons of a new transport system, or finding out personal information from your partner. These can be partially guided (for example, using a sheet with pre-written questions to ask a partner) or less guided (for example, *'Find three things you have in common with your partner'*). Activities based upon form are, for example, translating certain phrases, conjugating verbs, filling in blanks (cloze activities), or correcting one's own written work. Both these types of activities have their uses; the ultimate outcome, however, is for learners to be able to use the language in real-life.

The ratio between form-based and meaning-based instruction is likely to differ depending upon the kind of course learners are following. For example, in a specialist language department in a university, grammar or translation classes and spoken language classes are taught separately from each other. In a tutorial of Open University learners, one might well find that the learners have had to understand grammar points embedded in the course materials and undertake related course activities independently of the tutor and in advance of the tutorial. Face-to-face contact time is therefore largely a chance to clarify any queries and practise using the language.

Learning for progression

Planning also needs to take into account learner progression and development. This requires planning activities which are at the right level for learners and which develop their proficiency in the language. The learning spiral below shows how new language items are constantly added to the learner's existing knowledge base of familiar language.

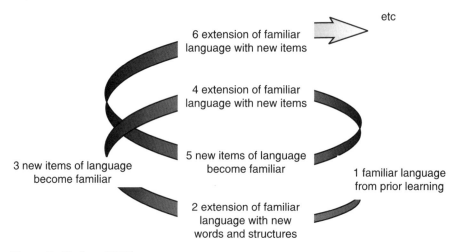

Figure 2: (Arthur, 1999)

Progression does not always feel as obvious to the learner as it might be to the tutor; indeed, progression can involve slipping backwards as well as forwards. If learners can see their improvements clearly, they will remain motivated. Feedback and evaluation from learners themselves can be incorporated in the planning of a course. One way in which this can be undertaken is through the use of checklists which can serve as ongoing self-assessment. Below is an example of a checklist which is used for a three-week phase of a Spanish lower intermediate course:

Spanish Stage 2 Summary Sheets.

Weeks 5–8 Talking about things that happened.

During this period you will have learnt the following (both spoken and written). When you go over this checklist, put a tick by the items you feel confident about, by those you are not sure of, and an X by the ones you don't know. This will help you to spend time on the items you need to practise.

Phrases	Confident	Not sure	Don't know
• talk about what you did	○	○	○
• ask what others did in the past	○	○	○
• talk about what others did in the past	○	○	○
• talk about what you had done at a given point in time	○	○	○
• ask what others had done	○	○	○
• talk about what others had done	○	○	○
• talk about what you used to do	○	○	○
• ask what others used to do	○	○	○
• talk about what others used to do	○	○	○
• talk about what you were like	○	○	○
• ask what others were like	○	○	○
• say what others were like	○	○	○

And of course you must be able to understand what people are saying to you!

Vocabulary:

Grammar:

Source: University of Sheffield, Spanish Stage 2, Summary sheet

Learners can also be involved in the process through evaluation of courses or parts of courses; feedback from these can then be incorporated into the planning of the rest of the course.

Evaluation is an essential part of the planning process. The tutor needs to step back regularly and reflect on how much learning has been achieved. Depending on the language level of the class, evaluation of learning can be undertaken by tutor and learners together. It can take a number of forms, such as an activity designed to evaluate learning, a short test, or even a team game. The tutor needs to be clear that the purpose of the activity is to evaluate learning. Involvement of learners in this process is also likely to help increase awareness of their own learning processes. They may even make recommendations for how they would like their learning to be organised – this can only be a positive thing from the point of view of the tutor.

Differentiation

No matter how carefully a syllabus or teaching session is planned, tutors need to be able to cope with unexpected difficulties or interruptions. In the classroom, learners, either individually or even as a group, may be unable to cope with given tasks; they may become demotivated or disengage from the learning process. In addition, they may respond with varying degrees of confidence and success. Acknowledging these differences is fundamental to the learning and teaching process. It is the skill of the tutor to be able to respond and make decisions there and then about whether to break off an activity and to do something entirely different, or perhaps tackle the same activity again, this time from a different angle.

Although it may not be possible to anticipate exactly which problems might occur, spending a little time considering potential difficulties learners may experience can help to ease the process. Some possible solutions to the difficulties could be a) to consider if there are other aspects in the scheme of work which can be covered more quickly than planned or to ask learners to undertake some of the planned activities independently; b) if the questions are relevant to the whole group, to abandon part of the class plan in favour of responding to the questions, or to take note of the questions and deal with them in a future class; c) either to accept that the whole plan cannot be completed, or to organise learners into study groups which work together and help each other out.

Every tutor will agree that not only do individuals differ within a group, but each group is in itself unique: in its overall atmosphere, for example, or in the way that the learners interact (or don't) with each other or with the tutor (see chapter 4). The need for an approach which caters for the requirements of all learners becomes all the more apparent when the focus moves away from the tutor to the learner. New technologies have also signalled a shift away from the traditional face-to-face contact of the classroom to distance learning, and a greater emphasis on independent and collaborative learning. Learners now have more opportunities for learning in ways which suit them.

The change in the term from **mixed ability** teaching to **differentiation** has been influenced by developments in psychology and learning theories. Mixed ability by its very definition tends to focus on the idea that some people have ability, whilst others do not. Differentiation does not necessarily polarise into more able and less able, but recognises differing needs and styles. Convery & Doyle (1993) state that whilst mixed ability teaching is more concerned with student management for teaching purposes, differentiation places the emphasis on the requirements of individual learners:

Differentiation ....is the entitlement of every learner to have his or her individual needs and abilities catered for, and the teacher's responsibility to find effective ways of managing those needs and abilities and to match them to appropriate teaching and learning styles.

Podromou makes the point that *'we constantly slip into the habit of thinking about (learners) in terms of their weaknesses rather than their strengths'* (1992). Certainly, thinking in terms of abilities emphasises this. However, if what actually works for learners can be emphasised through differentiation, then there is more chance that all learners will benefit. The tutor has a pivotal role in helping learners find the most effective way to learn and develop their potential. Planning for this will require tutors to know their learners, their learning styles and their needs, and organise learning to take account of them. By focusing more closely upon the learner, tutors find that they naturally plan for learner involvement in the class. Two common ways of differentiating are by group and by task.

Differentiation by group

One solution, if there are large numbers of learners at the same level of proficiency, is to place those learners with the same preferred learning style together. Thus learners can learn in the way that suits them most of the time. The question arises, however, as to whether this is in fact desirable even when it is practicable. One cannot be sure that reinforcing only one way of learning is in fact of most use to learners in the long run. Might it be better to expose them to other styles as well, in the hope that they might broaden their preferences or at least develop a tolerance of others' ways? Or is refusing to place learners in groups with similar learning styles a denial of their right to learn in their preferred way? In actual fact, most of the time it is impracticable to group learners in terms of their preferred learning styles, but it can still be very valuable to raise these issues for discussion with learners.

Differentiation by groups can also occur within one larger group. Small groups can be formed either on the basis of similar needs, or differing needs. Groups with similar needs can work together on similar activities at a similar pace, or groups with differing needs can support each other working through activities. In the latter case in particular, it is important to ensure that all members of the group benefit. Those learners who take on the role of helping their colleagues will also need to benefit. Two ways in which they might benefit from their role are:

- Through helping others learn, learners can themselves become more aware of the areas they were unsure of in their own minds and therefore be able to ask for clarification.

- They may also become more aware of their own learning styles and strategies through working with others. This can be useful in developing one's own autonomy.

Clearly, there are benefits to helping others learn. However, the tutor needs to keep an eye on collaborative work, to ensure that all members of the collaboration are benefiting.

Differentiation by task

Identifying exactly what learning is essential for all learners can allow for freedom to undertake follow-up activities which are relevant to individual needs. Learners can be given **core activities** which all members undertake; follow-up **branching activities** can then be organised which learners choose together with their tutor according to their needs (Ainslie, 1994).

Branching activities can be differentiated according to a number of criteria; for example, by task, by material, by interest, by length of activity or by skill. One such example might be a task that involves recounting an incident which happened. Core activities could involve listening to someone recount an incident and answering questions on it, discussing together the kinds of phrases required for telling such a story, and then telling each other about something similar which happened to them. Differentiation can occur in a variety of ways, some of which include the following:

- during the core activity, the tutor can vary the type of question according to the learner; for example, a factual, closed question is easier to answer than one such as *Why do you think this happened?* which requires the learner to interpret and give an opinion;

- some learners can be given vocabulary to help them with comprehension of the recording;

- learners who find this activity more difficult, perhaps through lack of vocabulary, can be required to fill in a grid asking them for specific factual information, such as *Who? When? Where? What happened?*

- some learners can undertake a role play, taking on the role of the characters in a recorded incident. Others, who need more of a challenge, can be given a few guidelines to make up their own incident, requiring them to be more creative with the language;

- learners who wish to have more writing practice can try summarising the story in their own words (it may be more appropriate to undertake this in independent study time rather than during the class).

Organisation of activities for differentiation does require a little more time, but the amount of extra time needed to differentiate effectively is often minimal. Most of the examples given above can be organised either instantly or with little more than a few minutes' preparation. Ensuring that all learners' needs are met in this way can help success and motivation.

Planning the use of resources

Today's language tutor may well find the number of resources available a little overwhelming. A glance down the list below illustrates this. With so many resources, how does one choose between them? Even tutors with few resources over and above a textbook may well find that learners have access to a number of resources at home, such as cassette players or computers with CD-ROM drives and internet access. Tutors can also take advantage of these resources even though they may not be available to them during the tutor-learner contact time. Some of the resources currently available to language learners are:

- Realia (Objects such as labels on packets, train tickets, maps, etc.)
- Coursebooks
- Audio/video cassettes
- World-Wide-Web resources
- E-mail
- Satellite TV and video recorders
- Language laboratories
- Visual aids (e.g. flashcards, transparencies, pictures etc.)
- Other tutors
- Other learners
- Native speakers from outside the class

Some of these resources are more suited to one learning environment than another. E-mail, for example, is far more suited to open and distance learning (ODL) than to classroom use, but coursebooks or World-Wide-Web resources could be useful for either.

Choosing authentic materials

Not all tutors have access to all of these resources. In any case, many tutors supplement resources and teaching aid with their own reading texts such as newspaper articles or sections of prose – texts which are termed 'authentic'. Basically, authentic materials are materials in the target language which are designed for native speakers of that language rather than created specifically for the second language learning market. McGarry (1995) notes that the use of authentic texts in the classroom can contribute to two main areas of concern for the tutor:

  (a) *the matching of language learning opportunities to the needs and interests of individual students;*
  (b) *the creation of the conditions under which students can most successfully exploit these opportunities.*

Examples include newspapers, magazines, brochures, TV and radio programmes. The language used in authentic materials is not graded for ease of learners' comprehension; however, becoming familiar with authentic materials from an early stage is an important part of preparing learners for encountering and using the target language outside the classroom. The fact that much of the language will be beyond them will give them the opportunity to develop the important skills of guessing and trying to work out meaning from context. Authentic materials can work for complete beginners, as long as the task they are given is suitable for their level. Some examples of language learning activities using authentic texts for beginners are:

- working out the score of a televised football match from listening to the commentary;
- listening out for family relations and occupations of participants on game shows;
- looking for the best hotel in a holiday brochure;
- working out the weather forecast.

For more advanced students, some activities might include:

- identifying the main themes covered on the front page of a newspaper;
- comparing football coverage in a UK paper with one from the target language;
- summarising the main points from an article;
- matching each person's viewpoint from a TV round table discussion;
- identifying the selling points of advertisements;
- summarising a radio news bulletin;
- using points put forward in a magazine article as a basis for debate.

Sometimes the problem is not a lack of materials but the fact that there are so many good resources available that it is difficult to decide which to use. Tutors can find they have to make the choice between a well-produced TV programme and an attractive magazine article, both of which cover the topic and language relevant to the learners. These choices are never easy to make, and there need to be clear criteria for selection. Two questions need to be asked: *'What will the learners be getting out of this?'* and *'How is it helping them to progress?'* Keeping these questions central to the decision-making process will ensure that choices are made which are commensurate with the learning aims and outcomes. Highly attractive materials are no use if they do not help to take the learners closer to the agreed outcomes.

Some issues for consideration when choosing materials are:

- Approach: What beliefs and values about language teaching and learning are demonstrated in this material?
- Content: What content does it cover? Is it compatible with the content which my learners need?
- Layout: Is it clearly and attractively laid out and easy to follow?
- Activities: What activities can be developed using this material? Are they appropriate to the type of syllabus?

- Progression: Is progression of learning catered for in these materials? Can they be adapted to help the learners progress?
- Authenticity: Are the activities meaningful and of the type one might have to undertake in real life? Are they culturally authentic? Do they stereotype the target culture?
- Involvement of learners: What will encourage learners? Will they exchange ideas with one other person? Will they focus on a grammatical item? Is this kind of involvement appropriate?
- Flexibility: Is the material flexible? Can it be used in a variety of ways, according to the needs of the learners and the time available? Is a variety of learning styles catered for?
- Equal opportunities: How does the material present people and information? Does it promote equal opportunities?
- Time: How long will it take to use this material? Is it time well-spent?
- Tutor preparation: What do I as the tutor have to know about the text and its content in order to use it effectively?

A particular resource is not necessarily communicative or useful in itself; it all depends upon how the tutor presents and exploits it.

There are many issues for consideration when planning classes. Some of the questions tutors ask themselves are:

- *How does the teaching session or tutorial fit into the overall scheme of work or study plan?*
- *What are the learning outcomes of today's session?*
- *What skills in particular will be practised?*
- *What is the balance between practising language already learnt and acquiring new language?*
- *How can I check on learner progress?*
- *Are there activities which accommodate the needs of individual learners?*
- *What strategies can I use to maintain learner motivation?*

References

Arthur L, *Teaching foreign and second languages* (The Open University, Institute of Educational Technology, 1999)

Convery A and D Coyle, *Differentiation – taking the initiative* (CILT, 1993)

Fry H, S Ketteridge and S Marshall, *A handbook for teaching and learning in Higher Education* (Kogan Page, 1999)

McGarry D, *Learner automony* (Authentik Language Learning Resources, 1995)

Nunan D, *Language teaching methodology* (Prentice Hall, 1991)

Nunan D, *Designing tasks for the communicative classroom* (Cambridge University Press, 1989)

Podromou M, *Mixed ability classes* (MacMillan, 1992)

Scrivener J, *Learning teaching* (Heinemann, 1994)

Skehan P, *A Cognitive approach to language learning* (OUP, 1998)

Willis J, *A framework for task-based learning* (Heinemann, 1996)

Wilkins D A, *Notional syllabuses* (Oxford University Press, 1976)

7

Skills development and learning activities

JANE WOODIN

Being able to communicate in the target language means being able to speak, understand, write and read the language, in other words to be able to use what is often termed by professionals in the language teaching and learning world as the **four skills.** Learning a language, however, also involves a range of other skills and competences, personality traits, learning styles and strategies. Furthermore, successful communication in another language requires an understanding of different cultural norms and codes of behaviour in social interactions, as well as constant practice with speakers of the other language in and outside the classroom. This chapter has as its particular focus:

- skills development in language learners;
- communicative activities for language learning;
- focus upon meaning and form;
- vocabulary development.

Developing the four skills

Listening and reading skills

All language tutors dedicate a lot of time to the development of the four skills. These may be practised in the classroom and tested **discretely.** However, in everyday communications these skills are not usually used independently of each other, for example when taking part in conversations we listen and speak and when writing notes from lectures, we listen and write. The use of the four skills in different combinations is often referred to as **integrated skills.**

Listening and reading skills are often grouped together as receptive skills. This does not mean that they are passive skills as they are sometimes (erroneously) called. The listener/reader is engaged in active processing of information, trying to make sense of the meaning of what is said or written. Some examples of real-life listening activities include: radio and television programmes, answer phone messages and conversations between native speakers.

Nunan (1991) defines the following as among the characteristics of listening activities: monologue/dialogue; planned/unplanned; interpersonal/transactional; familiar/ unfamiliar.

Aural texts can vary enormously in style and language. The kind of discourse used in a television news programme differs considerably from that in a telephone conversation between friends. In real life, as in language learning, the context of what is uttered will aid comprehension. The presence of the person who is speaking can also give clues to the listener. However, authentic listening contexts are not always easy to understand.

> *We tend to take listening for granted. Imagine, for example, that you are about to board a bus in a noisy city street. You continue talking to a friend and listening to her replies; you understand when the driver, whose voice you have never heard before, tells you what the fare is; you notice that a small child on the bus has started crying; you realize that the music that had been blaring out of the clothes shop by the bus stop has been switched off. All this happens – or more exactly, you accomplish all this – at the same time and without noticeable difficulties.* (Anderson and Lynch, 1988)

As language tutors we tend to overlook the fact that even in our own language the mastery of recognising different sounds has been developing slowly since our childhood. Tutors should certainly not expect second language learners to understand everything instantly. For example, learners sometimes report that they cannot distinguish between words, and so find that they cannot comprehend anything. These learners may require further contextual clues or some vocabulary support. Techniques to help them to develop good listening skills might include:

- providing a purpose for listening;
- giving reassurance that it is quite normal not to understand every word;
- finding out the difficulties students have with listening and helping them to overcome them.

Reading is different from listening in that it is not so constrained by time. With listening, listeners normally only have the chance to hear something once (although they may be in a position to ask someone to repeat what they have said). Facial expressions, intonation and other paralinguistic clues can be useful for the listener. However, one can look again and again at a piece of text, referring back and forwards to aid understanding. There are many different types of text, from road signs and instructions to newspapers, novels or magazines and the way in which a reader will approach a text will also vary. She or he will read **extensively** to get the overall gist of a text, and **intensively** for more detailed information. Reading need not be a solitary activity; in the classroom, long texts in particular can be divided up so that different learners read different sections and then compare information.

To sum up: when reading a text or listening to an excerpt involving spoken language, the learner or the tutor may choose to:

- skim a text quickly to get the main gist of it;
- scan a text for particular items of information;
- read or listen extensively, mainly for global understanding;
- read intensively, to extract specific items or information and for accuracy.

What follows is some advice a tutor might give to her students:

READING TEXTS

You can make use of various strategies to help you read a text more easily. Working on a text is rather like peeling an onion – there are layers of understanding. It is helpful to approach a text first globally and then systematically in sections.

- Scan the whole text – check how long it is and how many paragraphs there are. This tells you the size of the reading task.

- Look at the title and subtitles – these should tell you what the text is all about.

- Pick out words which are similar to English words (cognates) or whose meaning is immediately clear: this will give you an idea about the content.

- What other clues are there that tell you what to expect? Dates, for example, might indicate that the passage will be historical. Statistics will tell you more about its content. There might also be names you recognise.

- Look at the whole text and underline what you think are the key points contained in the text.

- Make some initial assumptions about its content.

- Then work your way through the text, look at each paragraph before you look at each sentence. Don't worry about any unknown words, but try to understand its meaning.

- Then look at the shape of the sentence. Where is the verb or the subject? Ask yourself 'who does what to whom?'

- Read each sentence trying to identify the carriers of meaning. That means you can leave out words which are not so important at this stage.

- Remember you do not have to understand each word to grasp meaning

- Finally, check if your initial assumptions need revising.

Arthur, 1999

Speaking and writing skills

Some learners find speaking the most difficult of all the skills. This may be particularly true of those who have spent very little time with native speakers. It is the productive skill which demands the most spontaneity of learners; this can cause problems for learners who are overly concerned about making mistakes.

Speaking requires a lot to happen at once. Learners need to think about what they want to say, how they are going to say it, what language they are going to use to say it, whether that language is correct and how the person they are speaking to is going to react to what they say. Some examples of meaningful and realistic speaking activities for practice include: asking for information, leaving messages on the telephone, general conversation, explaining something and giving a talk. There are a number of ways to lighten the burden on the language learner when speaking in the target language. Anticipation of the situation in advance can help enormously. If the learner is about to engage in a telephone conversation, it is possible to prepare for this by familiarising oneself with the most common telephone language, or practising what to say beforehand. Practice with pronunciation, stress, intonation and drilling is also important in developing speaking skills. The language laboratory can be very useful in giving all learners the opportunity to focus on these aspects, but is not always available in many institutions. Similarly, group choral repetition can be effective, although it becomes boring if over-used. Opportunities for authentic communication need to be provided to help learners develop creativity and spontaneity. From time to time tutors need to concentrate specifically on speaking tasks. These aim to encourage learners to: ask questions; be creative; be fluent; pronounce clearly; use language appropriate to the situation.

With reference to the importance of pronunciation, a particularly complex area for most tutors, Grauberg (1997) writes:

> *The learning of pronunciation differs in several respects from the learning of vocabulary and grammar. The outstanding difference is that, as well as involving memory and cognitive processes, it brings into play our motorsensory capabilities, requiring training of our auditory perception and control of our vocal organs. The total number of vowels and consonants in any language is much smaller than even the most basic stock of vocabulary or grammatical rules (typically between 30 and 50), yet between them, these vowels and consonants make up every word that [students] learn. This has two consequences. The first is that serious weaknesses in pronunciation can significantly impair one's ability to communicate. Second, whereas vocabulary and grammatical knowledge are built up slowly and incrementally over several years, the whole sound system is encountered quite early. Teaching to discriminate between sounds, to pronounce words acceptably and connect sounds with letters must therefore begin early.*

In everyday life most of us speak a lot but we tend not to write very much. We tend to use the telephone or perhaps e-mail to keep in touch with relatives or friends. In a work context, however, some of us have to write formal letters, summaries, project reports, or undertake translations. In higher education, too, there is still much emphasis on essay writing or presentation of a research project as an integral part of learner assessment. Some examples of real-life writing activities include: writing memos/messages, letters, minutes of a meeting, notes from lectures/discussions and writing e-mails.

Writing has the advantage over speaking in that there is time to check what is written and make alterations. Inaccuracy in writing is generally tolerated less. Whilst writing may not be a learner's priority, examinations generally require learners to write, and writing can help to focus on grammatical aspects of the language. This is possibly the skill which is least developed in tutor-learner contact time; more often it is carried out independently by learners. However, Lewis (1996) suggests that writing and re-writing, group writing and peer checking are very useful for developing learners' written skills and awareness of language. Learners often find productive skills more difficult than receptive skills; they are required to be able to select quickly (particularly in the case of speaking) and accurately (particularly in the case of writing) appropriate language for the task in hand. However, as mentioned previously, in real life discrete skills are rarely used in this way and integrated skills are employed to carry out a task.

Communicative activities

Is it desirable to replicate real-life situations in language learning activities? General opinion is that it is useful to replicate similar types of situations in order to prepare learners for using the language outside of their learning environment (Ur, 1996). Widdowson (1990) feels that this falls short of what language teaching should be aiming for:

> To try and replicate the conditions of natural communicative use of language in the classroom is to deny the whole purpose of pedagogy, which is to contrive economical and more effective means for language learning than is provided by natural exposure and experience.

Communicative activities are particularly appropriate to the classroom context, because they mirror real-life activities in providing genuine reasons for communicating. Sidwell (1993) describes the two principal characteristics of communication as **choice** and **unpredictability.** The speaker has a choice about what to say, and the interlocutor(s) do not know what is going to be said. He therefore proposes that these characteristics be present in language development activities:

Consider the following activities, with a group of near-beginner learners of Italian who are practising descriptions of people:

Example 1: Learners describe themselves to their partner.

Example 2: Learners describe someone in the room to their partner and their partner has to work out who it is.

Example 1 is rarely carried out in real life (although one can imagine situations, possibly slightly contrived, where one might have cause to describe oneself). In terms of choice and unpredictability, there is very little of either if the person who is listening can see the speaker. Example 2 may not be carried out in real life very often, but it does happen in the context of someone not remembering who someone else is talking about, or describing a famous person such as a film star. In real life the partner might not guess who is being described, but they might imagine the person described, possibly to see if the description matched their image of that person. There is choice on the part of the speaker as to whom they choose to describe, and there is unpredictability on the part of the hearer who does not know what is going to be said. For this reason example 2 is a more communicative activity than example 1, and is likely to involve the learners more. There are genuine reasons for listening and speaking.

Sometimes just a small change can make all the difference to whether an activity is communicative or not. For example, asking someone what they are wearing when they are looking at you is not a communicative activity, because you can see for yourself, but asking them what they wear when they go out with friends is a communicative activity. It requires no more work on the part of the tutor, just an awareness of genuine reasons for communicating.

Communicative activities focus on meaning rather than accuracy. Grammatical accuracy will only matter if errors hinder communication. **Pre-communicative activities** may be used to prepare learners for communication. They are often guided and controlled by the tutor and could be guided role plays, semi-structured interviews, simple information gap exercises; these are followed by **communicative activities**, where the learners are encouraged to apply what has previously been practised. These include free conversation, role plays and simulations, creative writing, narrating, describing events, coping with spontaneous language.

When involved in communicative activities the learner is encouraged to initiate communication, express ideas, intentions and opinions, use language creatively, apply interpersonal skills and seek connections between themes and topics and his or her real life situation. The emphasis here is on contextualised functional language, adapted by the learner to his or her needs.

Focus on meaning and focus on form

Both focus on meaning and on form are important (see chapter 6 and chapter 3). How much focus on each is necessary will depend upon other factors, such as the age of the learners, their previous experience of language learning or their learning styles. Focus on form generally includes a closer focus upon accuracy in the language; focus on meaning tends to encourage fluency practice. Clearly, these are appropriate at different stages of task development.

There are many ways to focus on form or grammatical accuracy in the language class. Both Willis (1996) and Skehan (1998) propose that the point at which one needs to focus on form is after completion of the task. In this way, learners are involved in the analysis of the language they have just used and the relevant grammar points can be discussed at a time when they are still fresh in the learner's mind. Grammar can be taught inductively or deductively. An inductive approach involves learners looking at the language in context first and then trying to work out the rules for themselves (see chapter 13). The advantage of using an inductive way of teaching grammar is that it allows learners to make their own hypotheses which can also help them to remember the rules.

An example of an inductive approach to teaching the passive is as follows:

1. Tutor introduces the theme, for example health, to learners by inviting them to discuss their own attitudes to and experiences of health-related issues.
2. Tutor introduces passive sentences in the course of conversation.
3. Learners 'discover' and practise widely-used forms of the passive.
4. Learners sum up basic rules for the use of the passive with the help of the tutor.
5. Learners work on texts relating to the topic of health which included further examples of the passive.
6. Learners then apply, in free conversation, many forms of the passive.

This approach allows learners to think through the way the language is formed. They are actively involved; the activity is learner-centred in that it is the learners who are solving the problem.

A deductive approach to teaching grammar involves presenting a grammar rule and then asking the learners to apply it. The advantage of teaching grammar deductively is that learners have the language explained to them before they use it so they can feel 'safe.' They also have the chance to practise it immediately after having had it explained to them.

Here is an example of deductive grammar teaching: the future tense

1. Tutor hands out copies of letters from people writing about their future plans for the New Year.
2. From the letters tutor points out the different forms of grammar items and then from this explains the rules of the formation of the future tense.
3. Learners then practise the uses of the future tense through exchanging future plans with their partner and/or writing down their plans.

Although the grammar is presented in context, the approach is still deductive; learners have little room for any hypothesising. They may also find that they can understand the forms but not be able to apply them. Furthermore, grammatical points raised this way may be too complex for some learners to cope with all at once. A deductive approach can, therefore, create many unwarranted anxieties, particularly in learners with little grammatical awareness.

Advanced language learners only require to see an explanation of a particular grammar point and its uses before they are willing to try it out; however the vast majority of learners need to be able to become involved in working out the rules for themselves. All learners benefit from seeing and using grammar in a communicative context. Lists of independent sentences may provide momentary entertainment; they do little for developing an understanding of the use of structures. Skehan (1998) proposes that, particularly when working with adults, one needs to incorporate plenty of form-based learning to raise awareness of the way a language works, but that this should arise naturally:

> *What is needed is to consider approaches which, in the context of meaningful communication, draw attention to form in more inductive ways, or raise consciousness. We need to develop pedagogic interventions where learners focus on form naturally, rather than artificially.*

So how can we help to develop a focus upon meaning? Prescribed activities can give learners the opportunity to employ a range of strategies in order to achieve their goal. These strategies, usually called **communication strategies**, have been categorised in a number of ways; perhaps the most useful way from the point of view of the tutor is to consider them in terms of conceptual strategies, where:

> *... learners engage in some manipulation of the concept they are trying to convey, and linguistic strategies, where learners resort to their L1 or another L2 and to morphological creativity. (Ellis, 1994)*

Skehan (1998) states that there are many ways in which language learners can compensate for inaccuracies when attempting to get their messages across:

> *We rely on time-creating devices, context, prediction skills, elliptical language and a range of similar performance factors to reduce the processing load that we have to deal with during conversation. And the older we become, (up to a point) the more adept we can be at exploiting these resources.*

Whether it is useful to teach these strategies overtly is a debatable point. Bialystock (1990) thinks not:

> *The more language the learner knows, the more possibilities exist for the system to be flexible and to adjust itself to meet the demands of the learner. What one must teach students of a language is not strategy, but language.*

On the other hand, by placing learners in situations where they are required to use these strategies in the target language, one can ensure that they are getting the kind of language practice which they need to be able to communicate effectively.

Developing vocabulary

Traditionally, the teaching and learning of vocabulary has taken second place to grammar. Communicative language teaching has contributed to the raising of the status of vocabulary within the curriculum and has offered new insights into the ways in which words are used. The role of memory has also been emphasised and a number of techniques developed for aiding memory. McCarthy (1990) proposes that:

It is the experience of most language teachers that the single, biggest component of any language course is vocabulary. No matter how well the student learns grammar, no matter how successfully the sounds of L2 are mastered, without words to express a wide range of meanings, communication in L2 cannot happen in any meaningful way. And the vocabulary often seems to be the least systematised and the least well catered for of all aspects of language learning.

Learners often ask questions such as: *How should I best learn vocabulary*? Some ideas for vocabulary development are:

- Theme groups: Words related to the same theme are learnt together, for example household vocabulary, or shopping vocabulary.

- Formal groupings: Learners can be taught the meanings of words such as *tele* (distant) or *phone* (sound) and then given lists of vocabulary items containing these words and asked to guess the meanings of these compound words.

- Word families: Similar to formal groupings, words can be grouped into families, developed from a single root. e.g. *part, partition, particle, participant* etc.

- Mnemonic devices: These are tricks for committing words to memory, such as rhyming, or associating pictures with words.

- Collocations: Words which are commonly associated can be learnt together, for example, to appeal against the judge's decision, to appeal to a friend for help.

- Cognates: There are many words in Western European languages which have similar forms and meanings. Learners can be encouraged to make associations between languages, but at the same time to be aware of false friends.

(Adapted from Nunan, 1991)

What is certain is that different learners are likely to have different ways which work for them, and that some may also need support in finding new ways to learn vocabulary.

Translation and interpreting

Traditionally, translation has been used in higher education for teaching grammar in context, often using literary texts. It now has a wider variety of pedagogic applications and is recognised as an authentic activity, often undertaken in real-life. Translation can be approached in a product-oriented way (focusing upon the end product), or as a process-oriented activity (focusing on the process of translating). In either case, learners need to be aware of the context of the text to be translated in order to be able to translate it successfully. Translation can help to focus upon the similarities and differences between the two languages in question; it can also usefully demonstrate to learners the frequent inadequacies of literal translation.

Interpreting is again receiving recognition as a skill which is required for today's language learner. The immediacy of interpreting makes it particularly difficult for lower level learners. Short interpreting activities can help language learners to retain information in a conceptual form, and encourage learners to think in the foreign language. For example, they can be asked to summarise a French news bulletin in English to others or interpret for a native speaker visitor to the class. Jigsaw listening activities—where members of the group hear different but related parts of a text and then pool information—can also be undertaken as an interpreting activity.

Tutors know from experience how rewarding it can be to design activities which not only develop skills in the learner but also give them a sense of achievement. By reflecting on student development and sharing ideas and concerns with colleagues, tutors themselves are often able to solve problems or to refine teaching processes. It is part of the tutor's ongoing learning process.

References

Ainslie S, *Mixed ability teaching: meeting learners' needs* (CILT, 1994)

Anderson A and T Lynch, *Listening* (Oxford University Press, 1988)

Bialystock E, *Communication strategies* (Blackwell, 1990)

Ellis R, *The study of second language acquisition* (Oxford University Press, 1994)

Grauberg W, *The elements of foreign language teaching* (Multilingual Matters 1997)

Lewis M, 'Implications of a lexical view of language' in Willis J and D Willis, *Challenge and change in language teaching* (Macmillan, 1996)

McCarthy M, *Vocabulary* (Oxford University Press 1990)

Nunan D, *Language teaching methodology* (Prentice Hall, 1991)

Sidwell D, *A toolkit for talking* (CILT, 1993)

Skehan P, *A cognitive approach to language learning* (OUP, 1998)

Ur P, *A course in language teaching: practice and theory* (Cambridge University Press, 1996)

Willis J, *A framework for task-based learning* (Heinemann, 1996)

Widdowson H, *Aspects of language teaching* (Oxford University Press, 1990)

8

Learning strategies and learner autonomy

LESLEY WALKER

Constant developments in the fields of technology and global communication emphasise the necessity to develop in learners the skills and attitudes needed for lifelong learning. Flexibility and versatility are needed for the world of work as well as outside it. Society demands learners with a range of transferable skills, and the attitude and potential to develop and modify them. Consequent shifts in attitudes and methodology are changing teaching and learning in traditional modes of classroom tutor-led learning, as well as in open and distance learning. Crucially, as Dickinson (1992) points out, '*all learners **need** to learn to be independent of the teacher*'. However, it is simply not enough to send them off to the self-access centre or the language laboratory or library. What is needed is an approach to learning and teaching that promotes a heightened awareness among learners not only of the **skills and strategies** they use to learn a language, but also, most importantly, of those they will need, as lifelong learners, to develop the ability to manage their learning and take responsibility for its direction.

While supporting learners has long been one of the tutor's priorities, too much support may have led to dependency on the part of the learner. Many teachers and learners have been comfortable with this state of affairs. However, to paraphrase Race (1994) **being taught** often inhibits the very development of the ability to manage one's own learning. By contrast, flexible learning pathways can foster this ability.

This chapter will cover:

- a definition of learning strategies:
- the different categories of strategies and how they are used in second language learning;
- the possibility and potential of teaching learning strategies;
- the importance of learning strategies in the development of learner autonomy;
- supporting autonomous learners.

Learning strategies

In the search to develop and refine effective practice in second language learning and teaching, attention has been focused in recent years not just on how best to teach and support learners, but also on how learners learn. When it comes to learning a second language the strategies learners use spontaneously to promote their language learning can make the difference between successful and unsuccessful language learning. Successful strategies are the *'strategies employed by people known to be good at L2 learning'* (Cook, 1991).

According to Wenden (1987),

> ... in the literature, strategies have been referred to as 'techniques', 'tactics', 'potentially conscious plans', 'consciously employed operations', 'learning skills', 'basic skills', 'functional skills', 'cognitive abilities', 'language processing strategies', 'problem solving procedures'. These multiple designations point to the elusive nature of the term.

How then to understand and define learner strategies? *'Learning strategies are procedures undertaken by the learner in order to make their own language learning as effective as possible'* (Mitchell and Myles, 1998). O'Malley and Chamot (1990) exploit theories from cognitive psychology describing the process whereby knowledge is taken in and stored in short- and long-term memory, is reorganised and automatised. The process is applied to the field of second language acquisition, and learning strategies are defined as *'special ways of processing information that enhance comprehension, learning, or retention of the information'*. Learning strategies then apply to all aspects of our learning. In the context of second language (L2) learning, Cook (1991) defines a strategy as *'a choice that the learner makes while using the second language, that affects learning'*. O'Malley and Chamot (1990) group learning strategies into the following categories:

- metacognitive strategies: the strategies used to make decisions on the learning, to organise and manage it;
- cognitive strategies: strategies used directly to process the information being handled;
- social/affective strategies: strategies having to do with the learner and the learner's attitude to the target language, culture and speakers.

Let us examine a practical application of strategies in use: Imagine that a student has been assigned the task of giving an oral presentation in the next tutorial. He or she must speak in the target language on some aspect of the target culture. The following strategies might well come into play in the case of a successful learner:

- metacognitive: planning the content of the presentation and which resources to use to find the relevant information, deciding on the writing up, organising the structure of the speech, managing the time given to this project, monitoring the various stages and evaluating the finished product;

- cognitive: processing the information in the target language, using such strategies as summarising, rephrasing, memorising, and rehearsing;

- social: asking peers or telephoning tutor for information, advice or help; creating opportunities to interact with native speakers either face to face or by e-mail with a view to improving intercultural knowledge or simply to practise speaking, reading or writing the target language; joining a newsgroup or going into a chat room on the Internet to converse with fellow students or native speakers of the target language;

- affective: finding ways of dealing with nerves or lack of self-confidence, having a positive attitude to finding out more about target culture during the research phase.

The example given above shows the interplay of strategies required to complete a learning task successfully. The task involved does not have to be such an ambitious one. Strategies come into play at all levels of learning and in all four skill areas. As Oxford (1990) points out: '*Strategies are especially important for language learning because they are tools for active, self-directed involvement.*' Learners use such strategies in their interaction with language wherever and whenever it takes place.

Oxford offers a complementary perspective on the categories into which strategies can be grouped. She creates a separate category for memory strategies, makes social and affective two separate categories and adds to the list the category of compensation strategies, also known as communication strategies, which the learner uses to overcome gaps in his or her output. Moreover, she distinguishes between direct and indirect strategies. Direct strategies – memory, cognitive and compensation – describe interaction by the learner with the language itself, for example learning vocabulary by heart. Indirect strategies – metacognitive, affective and social – are brought into play at one remove and involve various approaches to learning, for example deciding **when** to learn the vocabulary, **which method** to use and, more generally, **how** to integrate tasks and strategies and **monitor** their effectiveness,

Strategy training

Many language teachers, good language learners themselves, recognising certain tricks (or successful strategies) in their own experience of learning a language, pass on tips to their learners. Current teaching approaches promote the use of study skills such as learning to take notes and using dictionaries. Many secondary school pupils are given homework diaries or planners to inculcate good learning habits. If tutors are now armed with a taxonomy of learning strategies, is it then possible for them to give their learners access to the secrets of good language learning via strategy training? Taking into account motivation and the question of learner personality, and also the learner's native culture, it may be that tutors can have little influence on the social and affective behaviours influencing the language learning of individuals. However, we do know that students who experience success in learning do obviously become more and more confident in their ability to learn. By helping our students to initial success through strategy use, we may be able to change the course of their experience of language learning and lead them to more positive experiences.

Most learners use strategies without really being aware of them and tend only to be conscious of them when meeting new material that needs to be processed or when meeting a problem that needs to be overcome. If learners of a second language can be made more aware of their learning process, they are more likely to learn how to make it more effective. According to Oxford (1990), '*conscious skill in self-directed learning and in strategy use must be sharpened by training*'. Chamot and O'Malley (1987) are convinced of the effectiveness of strategy training:

- *Strategies can be taught. Students who are taught strategies and are provided with sufficient practice in using them will learn more effectively than students who have no experience with learning strategies.*

- *Learning strategies transfer to new tasks. Once students have become accustomed to using learning strategies, they will use them on new tasks that are similar to the learning activities on which they were initially trained.*

In the various studies which O'Malley and Chamot conducted on strategy training, their research led them to confront such important issues as to whether strategy training should be separate or integrated into the language learning materials and whether tutors themselves need instruction in strategy training. In the studies themselves they reported only limited success. Furthermore, although progress was seen in some skills after only one week of training, no follow-up studies were undertaken to see if the effects lasted. Such mixed results cause some educationists to question the effectiveness of strategy training. Many are wary of interventionism. McDonough (1995), emphasising the variation in strategy use between individuals, points out that '*incorporating particular strategies, however sensible they are, into teaching texts can constrain rather than extend the learner's range*'. He also points out that '*strategies are not necessarily good in themselves: almost any strategy can lead to failure if used inappropriately*'. A less proficient learner guessing wildly might not be successful most of the time, while the good language learner using informed guesswork will have much more chance of success. For some learners new strategies will not be as effective as tried and tested approaches. It is also essential to take account of cultural differences when promoting the use of specific strategies in strategy use, and allow for choice. In one study (O'Malley and Chamot, 1990), Asian students in a control group used rote repetition in preference to a new strategy involving grouping words and '*imagining themselves interacting with the object while using its name*', and outperformed others who had implemented this strategy.

Cook (1991) questions whether some strategies need to be taught. We already use communication or compensation strategies in our first language whenever we come across a word we don't know or remember. However, he does believe that attention drawn to such strategies and their transference into second language interaction and transaction can be beneficial. Compensation strategies, such as relying on linguistic or other clues to guess what is being said, or using mime or gesture to get a message across, are very important to learners of a second language, because they allow them to remain engaged in the learning process and so prolong exposure to the target language, extending opportunities not just for understanding the target language but also for producing it. However, mere awareness raising of strategy use may not necessarily lead to more successful learning if the learner's own strategies are not effective ones.

In a review of the latest research on learning strategies, Cohen (1998) reports that:

> ... *both more and less successful learners at any level of proficiency can learn how to improve their comprehension and production of a foreign language,* [and that] *explicit instruction in the development, application, and transfer of language learning strategies is preferable to implicit instruction.*

For example, 80% of the students taking part in a study involving listening strategies felt that their listening had improved after strategy training. Students had '*learned new strategies for improving listening and adopted for their own continued use those they found most helpful*'.

Tutors interested in promoting strategy use may wish to start with Oxford's *Strategy Inventory for Language Learning (SILL)* (Oxford, 1990:284–5), where learners are taken through a questionnaire which invites them to analyse which strategies they use, from which category and how frequently. The following extract from SILL is from the part of the inventory, items 16–20, which helps learners to diagnose the use of their **mental processes,** in other words their cognitive strategies, and to think about how they learn. In this case, English speakers learning a new language are presented with statements about learning new material and invited to say how well each statement describes them:

I say or write new expressions repeatedly to practise them ⃝

I imitate the way native speakers talk. ⃝

I read a story or dialogue several times until I can understand it. ⃝

I revise what I write in the new language to improve my writing. ⃝

I practise the sounds or the alphabet of the new language. ⃝

1. Never or almost never true of me
2. Generally not true of me
3. Somewhat true of me
4. Generally true of me
5. Always or almost always true of me

Read the item and choose a response (1 through 5 above) and write in the space after the item.

Other possible techniques for identifying and diagnosing students' present strategies are interviews, students thinking aloud as they work through a task, diaries and journals. Making learners more aware of the strategies they already use and others available to them might be all some of them need to implement additional effective ones. A straightforward and practical model for strategies-based instruction (SBI) can be found in Cohen (1998):

> *In a typical SBI classroom strategy training situation, the teachers:*
>
> 1. *describe, model and give examples of potentially useful strategies;*
>
> 2. *elicit additional examples from students based on the students' own learning experiences;*
>
> 3. *lead small-group/whole-class discussions about strategies;*
>
> 4. *encourage their students to experiment with a broad range of strategies; and*
>
> 5. *integrate strategies into everyday class materials, explicitly and implicitly embedding them into language tasks to provide for contextualized strategy practice.*

There are many exercises, which develop wide strategy use in all four skills in Oxford (1990) from '*guessing the meaning of reading passages*' to '*taking your emotional temperature*'. Alternatively, tutors may refer their students to handbooks such as The Open University's *Language Learner's Good Study Guide.* Tutors may also have their own agenda and knowledge of particular effective strategies they wish to transfer. The time factor is of course important. It is already difficult to cover the syllabus without having an additional area of study to explore. And yet, as good language learners, tutors can also appreciate the benefits of effective strategic use. Working with learners in a real or a virtual classroom, tutors have to acclimatise themselves to a culture of change and to be flexible in their approach. In addition to teaching, they have to develop methods to facilitate learning and embrace positively the growing need to acquire or develop the skills necessary for learner training.

Learning strategies and learner independence.

Let us return briefly to the study (Cohen, 1998) where students reported improved listening skills after strategy training. They also noted in their diaries that they:

> 2. *became aware of what and how to learn;*
>
> 3. *improved their ability to evaluate their strengths and weaknesses as listeners in the foreign language;*
>
> 4. *began to set learning goals for themselves; and*
>
> 5. *developed a (more) positive attitude toward learning through listening.*

Awareness of the learning process, and ability to self-monitor and to set goals, are all examples of metacognitive strategies. The above is a clear example of how the teaching of listening strategies led to an awareness of their use and a decision on the part of the learner as to what and how to learn. Learning goals were set, with students evaluating their ability. It also demonstrates how *'learner-training shades over into self-directed learning where students take on responsibility for their learning'* (Cook, 1991). It is the effective use of metacognitive strategies that holds the key to learner independence inside and outside the classroom. Without the development of such strategies a learner will always be dependent on a teacher figure. Tutors need to help the learner to develop the capacity for self-directed learning.

> *Poor students are those who depend most on the teacher and are least able to fend for themselves. The students must be encouraged to develop independence inside and outside the classroom.* (Cook, 1991)

According to Holec (1981), to take charge of one's learning is *'to have, and to hold, the responsibility for all decisions concerning all aspects of this learning'*. Taking Holec's model, the complete autonomous learner:

- determines objectives;
- defines contents and sequences;
- selects methods and techniques to be used;
- monitors the acquisition procedure (rhythm, time, place);
- evaluates what has been acquired.

In traditional set-ups, the tutor manages these operations through all stages of the learning process. Moreover, learning objectives are rigid and apply to a whole group. **Omniscient** tutors define materials, together with the choice of methods and techniques. Monitoring and evaluation are also conducted externally. However, as we have seen, learner autonomy can and should be developed through the integration of learning strategies into a learning environment, where students are constantly required to take decisions on their learning and to implement them.

To best prepare our learners for a possible scenario where aims, material, methods and evaluation, as well as the monitoring process, are put into their hands, we should aim to develop the capacity for autonomy whatever the learning context. For many learners, this will begin in the classroom; for those learning at a distance, it is through the course materials that autonomy will be promoted and developed. Lifelong learners need to develop the capacity to analyse their learning needs and set learning goals, so that they can decide on the materials and methods to be used. They need to know how to monitor and review the learning process, evaluate the effectiveness of their procedures, and manage their time. Finally, they must become competent in assessing their progress in order to be able to set the next goal. Focusing on tasks, planning for organisation, reviewing and checking are all metacognitive strategies. We can help our learners to develop these strategies by appropriate training.

For example, after completing a simple needs analysis exercise to diagnose areas of strengths and weaknesses, learners can be directed to, or can select for themselves, tasks and activities to practise particular skills, or more generally to build confidence. In this way, they begin to take on some responsibility for their own learning. A sequence of activities can then be evaluated after a set period of time. Diagnosing, evaluating and recording processes are all features of metacognitive competence and part of autonomous learning.

In open and distance learning contexts the process may be more complex, even though Race's flexible pathways (see p83) have obvious application. Merely because open or distance language learners have more opportunity to decide the place, time and rhythm of their learning *'we cannot'*, as Hurd (1998) points out, *'make any assumptions about them with regard to levels of autonomy'*. Many adult learners resist autonomy, preferring the framework of being told what to do and how to do it. On the other hand, more mature learners may well be metacognitively aware. Tutors need to be aware of learner variables and all learner types, taking care not to patronise. Thorpe (1995), writing on the challenge facing course design, says:

> We need to develop procedures and approaches which generate learning and develop self-aware learners and which also avoid either giving learners all the responsibility and no power, or leaving them to sink or swim.

Supporting learners

Some learners, because of such factors as motivation, personality and learning styles, will develop some form of independence more readily than others. Little (1990) remarks that accepting responsibility for their own learning may be the last thing learners want. Being controlled is often a much cosier, less stressful or threatening situation than taking control. So by what means can we move our learners away from dependence on the teacher, through various stages of interdependence to a situation in which they begin to take a more active part in their learning?

Many of the course materials written for open and distance learning programmes already encourage students through interaction and reflection to become more aware of the kind of learners they are and of their own learning process. At the same time as helping them to develop an awareness of effective learner strategies to meet their individual situation, more concrete help is provided through the different forms of learner support, for example course and project guides, feedback to accompany model answers in course books, and transcripts of audio-visual material. Feedback from tutors is also of crucial importance and is looked at in more detail in chapter 15.

In the present culture of developing lifelong learning skills, many institutions now have self-access centres where all facilities for independent learning are provided, including self-help leaflets and *how to use* instructions. The tutor can advise the learner on which materials and methods to use. For example, listening skills can be developed by video or satellite TV exercises; individual grammar practice by interactive grammar exercises on the web. Students can be guided from directive learner-training tasks to aid metacognitive development, through directive tasks concentrating on language development to non-directive tasks with no specific activity attached (Sinclair, 1996).

Another device for helping the independent learner structure his or her learning is the learner diary. A learner diary can help the learner to prepare, plan, organise and evaluate his or her independent learning. Here is an extract from a Tandem Learner Diary, as used in the Modern Languages Teaching Centre at the University of Sheffield. The writer meets regularly with a native speaker and is using the meetings to help her prepare for study abroad in the following semester.

Date: *May 1999*

Today's goal: *Extend cultural knowledge*

Topic: *Banks in France*

New words and expressions acquired

épargner: to save money *un compte bancaire: bank account*
un encouragement: incentive *un crédit bancaire: bank loan*
un code: PIN number

Cultural information

French banks do not offer as many incentives for students as English banks. However students at Grandes Ecoles are offered bigger loans as such students are the desired clientele of the future.

Grammar practised

re-used many structures using pronouns from last week's meeting (e.g. le mot auquel je pensais)

Did I achieve my goal or not?

Yes. This meeting made me feel much better prepared for managing my money and dealing with banks next year.

Next Step

I have gathered a lot of cultural information over the past few weeks. So next week I hope to concentrate on a different aim, to improve my use of the future tense. I will practise this by talking about what I plan to do after my degree and ask my partner the same. So this will give us a chance to find out a little more about one another and our aims for the future.

Observation of learning strategies used

I felt that I had planned just the right amount of material. In earlier meetings this was something I found hard to master.

Researching the subject in advance really helped me as it meant that I could contribute to the conversation more.

Today I was really aware of how my independent study skills have progressed over the module.

The use of the diary encourages learners to acquire the habit of planning ahead and deciding on what materials to use. The experience of doing so leads to proficiency in recognising suitable material and the ability to manage time. Tutors will recognise this stage from their own planning of lessons and choice of appropriate materials. Reflection in the diary on the process of learning will help the learner to develop his or her monitoring and evaluation strategies. The **next step** is designed to promote learner control of the learning, and responsibility for it by planning and consolidating. Finally, raising awareness of all strategies used will help the learner to recognise, develop or acquire effective strategies. If the element of a learner contract is added to the keeping of the diary, or if it is used as part of the assessment process, then the anxious learner will benefit from the knowledge that the tutor is committed to the process as much as he or she is.

The tutor working in such a relationship will also need to acquire new skills in order to be able to give learners good advice on their learning. In order to facilitate the change of emphasis from tutor-led to independent study, some centres are now employing language advisers or counsellors. Advisers, in many cases trained and practising language teachers, support independent learners through the process of analysing their needs and setting realistic goals. They also help in the choice of appropriate learning resources, as well as giving advice on self-evaluation or assessment. The large numbers of students who are on taught courses can benefit from the individual attention paid to their needs with the development of appropriate strategies, just as much as the few on self-study programmes. The importance of psychological as well as linguistic preparation is underlined by Esch (1994) who lays down effective ground rules for supporting independent learners and touches on the role of teacher turned adviser. The project, *Strategies for Managing an Independent Learning Environment (SMILE)* funded by the Fund for the Development of Teaching and Learning (FDTL)[1] and based at Hull University, has investigated all aspects of language advising and highlighted the need for further research and development to ensure the professionalisation of this role.

Language learning requires interaction with other people. The learner is not dependent or less independent because he or she seeks this. Students in self-help groups help each other to learn. A good tutor will want to set up such partnerships to work in the classroom and beyond. As we know, the good language learner seeks out native speakers for language practice. An ideal situation for the learner working towards independence is tandem learning. Tandem learning involves a partnership of two native speakers, learners of each other's language, who learn from each other and help each other to learn. By helping someone else to learn and being an expert in one's own language, even the more inhibited learners or learners with low self-esteem can gain self-confidence, at the same time as learning a language. This one-to-one collaborative learning exercise is very effective. Learners working in tandem, face-to-face or by e-mail, enhance language skills as well as learning strategies. Their enthusiasm for the method lends proof to the statement made by Bill Lucas, chief executive of the Campaign for Learning in the *Times Higher Education Supplement* (July 1999) that '(...) *learners tend to be more motivated when they have ownership of the learning and greater control over the choice of task and learning styles'*.

Language teaching for the 21st century presents tutors with more of a challenge than ever. Tutors can be confident of a job well done if, like Knowles (1987), they see their mission as '*helping individuals develop the attitude that learning is a lifelong process, and to acquire the skills of self-directed learning*'. Successful learning strategies lie at the heart of such skills.

References

Chamot A U and J M O'Malley, 'The cognitive academic language learning approach: a bridge to the mainstream' in *TESOL Quarterly*, 21 (2): 227–49 (1987)

Cohen A D, *Strategies in learning and using a foreign language* (Longman, 1998)

Cook V, *Second language learning and language teaching* (Edward Arnold, 1991)

Dickinson L, *Learner training for language learning* (Authentik: Learner autonomy series 2, 1992)

Esch E, 'Learner support: interacting with learners' in Esch E (ed), *Self-access and the adult language learner:* 50–53 (CILT, 1994)

Holec H, *Autonomy in foreign language learning* (Pergamon Press, 1981, first published by Strasbourg: Council of Europe, 1979)

Hurd S, 'Autonomy at any price? Issues and concerns from a British HE perspective' in *Foreign Language Annals* 31, 2: 219–230 (1998)

Knowles M, *The modern practice of Adult Education* (Association Press, 1976) quoted in Wenden A and J Rubin (eds), *Learner strategies in language learning* (Prentice Hall, 1987)

Little D, 'Autonomy in language learning' in Gathercole I (ed) *Autonomy in language learning* (CILT, 1990)

McDonough S H, *Strategy and skill in learning a foreign language* (Edward Arnold, 1995)

Mitchell R and F Myles, *Second language learning theories* (Edward Arnold, 1998)

O'Malley J M and A U Chamot, *Learning strategies in second language acquisition* (Cambridge University Press, 1990)

Oxford R L, *Language learning strategies: what every teacher should know* (Heinle and Heinle, 1990)

Race P, *The open learning handbook* (Kogan Page, 1994)

Stevens A et al, *The language learners good study guide* (The Open University, 1995)

Sinclair B, 'Materials design for the promotion of learner autonomy' in Pemberton R et al, *Taking control: autonomy in language learning:* 149–166 (Hong Kong: University Press, 1996)

Thorpe M, 'The challenge facing course design' in Lockwood F (ed), *Open and distance learning today* (Routledge, 1995)

Wenden A, 'Conceptual background and utility. An introduction to learner strategies' in Wenden A and J Rubin (eds), *Learner strategies in language learning* (Prentice Hall, 1987)

Notes

1   www.hull.ac.uk/lansinst/smile

PART 3

TECHNOLOGY AND LANGUAGE LEARNING

No one can really envisage a life nowadays without the computer. In offices and other arenas of public life computers have become integral components of everyday activities. At home, too, an increasing number of people shop via the Internet and use e-mail to keep in touch with family and friends. Furthermore, the Internet is a useful, additional tool for information gathering and data collection. Rapid advances in modern technology, however, can also divide: not everybody owns a computer, not everybody has the will or skills to apply it with confidence. Most educational institutions are concerned with the integration of a wide range of IT applications into the teaching and learning process, particularly in the context of telelearning and greater autonomy in distance learning – all of which have long-lasting implications for language tutors. Can IT help us teach more effectively for the benefit of the learners? What pedagogic and practical aspects issues have to be considered?

Chapter 9 gives an overall outline of different kinds of technology used in language teaching and offers an overall theoretical framework in relation to the use of, among others, audio-tapes, video and computers. It looks at a range of questions to be asked when considering the use of technology. Computers and language learning are discussed in chapters 10 and 11. Word processing, e-mail, the World Wide Web and CD ROMs are critically evaluated for their use in the learning process in addition to other more recent software designs such as thesauri, translation packages and concordances together with their integration into the curriculum. Chapter 12 raises questions about the future uses of technologies to support independent learning, such as networking and various modes of conferencing in the light of the emerging Virtual University. It concludes by stating that at this point in time we can only speculate on the possibilities for the language learner of personalised learning resources.

9

The role of technology

VICKY WRIGHT AND SU WHITE

Language teachers over the centuries have relied on some sort of tool to aid and enhance the teaching/learning process. We have used stick and sand, quill and ink, chalk and slate, the printed word and picture, the blackboard and the whiteboard, the flannelgraph and the flashcard along with the various pieces of 'realia' which bring an authentic feel to the classroom. However, it has been the 'machines' which matured during the latter part of the twentieth century, which have had the greatest impact on teaching practices. Radio and television (terrestrial, satellite and now digital) along with the photocopier, the overhead projector the audiocassette and the video player have all revolutionised what is possible both inside and outside the classroom. But it is the networked personal computer integrating all that has gone before it in a single digital environment – with text, graphics, audio and video – which promises the biggest impact of all. Its advent even raises the question of whether an interactive language machine of the future, which responds to what we say and translates automatically from one language to another, can replace the language teacher, and whether we will ever again need to learn more than one language.

The 'one stop shop' is set to be the technology of the future – the fridge or the microwave will 'intelligently' order the shopping when food items run low or heat a meal before the householder returns home – the PC and TV have already become multifunctional, and are set to develop into far more sophisticated machines. But if we as teachers are to cater for a wide range of needs, interests and learning styles and for a range of budgets, there needs to be some consideration of appropriate technologies for the learning context.

Supporting the learning process

Technology in its many forms has much to offer the language learner and teacher today. The classroom audio and video cassette player (and its more recent digital relations), multimedia applications and online learning environments, are doing much to stimulate new approaches to teaching and learning, but we can usefully bring our existing expertise and knowledge to evaluate changes which we propose to bring

97

about. Laurillard (1994), whilst describing a general move to embrace new media, advises that this *'technological pull'* needs to be balanced by an *'equally powerful pedagogical pull that keeps it on the track of the educationally beneficial'*. She gives the example of schoolchildren using a CD-ROM encyclopaedia to carry out research. They are motivated to persevere in a way they would not have done with a book, but without support they may not be able to evaluate the information they retrieve, nor integrate the fragments of knowledge they end up with. This could be equally true of language learners surfing the web to carry out research for a classroom project. They will need help turning the information into knowledge.

Before we rush to adopt the latest technologies, we need to consider how these, and those we use already, will support the learning process. Laurillard (1993b) provides a useful framework for evaluating 'educational media' – such as print, audio, video and computers – in terms of how they support a conventional view of the teaching and learning process. In this view, the process is seen very much as an active dialogue between teacher and learner. It consists of a repeated cycle of four phases: discussion, interaction, adaptation and reflection. But no one educational medium in her view is able to adequately support the whole cycle and thus fill the role of the teacher. Video, for example, is good as a presentational medium conveying better than print a vicarious view of the world, but is one-sided in the discussion it allows. Computer or telephone conferencing might support a more balanced dialogue in the presentation and discussion stages, but might lack visual images or sound. Interaction could be supported by well-designed specialist software but, in Laurillard's view, few media support and encourage adaptation (learners adapt their view of the world and thus 'learn') and reflection (learners reflect on learning process and integrate new knowledge with previous knowledge) in the way the teacher can.

Laurillard's model is perhaps particularly useful because it encourages us as teachers to stop and reflect on the learning process as a whole and the ways in which technology might support it. Without this reflection, technology might all too easily be seen as a panacea which will not only enrich the learning experience but also solve the problems of large classes, motivate reluctant learners and facilitate distance learning.

Developments in technology are taking place alongside a move towards more learner-centred approaches in language learning, including resource-based learning. There is a growing wealth of resources available, from dedicated language programs, world-wide digital radio and TV transmissions to the growing presence of the internet. But these benefits can only be maximised by careful evaluation, and their use should be fully integrated into the overall teaching programme if effective learning is to take place.

Interaction

When considering the contribution of different media or technologies to the overall learning process, it is also worth focussing on the degree of interaction (either person to machine or person to person) that any one medium can support. Hall et al (1999) suggest that at one end of a continuum (see Figure 1), there are more passive technologies – audio tapes perhaps or certain computer programs – which are concerned solely with presenting content, demanding nothing of the learner and providing no feedback. Moving through increasing levels of interactivity to the other end of the continuum, there are those which are predominantly concerned with the learning process. These demand considerably more of the learner and provide discussion and feedback of either a more closed (e.g. on predictable answers) or more open nature (as in, for example, a teacher mediated electronic discussion group). All have their role to play.

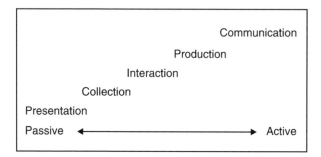

Figure 1: Possible levels of interaction

It is the relatively simple, easy to use, presentational technologies which have been used to great effect in the language classroom. The video or audio recording, the overhead projector which are used to introduce or practise a language point or bring in a hint of the target culture. As we encourage greater learner autonomy and the skills and strategies which enable learning to go on beyond the classroom, learners will demand more of technology and will expect a greater degree of interaction and electronic tutorial support. This will be especially important for the home-based or workplace learner.

Options

When you are considering which technologies to use, there are a number of pedagogical and practical issues worth bearing in mind. Some may be more or less important depending on a particular teaching and learning context. Pedagogical criteria should, if possible, drive the selection process although practical issues can impact on the possibility of achieving pedagogical objectives. It can be useful to identify any possible impediments so they can be dealt with effectively.

Tables 1 and 2 raise some of the pedagogical and practical questions which are worth posing and resolving at the planning stage and, subsequently, when technological provision is being re-evaluated.

Table 1: Pedagogical questions to ask when considering use of technology

For each technology type you are considering, answer the following questions. To establish appropriate selection criteria, decide on the relative importance of each factor and rank it accordingly. Add any other factors you think appropriate.

Factor	Question	Rank
Range	Is the technology useful for learners of any language level and any age? Can it cater for a range of interests and needs?	
Language activity	What type of learning activities does it support? Is it best used for intensive or extensive work?	
Interactivity	How interactive is it? Is its main use presentational? Is any form of feedback possible?	
Approach	Does it support a range of approaches? Are both teacher led and student-centred activities possible?	
Range of media	Which media (e.g. written text, sound, still and moving image) are supported? Is an integrated approach possible or desirable?	
Learning environment	In what ways does the learning environment provided by the technology enhance the learning experience? Is it the best available?	
Learning outcomes	How far will it support intended learning outcomes? What additional benefits are there (e.g. the development of IT skills)?	
Teacher time	Does it release the teacher from certain activities? Does it 'save' teacher time?	
Appeal	Does this technology have appeal value? Are learners therefore motivated to extend their learning?	
Learner training	Will learner training be needed before the technology can be used effectively? What form could it take?	
Learner support	What learner support will be needed when in use? Will this involve teacher, technical or resource manager time? Will 'help' materials need to be developed?	
Staff development	Will teachers need training before they can use it at its full potential? Will there be initial reluctance to use it?	

Table 2: Practical questions to ask when considering use of technology

For each technology type you are considering, answer the following questions. To establish appropriate selection criteria, decide on the relative importance of each factor and rank it accordingly. Add any other factors you think appropriate.

Factor	Question	Rank
Cost	What is the initial outlay? Is the equipment (e.g. PC, language laboratory) upgradeable at a later date to a higher specification? What is the additional cost? Does it save money or are there other benefits? Is it value for money?	
Quality	What is the quality of performance? For example, is there good sound delivery? Is it good enough for the intended teaching/learning aims?	
Maintenance and technical support	Is it easy to maintain? What are the associated costs? Is nearby technical support advisable and is it available?	
Life span	What is its expected working life? Will it be quickly superseded by a better model? Does it matter?	
Reliability	How reliable is it? If it breaks down can teaching/learning continue?	
Security	Can it be easily stolen? Are there ways of making it secure but still easily accessible?	
Ease of use	How easy is it for either the teacher or the learner to use? Is it easily stored or transported? Is it a familiar technology – in the way, for example, that the personal stereo has become ubiquitous?	
Reach	How many teachers and/or learners can this technology support? Can individuals and groups both use it? Does it provide for learners with special learning or physical needs?	
Flexibility and accessibility	How flexible is it? Is there a repeat, recording or save function? Can it be used in class, for self-access, for distance learning?	
Availability of materials	Are learning materials readily available? Can they be adapted or will they need to be developed from scratch?	

Pedagogical issues

The first issue when considering any equipment purchase on pedagogical grounds is to consider how it contributes to the **learning process**. What learning activities does it support? Perhaps a simple free-standing audio player is more appropriate for developing listening skills in the classroom, self-access centre or home than the multimedia environment of a personal computer which some might find distracting. The computer might be ideal for others who want access to a range of resources at the same time – for example, to the transcript of the recording, a dictionary, an electronic notebook and so on. In some cases the computer might be more useful for intensive listening exercises (easy to find one's place) and the portable player might be more useful for extensive listening activities (easy to sit back and focus one's attention).

There also needs to be a focus on the desired **learning outcomes**. It seems obvious, but if one of the aims of a course is to develop not only language competence but information technology skills, learners will need easy access to computers and activities will need to be designed which incorporate IT use. However, some caution is advisable. It is important not to attempt too much when the technology itself may be relatively unfamiliar. Piper and Wright (1999) report on a study observing language learners using the Internet to locate foreign sites at a time when the World Wide Web (and the mouse-driven computer) was relatively new to students. It showed that although learners appreciated the possibilities, very little language learning was actually taking place. Too much was new; study and search skills were being stretched in a new medium, the learners were not confident with the computer and they had no spare capacity to reflect on how they could develop (or even use) their language skills. See also the section on 'networked technology' in chapter 12.

When looking at the uses of technology, it is also important to ask how the technology enhances the learning environment for the learner and which media are really needed for what purpose. A well-designed resources centre offering a range of conventional media (print, video, audio) and a dedicated computer – with possibly a language advisor close at hand – will provide a flexible learning environment catering for a variety of interests, needs and abilities. The multimedia PC may offer a similarly stimulating and rich one-stop learning environment (more cheaply) but might also provide access to online discussion groups and other resources. However, perhaps there will be no need to provide access to a wide range of expensive resources if learners only want to improve their speaking skills.

Time for **learner training** must not be forgotten and may have to be built into a course if the equipment is unfamiliar. Learners may have the basic confidence to use equipment but often do not use it to its full potential unless shown how. How many language students will think of using TV subtitles for the deaf as a learning tool when watching foreign language television on their own if it has not been suggested to them? If learner training is important, staff development is equally important. Teachers will not embrace new technology unless they become familiar with its use and possibilities. At the beginning of the twenty-first century, the move to give all UK schoolteachers access to home computers and IT training is to recognise that confidence and skills need to be acquired.

Practical issues

When considering practical issues, cost is likely to be important but may well be set against other factors such as cost savings and benefits in other areas. For example, videoconferencing using ISDN telephone lines was introduced for fashion students at a school of art prior to an exchange visit to a partner college in Spain (Light et al, 2000). The Spanish students received English language classes during videoconferencing sessions, and students and staff in both countries collaborated online and planned for the actual exchange. Cost of equipment and telephone time could be set against real savings in extra travel expenses for staff, extra learning time for students and the unquantifiable benefits of getting to know and speak to students in another country.

Other practical issues governing the choice of technology or particular products should include an evaluation of its **quality** and how it matches general and specific teaching aims. This involves asking such questions as:

Is the television monitor big enough for everyone in the classroom or language laboratory to see?

Do I have access to a teaching room with blackouts to avoid too much sunlight interference?

Is the sound quality clear enough that everyone can hear the recording clearly?

Is the digital image on the computer screen recognisable?

Is the lip/mouth synchronisation on that new computer program or videoconferencing system good enough that it gives the learner benefits that they would not otherwise have?

Further questions might address the **durability** of the piece of equipment and the frequency of use. If teachers and learners are going to use a piece of equipment – a TV, a computer or audio recorder – on a regular basis, is it worth buying the heavy duty but more expensive educational model, or the cheaper domestic version from a High Street store? The question of reliability and maintenance is also worth examining. Is the maintenance contract on that old tape-based language laboratory so expensive that it might be worth investing in a number of personal computers which might be able to do the same job? More radically, could the equipment be replaced and purchase and maintenance costs shared with another institution/college/school?

Reliability of equipment may also be a problem if there is no local **technical support**, and it is worth considering whether teaching/learning could continue if it fails. In the art school (described by Light et al, 2000), problems with equipment and line connections were sufficiently frequent to de-motivate both learners and teachers.

When equipment is bought in the first flush of enthusiasm, it is vital to consider how **easy** it is **to use**. The audio cassette player, although it probably did not deliver the same sound quality as the reel to reel tape system, became the system of choice for those who wanted ease of use. The cassette recorder and cassette tape, in their turn, are giving way to other more flexible digital systems as did the vinyl disk before them. As a general rule, it is true that equipment that is difficult to get to know will not be used enthusiastically by learner or teacher.

Finally, one of the most important practical issues to consider is the **availability** of learning resources. When CD-ROM drives in personal computers were introduced, the technology was far in advance of the supply chain. The numbers and variety of educational CD-ROM packages were so limited that PC users were tempted to buy any program for novelty value without too much consideration of educational value (see chapter 11).

Fit for the purpose

Ultimately, the technology chosen has to be able to achieve the appropriate ends. Whilst travelling off the metalled road in the desert of Niger in the late eighties, one of the authors was shown around a village school by its teacher cum principal. The tour ended in front of a large wooden cupboard outside the school building and the doors opened to reveal a large television set. Despite its pride of place, the school and the village had never been able to make use of the set as the solar panels planned to power it had never been adequate, and the nearest electricity source was some fifty miles away. The project that was to bring educational television to the village was doomed to failure – unlike the school vegetable garden. It is only recently that a technology which uses inexpensively generated sources of electrical power has come to the fore. We have the wind-up radio, but at the time of writing we have yet to see the individually wind powered or wind-up television.

Encouraging use inside and outside the classroom

Learning materials and resources to be used, and technology is no exception, have to be built into the learning programme in such a way that the learners themselves understand its use and the associated learning objectives. In a formal learning context, this means that what happens outside the classroom in the self-access or resources centre needs to be fully integrated into the language curriculum or learners will not prioritise their independent learning (c.f. the findings of the FDTL *Ciel* project[1]). Very often this means that formal assessment of activities needs to be addressed. In independent learning time, students at one UK university worked through a number of self-marking Spanish grammar exercises which were freely available on the web[2] and the marks were automatically submitted to their tutor by the system when they were happy with their score. Learners and tutors both reported how pleased they were with the success of the scheme. Tutors were able to focus on different teaching points in the classroom but were able to keep a track on the progress of their students. Learners were motivated to work with the exercises because they could see their progress and knew their teachers were monitoring it.

However, we cannot always be totally confident about learners' independent use of resources. A study of UK Open University language students (reported by Stevens, 1999) found that learners were not necessarily using the components of their course as had been planned by course designers and which had been integrated into the course, unit by unit. In particular, they often found it easier (and possibly more coherent) to watch all the video sequences at one sitting before moving on to use the other materials.

References

Hall W, S White and B P Woolf, 'Interactive systems for learning and teaching' in Furht B, *Handbook of multimedia computing* (Boca Raton, Fla: CRC Press, 1999)

Laurillard D M, 'Multimedia and the changing experience of the learner' in M Ryan (ed), *Proceedings Asia Pacific Information Technology in Training and Education Conference and Exhibition*, APITITE 94 Brisbane, Australia, 1: 19–24 (1994)

Laurillard D M, *Rethinking university teaching: a framework for the effective use of educational technology* (Routledge, 1993b)

Light V, P Light and V Wright, 'Seeing eye to eye: an evaluation of the use of videoconferencing to support collaboration' in *European Journal of Psychology of Education,* Special Edition: learning to collaborate and collaborating to learn (2000)

Piper A and V Wright, 'The contribution of the Web to foreign language learning: an evaluation of the use of the World Wide Web by undergraduate students' in Hogan-Brun G and U O H Jung (eds), *Media, multimedia, omnimedia* (Peter Lang, 1999)

Stevens A, *Resources for independent language learning,* Plenary session at Ciel workshop, November 1999 (1999)

Notes

1   Higher Education Funding Council for England project funded 1997–2000, to promote the integration of independent learning with the taught language curriculum at university level. Details at http://ciel.lang.soton.ac.uk/

2   www.studyspanish.com/tutorial.htm

10

Computer-based applications and their use

VICKY WRIGHT AND SU WHITE

> 'Blimey! Can't believe so much time has gone by.'
> 'I like the electronic dictionary 'cos I never got the hang of the alphabet.'
> 'You can do the mouse next time.'

(Quotes from language learners observed working with computer-based multimedia materials)

This chapter will give an overview of the development of computer assisted language learning over the last few decades and present some of the more commonly available computer-based applications, such as word processing, e-mail, the World Wide Web and multimedia resources. It will look at how they might be used by language learners and at some of the research being carried out into their educational effectiveness.

Historical perspectives

Only around since 1975, at a time when the first BBC computers were being adopted for widespread classroom use in the UK, the now pervasive personal computer is the most recent addition to the technologies available to language learners and teachers. However, computers have been used in some form by language teachers since the 1960s. Warschauer (1998) usefully divides the history of computer assisted language learning (CALL) into three main stages of development which correspond neatly with three key pedagogical approaches to language teaching:

1. behaviouristic CALL;
2. communicative CALL;
3. integrative CALL.

Not all stages fit neatly into the suggested time periods and current usage has adopted many practices from earlier paradigms.

1. Structural approaches saw CALL being informed by behaviourist models of learning. This paradigm, dominant in the 1960's and 1970's, viewed the computer

106

as '*a mechanical tutor which never grew tired or judgmental and allowed learners to work at an individual pace*'. Its most significant feature was the repetitive drill and practice exercise, known pejoratively as 'drill and kill'.

2. Communicative CALL in the late 1970s and 1980s aligned with cognitive/constructivist theories that stressed that learning was a process of discovery. The emphasis was on language use rather than language forms, with grammar being taught implicitly rather than explicitly and the target language in use as widely as possible. Software developed included text re-construction programs (mostly variations on gapped texts and jumbled sentences) and simulations. The perceived advantage of much of this software was the language and discussion generated amongst learners working together as much as the practice provided by the software itself.

3. By the late 1980s and early 1990s, general learning theories which took a social or socio-cognitive view of learning (where learning is a social activity inseparable from the social context in which it takes place) were leading to a broader view of communicative language teaching which highlighted collaborative learning and language use in authentic contexts. Task-based and resource-based learning approaches stressed the use of authentic environments which bring together learners and integrate language skills. Technology was beginning to be seen as an integrative part of this learning process. No longer just an add-on to the learning environment, technological tools were to play a central role and would no longer mean just a once a week trip to the language laboratory for isolated language exercises.

Convergence

In the late twentieth and early twenty-first centuries, now referred to as the 'information age', a number of strands have converged to further embed the use of technology in education generally:

• technological advancements which have brought in the multimedia computer, high-speed networks and interactive digital TV;

• learning theories which focus on the social interactive aspect of learning (see above) and which place teachers in a facilitating role;

• communicative language learning pedagogies which highlight the value of authentic activities;

• general learner-centred pedagogies which see knowledge acquisition as a process (not as an end in itself) and stress the importance of key learning skills and strategies;

• the wide-spread political agenda to promote lifelong learning and widen access for all sectors of the community;

- financial constraints brought about by ever-increasing costs of conventional delivery which have led to the viewpoint that technological solutions are potentially financially advantageous (c.f. National Committee of Inquiry into Higher Education, 1997: Appendix 2).

Computers have become central features in home, library, school, college and university, their power has increased, and their cost in real term has fallen. However, there is still little evidence to support assumptions of significant cost-saving benefits for computer use in the classroom or self-access centre through reductions in teaching time. In fact, many initiatives have found that the reverse is the case – computers are relatively cheap but the software is never entirely fit for its purpose and costly development and user support time has to be costed in.

Language learners are particularly benefiting from many of these developments which bring affordable access to computer-based tools, multimedia software and the global resources of the internet.

Computer-based applications

Word processing

Computer word processing allows quick and easy revision of the written word and many writers now compose with more confidence, knowing that text can be easily moved around, corrected and deleted. Language learners benefit from the comparative ease with which documents can be drafted and re-drafted since it encourages them to focus on the process of writing (see Piper, 1987, Jarvis, 1997). They are able to work through a series of drafts, either on their own, with peers or with a teacher, until they are satisfied with the structure of the text and the development and sequence of their ideas. Dialogue around the developing text can be set up between learners, and between learners and teachers if the document is either printed out or sent as an e-mail attachment. At the more detailed level of the sentence, easy correction should encourage comprehensive proof-reading for errors in spelling, punctuation and syntax.

A foreign language word processing package purchased from one of the big software companies (often bundled with a full suite of office software, such as spreadsheets) will provide the additional benefits of the target language environment. The normal commands and the 'Help' files are all in the target language and learners should soon acquire the new technical vocabulary. A similar effect can be achieved if learners access the World Wide Web through a foreign language version of their normal web browser. Although a more authentic feel can be achieved with a foreign keyboard, which usually has dedicated keys for special or accented characters, it is not strictly necessary. These characters can normally be typed in either the English language or foreign language word processor using a sequence of function keys and numbers (depending on the particular package) or the 'Insert Symbol' option on the toolbar. A list of useful key strokes placed next to the computer might help learners learn the most common of these.

When using foreign language word processors, learners usually have access to a spelling and grammar checker and a thesaurus. Some may argue that these tools give learners unfair support, but most checkers are unable to offer more than suggested alternatives to individual words and phrases and only serve to prompt the learner to consider carefully. It can also be argued that these tools will become commonly available in the workplace and we must give our learners practise in using them.

E-mail

Electronic mail, bulletin boards, and discussion lists allow learners and teachers to communicate independently of space and time via the Internet. E-mail is cheap and easy to use and can provide a broad range of activities for language learners, although there is as yet limited research into its effectiveness. Learners can work together on activities over a period of time, on projects or stories, for example, which can be posted to a bulletin board or class distribution list. E-mails need not be restricted to text since sound and picture files can be attached to the e-mail.

Learners can also work on e-mail diaries which are sent to the whole class, or if the diaries are of a highly personal nature, to the teacher alone. The medium seems to encourage learners to invest more in the communication process than they might in face to face learner/teacher interaction, perhaps because e-mail is seen as an equalising medium by both parties. E-mail diaries may be significantly longer than an equivalent, conventional piece of writing and far more personal in terms of how much the writer is willing to reflect and reveal of himself or herself. A number of teachers have reported on the level of comment and detail to be found in e-mail diaries. It is interesting that this degree of openness (about family, friends, feelings, other learners and teachers) does not often carry back to the classroom and seems to be reserved solely for e-mail communication.

E-mail can provide multiple benefits for language learners if they correspond with a target language partner. Each partner can correct the other's work and send information about his or her country. In a tandem e-mail partnership (Little, 1996) these possibilities can be enhanced if both partners are sufficiently autonomous to be able to plan, monitor and evaluate their learning and know how to exploit the native speaker competence of their partner. It is recognised that this is not an easy task and that learners will need a lot of support and guidance from teachers. Learning advice on the e-mail *International Tandem Network* web pages[1] includes tips on: how to get started; what learners should talk about; when to use which language; how to correct the partner's texts; how to learn from the partner's texts; how intercultural learning can be promoted; how to translate in tandem; how to write letters in tandem.

The *Tandem Network* makes the following suggestions to learners on how they might benefit from an e-mail tandem partnership:

- *You can improve your knowledge of the foreign language. And you can learn lots of new things about your partner, your partner's mentality, beliefs, ideas, country, culture, etc.*

- *You learn by using your partner as a model – what he or she writes has a similar function to texts in a language learning book. You learn, for example, new, useful phrases and vocabulary. Also, he or she might use expressions and sentence structures which you once learned and thereby remind you of that which you had learned before.*

- *You learn by your partner helping you to understand that which he or she has written. For example, when you are still having difficulty understanding even after using a dictionary, then you can just ask your partner.*

- *Your partner aids you in learning by helping you to express what you wish to say. You could, for example, write something in your native language and then ask your partner how he or she would express it in the foreign language.*

- *You learn by your partner's corrections of your texts. But you determine yourself what and how your partner should correct.*

- *You profit from what your partner knows by asking him/her questions, by reading his/her accounts of things and by discussing various topics.*

E-mail exchanges can be a motivating addition to the curriculum. They can be institution to institution and a fairly formal arrangement, perhaps with joint topic work, or they can be on a 'one to one' individual basis. There is an obvious enthusiasm for working with native speakers of the language being learnt, and at the time of writing there were over thirty different language combinations (or sub-nets) available on the *Tandem Agency* web pages.

The World Wide Web

> The web is easier to search for specific stuff rather than leafing through millions of pages but it's complementary – it doesn't stop me using other language learning resources.

(Quote from a language learner observed working with the World Wide Web)

The World Wide Web is the hypermedia arm of the world-wide computer network, most commonly referred to as the Internet. It was invented by Tim Berners-Lee as recently as 1989 while he was working at CERN, the European Particle Physics Laboratory near Geneva. With a background of system design in real-time communications and text processing software development, the World Wide Web[2] was set up as an initiative for global information sharing

Accessed via a web browser such as *Internet Explorer* or *Netscape*, World Wide Web links (followed by clicking on 'hot links' or highlighted text) to authentic multimedia resources around the globe seem to offer possibilities unimaginable by earlier generations of language learners and teachers. Crompton (1999a), for example, reports that there are over three hundred thousand language journals – newspapers, magazines and periodicals – available in Spanish alone on the web. To this can be added other resources such as Internet radio and television, access to an online world of commerce, art and culture and growing libraries of documents from governmental and non-governmental organisations. A range of specific language learning resources such as dictionaries, online grammars and courses add to these possibilities to create a virtual learning environment.

Learners appreciate the potential of the web but do not always find it easy to use as a language learning tool without support and guidance. Piper and Wright (1999) report how a group of 92 university students viewed its use for language learning. A minority identified particular language skills and sub-skills on which the resources of the web could help them focus, seeing it as a useful source of reading practice, vocabulary and grammar development. Others mentioned online language courses, bulletin boards and discussion groups which could be used for writing practice. One learner mentioned the usefulness of bilingual sites where documents exist in both the target language and English. This was thought to be a valuable source of translation practice, but it was too tempting to read just the English version since '*it is faster to read and easier to understand.*' The majority of learners, however, saw the web as a unique source of up-to-date information about the countries whose languages they were studying. Most learners felt that the web as an open resource was not a learning tool in its own right but a complement or addition to formal teaching. Classes were described as more structured, giving feedback and providing opportunities for real interaction.

The obvious need to provide a more structured learning environment in which to exploit the potential of the web has led to a number of developments since the study described above took place in 1996 – although research by Rosell-Aguilar (2000) reported many similar reactions from students. Web pages are now being designed by teachers with specific groups of learners in mind so that links to useful resources are easier to find. Course modules are being placed on the web for learners to access and are being designed to give automatic feedback (both formative and summative) on the learner's progress. Free web sites are appearing which will automate the preparation by the teacher of simple text-based exercises (see for example the *Castle Toolkit* web-site[3]). However, as with any new medium, the design and use of materials accessed and delivered via the web will need to be explored as we discover its strengths and weaknesses.

Crompton (1999b) describes grammar practice materials which were re-purposed from print format and made available over the web to a large group of learners of Spanish. Moving them online had several management advantages in that they were easier to distribute and could be readily updated. They could also be linked to relevant resources, such as newspapers, for particular exercises. The study concludes that learners generally benefited from the web-based format, but unexpectedly they preferred to keep written record sheets of their work rather than online versions and spent more time on short exercises than longer ones. The study also concluded that unsophisticated presentation and a simple range of activity types are not sufficient for learners used to the player interaction of highly developed computer games.

Work by Richter (1999) summarises a number of key principles underpinning the facilitation of learning with web-based materials:

- interactivity with feedback;
- adaptability to the needs of the user;
- instructional design – interactivity needs to include structured activities which practise, consolidate, process, contextualise and apply acquired knowledge;
- communication facilities to enable flexible, adaptive feedback by human interaction (user/user, user/tutor communication);
- skills to use the tools of the learning environment, e.g. browsers, e-mail, web searches, web-publishing.

The last point is crucial since the majority of learners in the Internet study described by Piper and Wright (1999) had very poor search skills and many lacked confidence in their IT skills. A number lacked confidence in their linguistic ability, preferring to search for what they wanted through the medium of English.

Richter usefully defines three modes of learning/teaching with varying amounts of tutor support, which are possible using the web:

1. use of resources in the form of special link collections (no tutor support);
2. use of on-line seminars as a delivery mode for class teaching (tutor support and feedback, possibly via e-mail);
3. use of specially developed open learning courseware (no human feedback).

Whichever mode is used, the learner unused to setting his or her learning objectives and lacking the independent learning skills to take forward their learning will need considerable support and guidance from a real, as opposed to a virtual, teacher. How effective the web is as a general or specific learning environment will emerge fairly quickly in the first years of the twenty-first century.

Multimedia

Whether delivered by CD ROM, DVD (Digital Versatile Disk) or over the Internet, language learners now have the opportunity to access and control multiple media (text, sound, graphics, video, animations) in a single multimedia computer environment. Multimedia courses (and other multimedia tools and resources such as encyclopaedias, electronic dictionaries and films) give the learner the opportunity to '*explore, discover, ponder, search, question, answer and receive feedback*' (Brett, 1998). Intuitively, it seems that such an environment must enhance language learning and bring added value which may be greater than the sum of its parts. Brett suggests that, although research into the effectiveness of multimedia is in its infancy, support for it comes from three main areas:

The first is in the area of intuition itself. As teachers we can see benefits in a medium which is flexible and potentially interactive medium, able to cater for individual learner differences and provide access to a wealth of authentic materials.

The second is from Second Language Acquisition (SLA) research and theory (Doughty, 1991). The concepts of negotiation of meaning (e.g. Pica, 1994), of noticing (e.g. Schmidt, 1990), motivation (Crookes and Schmidt, 1992) and learner autonomy (Dickinson, 1987) have particular relevance since they suggest that a multimedia environment provides necessary language input, the potential for interaction and negotiation and a range of support features which aid comprehension.

The third is from the limited empirical research which has been carried out. Although difficult to draw conclusions, given the novelty factor and the variety of software available, results have been positive. Individual studies have shown that listening skills, pronunciation and vocabulary gains tend to be higher in learners working with multimedia compared to conventional media. Learners are also more likely to show positive attitudes to learning. However, some learners, confronted by too many media, may be distracted from their purpose and may do less well. Others may benefit from having a freer choice.

Several small-scale studies (Piper and Wright, 1999) have investigated how learners work in a relatively open hypermedia environment in which they are free to choose their own pathway through the materials. Pairs of learners working with linked multimedia modules (e.g. authentic documents, transcripts, interactive activities, and links to dictionaries, reference grammars and the internet), developed using an authoring platform or computer environment called *Microcosm* were observed and found to vary widely in the way they chose to work.

Figure 2 shows how language learners might choose to work with the resources available:

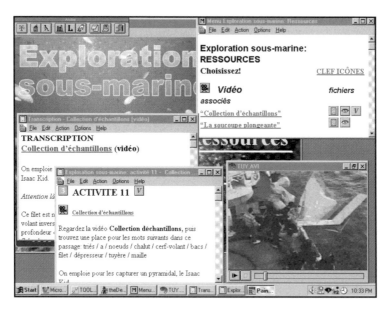

Figure 2: Screenshot from the Microcosm, hypermedia French application

Each of the pairs stated their learning aims before they started work and reported on what they had learnt at the end of the observation period. Some pairs were observed to focus primarily on **content** – threading their way through the resources, following up items that interested them, using the dictionary as they needed and doing the accompanying activities as they occurred. Other pairs chose to focus primarily on perceived language needs and to select from the list of activities according to the **skill** they wanted to practise. All learners felt that they had made gains which might not have been possible using separate resources. Although the majority of learners claimed to have achieved their learning aims, and some were surprised to find that they had made progress in unexpected areas such as IT skills, learners and teachers need to be aware of the potential dangers of this type of open (and possibly unstructured) environment.

Multimedia does not just offer benefits in the area of language learning. The work of Kramsch and Andersen (1999) suggests that multimedia CD ROM technology is a particularly powerful tool when used to teach language in its authentic, cultural context. The computer gives learners access to video footage and other cultural materials (photos, commentaries, transcripts, etc) which give learners a real sense of the socio-cultural context in which the language is used. However, learners faced with a rich resource of this nature are seen as being faced with the double task of having to interpret both the cultural and the linguistic features (and the interaction between them) to arrive at an understanding of language in use.

References

Brett P, 'An intuitive, theoretical and empirical perspective on the effectiveness question for multimedia' in Cameron K (ed), *Multimedia CALL: theory and practice* (Elm Bank Publications, 1998)

Crompton P M, 'Integrating internet-based CALL materials into mainstream language teaching' in Cameron K (ed), *CALL and the learning community* (Elm Bank Publications, 1999a)

Crookes G and R W Schmidt, 'Motivation: reopening the research agenda' in *Language Learning*, 41, 4: 469–512 (1992)

Dickinson L, *Self-instruction in language learning* (Cambridge University Press, 1987)

Doughty C, 'Theoretical motivations for IVD software research and development' in Bush M, A Slaton, M Verano and M E Slaayden (eds), *The interactive videodisc, the 'why and the 'how'*, CALICO Monograph, 2 (Provo, Utah: Brigham Young University, 1991)

Jarvis H, 'Word processing and writing skills: practical applications to language teaching text books' in *British Journal of Educational Technology,* 28, 3: 165–175 (1997)

Kramsch C and R W Andersen, 'Teaching text and context through multimedia' in *Language Learning and Technology,* 2, 2: 31–42 (1999)

Little D, 'Learner Autonomy and Learner Counselling' in Little D and H Brammerts (eds), *A guide to language learning in tandem via the internet,* CLCS Occasional Paper 46 (Trinity College Dublin, 1996)

Pica T, 'Research on negotiation: What does it tell us about second-language learning conditions, processes and outcomes?' in *Language Learning,* 44, 3: 493–527 (1994)

Piper A, 'Helping learners to write: a role for the word processor' in *English Language Teaching Journal*, 41, 2 (1987)

Piper A and V Wright, 'The contribution of the Web to foreign language learning: an evaluation of the use of the World Wide Web by undergraduate students' in Hogan-Brun G and U O H Jung (eds), *Media, multimedia, omnimedia* (Peter Lang, 1999)

Richter U, *Web-based language learning in a classroom context: a case study,* Paper given at ALT-C 99 Conference, Bristol, September 1999 (1999)

Rosell-Aguilar F, *Language learning with the Internet: a Spanish example,* Presentation at the CIEL workshop on ICT for language learning, LSE, March 2000 (CIEL, 2000)

Schmidt R, 'The role of consciousness in second language learning' in *Applied Linguistics*, 11: 129–158 (1990)

Warschauer M, 'Computer-mediated collaborative learning: theory and practice' in *Modern Language Journal*, 81 3: 470–481 (1997)

Notes

1   www.slf.ruhr-uni-bochum.de/

2   www.w3.org/People/Berners-Lee/

3   www.le.ac.uk/castle/

11

Integrating IT into the curriculum

VICKY WRIGHT AND SU WHITE

Delivery and platform

Early text-based CALL (Computer Assisted Language Learning) software was for the most part delivered on floppy disk and run on standalone computers of varying types or platforms (e.g. BBC, Apple Macintosh, IBM PC). Multimedia packages need higher capacity delivery modes and consumer expectations, combined with commercial demands, are leading to the development of ever higher capacity disks for what are currently standard (e.g. IBM PC and Microsoft Windows compatible) platforms. A comparison of the storage capacity of computer disks to emerge over a short period of time at the end of the twentieth/ beginning of the twenty-first century shows how this is the case. The floppy disk holds 1.44 megabytes (MB) of information, while at the time of writing the standard CD ROM holds 650 MB, enough for 74 minutes of audio recording, the text of an encyclopaedia, between 15 to 20 hours of digitally compressed audio and a small amount of digital video (of rather low picture quality, not necessarily full screen). High density CD ROM disks store 1.2 gigabytes (GB), double the capacity of a standard disk. The DVD (digital versatile disk) has been developed so that it can store and deliver high picture quality films of around two hours in length together with film related information, additional clips and web links. This requires a storage capacity of 7 GB. The next generation of video recorder, the digital video recorders, will probably record some twenty hours viewing time onto hard disk. The increase in picture quality and storage capacity which has accompanied the most recent technological advances brings advantages to the language teacher and learner. The quality of the visual element is especially useful to the learner who is likely to be easily distracted by fuzzy images and poor sound/lip synchronisation.

Software delivered on disk can be used on standalone computers; programs can be copied onto the computer's hard disk or used directly from disk. CDs can be stored in CD towers or servers and delivered over a local network. This has the advantage of higher security but may have the disadvantage of a slower delivery, depending on the quality and bandwidth of the network. Delivery of equivalent software over the Internet is often very slow, although this depends on the nature of the connection.

Connections range from the low bandwidth modem commonly used by individuals with dial-up telephone access, through the faster ISDN lines, onto leased lines which may be used by small companies or organisations. At the top end are the increasingly high bandwidth connections available to schools, colleges and universities. There may be considerable cost implications associated with better quality connectivity.

Software design and evaluation

If computer-based activities for language learning are to be successful in terms of learning outcomes, software – whether designed in-house or bought commercially – should satisfy a number of basic design criteria. This is especially important when the suspicion remains that computer use is still, to a large extent, driven by technology rather than pedagogy. Blin et al (1998), in a review of language teaching courseware development, suggest that there needs to be greater analysis of the relationship between the software content and the supporting medium. Teachers/developers need to ask whether the content is pedagogically useful and whether the mode of delivery is appropriate, and at least as effective as other more traditional media and face to face classroom teaching. One problem is that software design is still driven by technological and interface considerations and this is compounded by the fact that teachers/developers are only just beginning to find out how learners actually use computers.

Blin et al. (1998) highlight key areas in software design and use. The most important of these are:

1. Software design methodologies which are informed by the relationship between...
   - an analysis of learners needs;
   - a model of language learning;
   - the platform or authoring system;
   - screen design, navigation, technical constraints.

2. Software evaluation methodologies which are informed by...
   - reliable testing with user groups;
   - design and measurement of appropriate criteria;
   - a measure of the value compared to other software and other media.

3. Implementation/integration of the software into the curriculum which is informed by...
   - the learning environment (e.g. self-access, classroom, distance learning);
   - its relationship to the curriculum;
   - the degree of learner control;
   - the degree of interactivity;
   - the role of the teacher.

The importance of the inter-relationship between the learning goals, the software itself and the teaching and learning context is also highlighted by Hemard (1997). Teachers considering adopting a particular piece of software or developing their own might find it useful to set out first an evaluation framework based on their own context. It is also worth consulting existing users and any software reviews (e.g. the web-based database maintained for the UK Subject Centre for Languages, Linguistics and Area Studies by the University of Hull[1].

The down-to-earth questions (see below) put by Laurillard (1993a) in a checklist for language software designers and evaluators will prove of further use. Not all are relevant to every program:

- Does the program never crash or hang?
- Does the program allow a QUIT option at all times?
- Does the program allow access to all parts of the program where appropriate?
- Does the program state its objectives briefly and clearly?
- Does the program make clear at each point what the learner is supposed to be doing?
- Does the program offer some kind of feedback to the learner?
- Does it avoid making definitive judgements?

The following might be added to Laurillard's list:

- Is the program appealing visually?
- Does it motivate the learner to want to work with it?
- Does it challenge the learner to move forward?
- Does it provide both formative (during the activity) and summative (end of activity) feedback and assessment?

The reader will want to suggest further questions.

Integration into the curriculum

If computer-based teaching and learning is to be adopted successfully in an institutional environment (school, college, university), experience shows that it will need to become either a core component of the language curriculum or integrated in such a way that learners (and teachers) feel that it is a necessary and useful component. Only then will they prioritise the use of the computer.

This can be done in a number of ways. Learners working in a well-resourced university language centre might use computer-based resources to support their independent learning outside the classroom in the following ways for the following reasons:

1. They use a dedicated language program (e.g. a grammar exercise, a pronunciation or translation package, a multimedia course) because it has been recommended by the teacher or is required work for the current work module.

2. They use computer-based based reference materials such as dictionaries and grammars to support their hand-written or computer-based work (e.g. translations, essays).

3. They use electronic newspapers, the web, encyclopaedias, foreign TV and radio stations to research information for an individual/group project or end of module task.

4. They watch foreign television/film on internet-based digital TV or DVD for general listening/viewing practice or to relax.

5. They surf the web for general language practice or to relax.

6. They use a course electronic bulletin board to add to the current discussion or to check on work set.

7. They send e-mails to foreign language pen-pals as a course requirement or personal e-mails to friends and family in this country and abroad.

They might carry out one or several of these activities in one session (and this is by no means an exhaustive list) or use foreign language word processors in the computer laboratories in order to complete work set. They might work on their own or in groups. They could equally well be working at a distance with some of the learning materials, if appropriate software user licences and copyright clearance are available for the CD ROM-based software, and the network connection is fast enough and of sufficient bandwidth to support multimedia applications.

Although the above scenario describes advanced learners working outside the classroom, many of the activities described might be carried out in the classroom or by younger or less advanced learners. The use of computers for task and project-based activities, for example, is growing as learners have greater access to computers in the classroom and the home. In some contexts, single computers will provide an additional focus for individual or group work in a classroom; in others, the institution's computer laboratory will replace any need for a dedicated language laboratory and will be used for whole class or individual work. In some cases, electronic materials may form the core of the course with all teaching and support being carried out online and at a distance.

Computer use for language learning will continue to expand as the use of computers expands generally, but is likely to remain in a supporting role rather than act as a direct replacement for face to face class teaching. For many users however, both learners and teachers, it remains an unfamiliar tool and support and training for those that need (and want) to acquire the relevant IT skills is a crucial issue. *ICT4LT* is a European-funded *Socrates* project[2] which has addressed the issue of IT training for language teachers and developed a series of on-line web-based training modules.

Overview of computer-based applications used for language learning

In the early 1990s, the *TELL* (*Technology Enhanced Language Learning*) Consortium of universities (funded under a UK higher education initiative, TLTP, to enhance the effectiveness and efficiency of teaching and learning with computers) developed a suite of language learning packages which had considerable impact on a sector where little foreign language learning software had been developed commercially except for English as a Foreign Language. Whilst under development the TELL[3] packages were classified into one of three categories: language tools, language resources and language courses. This seems a useful distinction to make and the overview of applications which can be used for language learning given in the lists in Table 3 continues to use these rough categories. The classification is for guidance only as some applications may fall into more than one category.

Many of the items in the list may not have been specifically developed for use in language learning (e.g. foreign language word processors) but can offer powerful learning opportunities when used imaginatively. Some indication of the range of educational possibilities offered is given, but the list is only a starting point for thinking about the use of technology. It is not exhaustive and, given continued developments in new technologies, some of the contents may date fairly rapidly. The reader is invited to review the list in the context of current developments at the time of reading.

Table 1: Computer-based language learning materials

Computer-based language tools	
Language tools help learners achieve their objectives and the list is growing as technology advances. Some are available on standalone computers some depend on networked access. They include:	
Word processors	Help learners focus on the writing process and facilitate drafting and re-drafting. If available, foreign language versions provide a target language environment. The foreign keyboard is not essential.
E-mail	Links learners and teachers and can provide a good source of writing activities, exchange of information and contact with native speakers.
Spell and grammar checkers/ thesauri	Usually incorporated into word processors but often available as add-ons in the form of multilingual proofing tools. Far from providing all the answers, they encourage learners to reflect.
Translation packages	Commercial packages are variable in quality but improving along with developments in natural language processing; will be common tools in the office of the future. Some web search engines (e.g. *Altavista*) provide a 'translate' option for foreign language web pages but can be used to translate small amounts of text entered by the user.
Concordancers	Promote 'data driven learning' (see Johns and King, 1991), permitting learners to search and query large collections of texts or

	'corpora'. Investigation of patterns in authentic written and spoken language possible, but packages not always easy to use.
Speech recognition and text to speech packages	Originally designed to facilitate reading and writing for those with disabilities, they convert speech to text and vice versa. Not yet 100% accurate, they offer wide-ranging possibilities for language learning and are beginning to be incorporated into language learning packages.
Online tuners	Locate global web-based radio and TV stations via a web browser[4] or via a self contained internet program sitting on the computer desktop. Provides cheap and easy access to foreign language stations. Picture and sound quality may be variable.
Web search engines	Useful for learners locating information for project work but demand fairly sophisticated research skills. Foreign language versions facilitate searches of foreign documents.
Internet portals	Web pages providing structured access to internet information and resources. Many foreign embassies provide a service.

Tools for teachers might include:

Commercial authoring programs	E.g. the *WIDA Authoring Suite* or the *Camsoft* programs which allow language teachers to input their own exercises into an existing template.
Testing software	E.g. generic software from *Questionmark Computing*. Can be used to create multiple choice tests/cloze tests etc.
Software writing tools	Generic 'toolbox' approach to design/writing of new learning packages. E.g. *Director, Toolbook, Visual Basic* and specialist web-design tools.

Computer-based language resources

Computer-based resources provide access to the target language or information about the target language and culture. Many are designed specifically with language learners in mind, the majority are not. A search of supermarket shelves or bookshops when abroad or in specialist shops at home will reveal growing possibilities. The list includes:

Encyclopaedias	Native language versions useful for topic work. If run locally on a computer they are easier and faster for locating items than the web. Likely to include graphics, statistical information, text, video and sound. Foreign language versions available.
The World Wide Web	Is often seen as a library of authentic multimedia resources from news reports to contents of art galleries. Offers a multitude of language learning possibilities encompassing most of the tools/resources/courses listed here. Difficult to guarantee reliability of documents; often difficult to navigate.

Newspapers	Available on CD ROM and over the Internet. CD versions can be built into an easily searchable archive, internet versions are more likely to be up to date.
Grammar reference	Electronic searchable grammars often linked with practice exercises. Available as a standalone package or on the web. Some web sites run free grammar clinics, responding to learners' questions.
Electronic dictionaries	Vary from easily searchable text-based packages to those with picture and video illustrations and pronunciation of head-words. Some web sites offer dictionaries or access to terminological databases/corpora collections.
Films on DVD	Played on a PC or standard TV, they often have subtitles or are dubbed in several languages and background notes. Easier to manipulate than standard video but would need to be projected for classroom use.
Books	Often abridged versions of full-length books As on-screen reading is tiring, the printed book might be preferable and cheaper.
Games	Games are motivating and vary from very simple text-based games to those, mostly designed for native speakers, which incorporate virtual reality effects. Many of these involve players as actors in a simulation game.

Computer-based language courses

Perhaps a little misleading, the term 'course' here denotes dedicated language learning software. It usually provides some degree of interactivity and automatic feedback and corresponds most neatly with the term CALL (Computer Assisted Language Learning). Packages will vary from those offering practice of particular skill elements, to full courses which provide a language learning curriculum. Software may be delivered on floppy disk, CD ROM, DVD or downloadable from the internet.

Focused practice	Found in packages aimed at providing a focus on one of listening / writing / reading / vocabulary /pronunciation or grammar. Often used to extend classroom learning since learners can work at own pace according to needs. Grammar and vocabulary activities are useful especially when offering alternatives to traditional text (i.e. with graphics or sound).
	Pronunciation packages should allow recording and playback. Many offer graphical representation of the way individual sounds are articulated through speech recognition technology which also compares learners with a model speaker.
	Listening practice software may offer transcripts and translations. Few packages offer opportunities for speaking/fluency practice.

Integrated approaches Are found in packages which combine various activities and may offer online tools, e.g. *TELL Encounters* which offers listening practice with options to participate in the scripted dialogue, transcriptions and translations, grammar reference and practice. An integrated approach is useful for the learner working without a teacher.

This chapter has given some insight into the type and variety of computer-based applications which can be used for language learning. Only trial and use will show how each can be implemented in any one context, but once again it should be emphasised that it should be primarily pedagogical considerations, rather than application type (or fashion), which determine choice.

References

Blin F, N Chénik and J Thompson (eds), *CALL courseware development: a handbook* (Hull: EUROCALL 1998)

Hemard D P, 'Design principles and guidelines for authoring hypermedia language learning applications' in *System*, 25, 1: 9–27 (1997)

Laurillard D M, *Program design principles* (The University of Hull: The TELL Consortium, 1993a)

Notes

1 www.lang.ltsn.ac.uk

2 see: www.ict4lt.org/

3 see: www.hull.ac.uk/cti/tell.htm

4 http://vTuner.com

12

Using technology to support independent learning: the future?

VICKY WRIGHT AND SU WHITE

This chapter identifies how the most fast moving current changes in the use of technology for language learning point the way to ongoing future developments. Major changes are seen to be driven by the growing ubiquity of networked technology. It is understood that the reader will not necessarily have access to the full range of facilities which are described.

The basics of networked technology are described, and the ways in which this technology has impacted on the traditional constraints of time and place for the learner. The text outlines a range of ways in which audio, text, video and conferencing can be used both to support directed and independent learning. These technologies can equally well be used to provide peer support and a channel for expert discussion between teachers supporting such learning. The chapter then goes on to discuss how such technologies can be integrated together within a single 'learning environment'.

Networked technology

Networked technology provides many enhancements to the capabilities of a multimedia computer system described in the previous chapter and has much to offer the language teacher and learner. The computer may be part of a local area network (LAN) which links all the computers in a language laboratory or self-access centre, or be part of some wider network such as a school or campus wide network. The computer network may be configured as an Intranet which presents a closed world of networked resources for some its pre-defined community of users, or it may allow full and open access to the global resources of the internet in a less managed way. In some city areas or geographical regions, systems may also be part of a metropolitan area network (MAN) which links on a regional basis, and frequently offers special sets of resources and information services within that region.

Computer-mediated communication

Within the classroom, networked computers allow real-time on-line written discussion between members of the class working all together or in groups. Warschauer (1997) argues that a medium which allows learners to plan, draft and re-draft and to respond quickly to others leads to significantly greater involvement and interaction than in a conventional class. As learners work together on a joint task, communication is enhanced. This reflects the point which was made by Papert (1980) that the learners engaged in a joint task, and talking about working with the computer enabled them to engage in their cognitive tasks to a greater extent. Computers facilitate collaborative interaction as *'the historical divide between speech and writing has been overcome with the interactional and reflective aspects of language combined in a single medium'*. The power of the written word for rapid interaction between young people is also in evidence in the fashionable use of text messaging using mobile telephony.

The distance learning environment

Earlier technologies supporting independent language learning made use of discrete technologies, such as audio or video broadcast and recordings, the fax or the telephone. The advent of increased use of networked technology has been accompanied by the integration of some of these supporting technologies, for example through the use of computer systems, to enable text, audio or videoconferencing. However, the introduction of such facilities is not necessarily trouble-free and problems may easily arise from operating difficulties or lack of familiarity with the principles of the equipment. One practical way in which such problems may be reduced is for teachers to make use of the technology through actively engaging in on-line activities prior to using the technology for teaching. For example, collaborative preparation of the materials can provide an opportunity to make real use of the computer systems, familiarising teachers with their capabilities, and gaining a realistic appreciation of how learning resources and activities will be rendered by the computer system. Despite the acknowledged problems, evidence of their pedagogical benefits in the area of language learning is strong (see Light et al, 2000 and chapter 9, 'practical questions'). Table 4 outlines a range of examples of how the various conferencing technologies (video, audio and text) can be used.

Table 1: Conferencing techniques

Conferencing allows both same language and bilingual groups of learners to work together and remote groups to join a class with a teacher. Video and audio conferencing must be synchronous, with the learners accessing the computer network at the same time. However, text conferencing can also be asynchronous, with participants writing to the conference at different times.

The teacher will need to use skills and judgement, developed for the classroom, to manage interactions in the conferences. Areas to be particularly aware of include dealing with silence, the lack of visual or audio cues, error correction strategies, and the way tutors balance interventions against learner autonomy

Audioconferencing	A dedicated conference telephone can link a number of learners together; a telecommunications company will also set up a conference for a small fee. Many domestic phones offer a three-way facility without the need for special equipment and many schools, colleges and universities have installed communication systems which support multiple telephone conferencing. Internet telephony offers the possibility of inexpensive global communication. Many people prefer the anonymity of the telephone – risk-taking may be easier for language learners when they cannot be seen.
Suggestions for successful audio conferences:	A number of the suggestions for successful video conferences are equally true of audio conferences: • Sessions are most effective if there is a focus. OU students who were given tasks to prepare in advance of sessions with a tutor participated more effectively than those who were not (Stevens, 1999). Adequate linguistic preparation will help learners overcome lack of visual clues. • Possible language activities include role-plays, collaborative projects and interviews. • When there are no visual clues, it is important that speakers name the person they are addressing. A nominated chair to manage proceedings is effective. His/her role can be to initiate new conversational strands should silences arise. • If participants have not met before, a short description/biography could be circulated. These could be made available via e-mail or on web pages. • If groups are working collaboratively, an agreed written record of discussions and any decisions is useful. • Even using standard telephone conferences, documents can be shared prior to the conference either by e-mail, web publication or in paper form. • With Internet based conferences, documents can be made available for sharing in an on-line resource centre.

Videoconferencing

Communications can be via the telephone network using specialised equipment or via a computer network using dedicated software.

High quality electronics has made desktop conferencing from individual PCs workable. For large-scale conferencing a studio might ensure suitable lighting and acoustics; images can be projected for large group participation. The quality of the network in terms of speed of transmission and volume capacity will determine the sound and picture quality.

Conferences can be multi-point (many sites) or point to point (single site to single site) with one to one (learner/learner or learner/teacher) or one to many (teacher/learners) combinations.

Experience suggests that videoconferencing is most effective when participants have met – however, many users talk about the benefits of being able to 'contextualise' their interlocutors in terms of appearance, gestures and surroundings.

Suggestions for successful videoconferences:

- Learners working together will need to be set tasks (e.g. joint projects) or will need to decide what they want to achieve in advance in order to give some purpose to the session.

- Interaction is more effective in pairs or small groups; every member of the group should participate.

- A teacher-led session (one to many) might be followed up more successfully off-line.

- Participants need to speak clearly, taking into account any time delay.

- Speak one at a time – hand over 'speech turns' by naming the person you are talking to. A nominated 'chair' at each site might be useful if groups are working together.

- Rapid movements are likely to cause blurred images.

- Eye contact is important in face to face interaction, so the remote image will need to be positioned just below/next to the camera so that participants are looking into the camera when speaking.

- A shared collective writing space on the screen know as a whiteboard can be used to write points that need to be saved or are hard to hear (e.g. phone numbers, addresses) and for writing collaboratively. Other applications/documents can also be shared.

A nearby telephone will allow participants to make last minute changes to meetings easily.

Text conferencing	Text conferencing grew out of the activities of early games playing programs and some systems will be referred to as MOOs. Can be in real time or asynchronous, local or global. Web-based bulletin boards or e-mail lists run by a list server allow multi-user conferences. Web-based chat rooms allow synchronous discussion so that groups of learners or learners and teacher can arrange to meet at a pre-arranged time. Class members can be e-mailed to be given appointment times. A single to many conferences can be mixed mode with teacher/speaker visible through a web camera and participants communicating via e-mail or chat room. Sound, picture and written attachments can be sent with the document.
Suggestions for successful text conferences:	Again many of the tactics appropriate for audio and video conferences may be applied in the context of a live text conference. Possible activities are: • group or paired writing tasks; • role play; • virtual class work e.g. follow-up activities to an on-line lesson; • learners clarifying points of uncertainty with the teacher. Where a customised text discussion tool is not available, it may be possible to replicate some of the tasks using email discussion lists or even one-to-one e-mail.

The pedagogical strengths of computer technology in the classroom and the ability to use computers, software and electronically stored resources irrespective of time or place has provided technology with a special role in supporting open and distance learning. Since the establishment of The UK Open University in the late 1960s, study initiatives which in some way take advantage of available technology have become increasingly widespread. This development recognises and makes use of the continuum which exists between the classroom, the self-access/open learning centre and the home or workplace.

The increasing use of technology in general, and computers in particular, for language learning has been accompanied by a move to harness their ability to enable, support and even enhance the opportunities for the learner to access materials and work independently, both within conventional educational environments and at a distance.

Typically, computer-based open learning is supported over a local area network or intranet, with perhaps some additional accessibility for learners to do part of their study from their home or workplace. In both open and distance learning, the use of conventional resources may be integrated with a multiple media approach which sets the use of papers, video and audio resources alongside the computer-based resources. In distance learning this may particularly be the use of a local CD-ROM containing some part of the learning resources, with updated and interactive components provided by live access to the Internet.

We are seeing the convergence of the technical, pedagogical, political and financial will (see chapter 10, 'convergence' above) and the integration of the broadcasting, publishing and computer industries predicted by Negroponte (1995). This convergence provides the means to change the learning environment, accelerating the integration of different components of the various channels and media which provide resources and support learning processes.

In the context of such changes, language teachers can take the opportunity to integrate the components of these technologies of print and publishing, broadcast and motion picture, computer and communications to bring together the 'virtual language learning resource centre' and the 'virtual language classroom in order to build virtual language learning environments.

The key driver for such changes can be seen in the development of networked learning, enabling the exploration of ways in which learners might engage in learning, independent of location or independent of time. The emergence of virtual learning environments was accompanied in the USA in the late 1990s with the development of 'For Profit' educational establishments such as the University of Phoenix. These institutions initially offered niche market courses, frequently for the completion of degrees or for shorter post experience, vocational study. At the same time numbers of large-scale companies began to talk about and set about creating corporate universities, which made use of multimedia technology and global communications. A useful account of the growth of such environments and the potential globalisation of education is given by Marchesse (1998) and a detailed discussion of the potential implication for higher education in the UK followed from Newby (1999). These developments have not however been restricted to higher education. Major companies such as IBM and Microsoft have active school level educational collaborations which include the use of virtual learning environments.

It is the visions of the global university or global learning environment to which the full-scale view of virtual learning environments is most relevant, but cut down versions may be applied to small groups or more informally organised learners. Organisations starting from scratch have had the impetus to streamline and integrate their administration. As well as typically providing for access to learning resources and interactions between learner(s)/teacher(s) and learner(s)/learner(s) via a single computer desktop, such environments are also able to integrate elements of classroom and student management such as student registration, tracking and assessment. These environments go by various descriptors and accompanying acronyms, including managed learning environments and web-based learning environments.

Components

Essentially the virtual learning environment provides a set of tools for the teachers and/or class administrators. They can enter information about students and link to learning and information resources to fill or 'populate' the environment. From the learners' point of view, the environment will have some kind of visual or iconic representation of the different processes and activities which are available to them as part of their programme of study. Figure 3 below shows a graphic depiction of the 'Virtual U', a virtual university which emerged from work by Linda Harasim at Simon Frazer University in Canada.

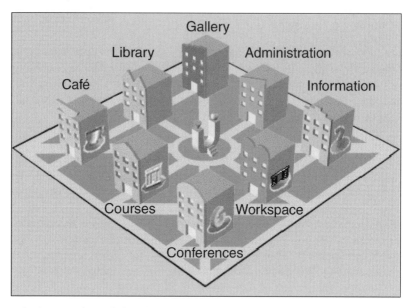

Figure 3: An overview of the Virtual U

The most sophisticated systems create environments which effectively provide and manage virtual schools, colleges and universities incorporating the whole gamut of administrative processes of registering, tracking, accrediting the learner and ultimately awarding qualifications. The suites of computer programs which manage and present these systems are by their nature and complexity large and expensive.

Within these wide-scale virtual systems and within smaller class or programme based systems, there is a need to provide the learner with a graphic overview of the system, along with a course or module scale view of the environment. Again there is a range of ways in which the environment can be presented to the learner. Some systems mix text-based lists with icons or a 3D view of a study room. The graphic representation of a learning environment via a study area metaphor is illustrated with an example from the Virtual U shown below in Figure 4.

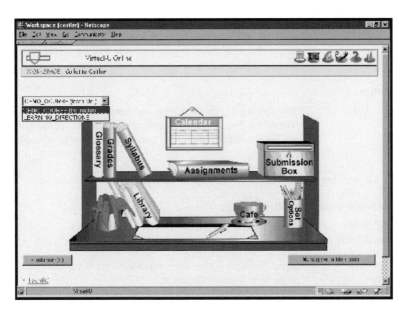

Figure 4: The study area metaphor from the Virtual U

Each environment needs to accommodate a number of academic, administrative and social functions. These functional components can be subdivided into four areas: course management, back office, self-access/independent study and learner interactions. They are itemised in Table 5 below. Individual readers will be able to identify which items within the components are most relevant to their own teaching context.

Table 2: Components of a virtual learning environment

Course Management	
Registration	Ideally systems have direct on-line registration by the learner, although this will depend upon the context in which the system is used.
User tracking	Provides information for student information database indicating progress through the course. Sophisticated systems may alert learners or tutors of unexpected levels of progress.
Messaging system	For tutors to broadcast messages to learners and to mail learners in specific sub groups.
On-line file exchange	For remote submission of assignments and distribution of files. between instructor and learner.
Assessment tools	For self-assessment tests, formative tests and summative tests

	Results from tests can be fed back into student information database. If the system is to be used for summative testing, then issues of unique student identification and encryption of responses have to be addressed.
Back Office	
Database reporting	Information on grades fees, courses/modules attempted or completed. The system can generate reports for periodic review, can also be used by learner or tutor to give snapshot of progress to date.
Course site statistics	Information on number of hits per page and for whole site
Self Access/ Independent Study	
Syllabus, course description pages	Predominantly text based.
Open learning resources/study packs	Structured texts – effectively digital versions of traditional OU style paper based course materials
On-line courseware tutorials etc	Texts, exercises, transcripts, facsimiles of authentic documents, audio and video.
Student notepad	On-line note taking facility integrated into courseware.
Learner Interactions	
These may be:	1. one to one between learners or learner and a tutor 2. one to many between tutor and learners 3. one to many between learners Interactions may be in real time – synchronous, in the same time or at different times – asynchronous. The time/place options are illustrated in Figure 4.
Real-time chat	
Videoconferencing	This tends to be desk top videoconferencing rather than large scale broadcasts with limited audience participation.
Audio conferencing	Use of Internet telephony has created integrated audio conferencing.
Text conferencing	Text based discussions, often used as preparation or follow up to focused learning topics scheduled within the course structure. This will be unstructured, ad hoc chat. Structured discussions are accommodated by bulletin boards and threaded discussions.
Whiteboard	This is a shared space for live writing, drawing on or working on specific computer programs. These devices provide an opportunity for shared working – for example two individuals working collaboratively (at the same time) on a word processed text.

	Whiteboards may well be used in conjunction with audio or videoconferencing.
Threaded discussions or bulletin board	These applications were the original unique appeal of the Internet, before the advent of the World Wide Web. These may be closed to the learning environment or part of the wider Internet community. Although discussions do sometimes take place in real time, they are generally used for asynchronous discussion.
Messaging system	Simple e-mail system enabling learners to identify fellow learners and contact them directly. Learning environments may provide e-mail lists by name, course etc. Learners may have e-mail identities within the environment which are in addition to their usual Internet-wide identity.
Collaborative work groups	Learners may be allocated into working sets, supported by group e-mail names and integrated into the messaging system and threaded discussions.

Within a learning environment, as within a conventional language learning context, it is not uncommon for only a selection of the available tools and techniques to be put to use. Many virtual learning environments are created which do not make use of the course management components, particularly the heavier administrative functions. User tracking, messaging systems, on-line file exchange and some kind of assessment tools are all powerful and useful aspects of an integrated on-line learning environment. The theoretical benefit of such tools can be recognised by most teachers, but may also be identified as inappropriate for their current situation, given the existing support and administration structures and procedures which are in place. However, teachers may still appreciate the potential benefit of additional and detailed information which such systems can provide, such as individual and group progress tracking and summarising of assessments.

E-Learning Virtual learning environments, at their best, can be used to integrate disparate activities such as listening, reading or grammar exercises alongside a live tutor-led (video or audio) class conference or alongside an 'offline' text discussion via a bulletin board or threaded message system. The different aspects and capabilities of synchronous (same time) and asynchronous interactions (different time) are illustrated in Figure 5 below.

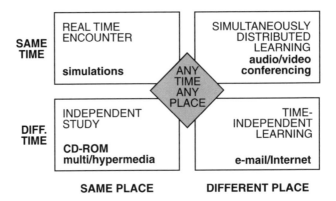

Figure 5: Time and place in learning

For some teachers it will be the ability of the virtual learning environment to 'contain' the learning resources and thereby focus the learner which is its greatest strength. For others, it will be the opportunity to set a closed, defined set of resources alongside the open unbounded resources of the World Wide Web which is particularly powerful. This contrasts with previous views that, although the web offered a wealth of learning opportunities, particularly for language learners, guides and signposts were needed to prevent learners being lost in hyperspace. The well constructed virtual classroom prevents this from happening.

Many teachers and learners, reluctant to give up the human face-to-face interaction of the classroom, may be swayed by the view that a virtual learning environment can provide tools with which to remove some of the barriers to learning. For many learners, the mere act of managing the learning activities which contribute to the learning process – whether it be using the self-access centre/library or getting together with other learners for group activities and practice – can be problematic in conventional settings. The virtual environment enables the collection and integration of components which go to make up the learning process in a way which has not been possible in conventional face-to-face settings. The ability of virtual learning environments to integrate on-line synchronous and asynchronous interactions, alongside learning resources (text, graphics, audio and video), including assessments, simulations and conventional CALL, is probably its single most convincing strength.

There have been two types of moves towards creating virtual learning environments, the first to concentrate on assembling a set of tools, the second to provide an environment with content to support the learning process. Commercial companies and academic institutions alike have worked to create the environments and the tools. Emerging products have included initiatives such as Blackboard.com and Lotus Learning Space from the commercial stable and WebCT, Merlin and Colloquia from the academic community.

Probably more interesting are those initiatives which aim to provide populated learning environments. One early implementation of virtual learning environments for language learning was the Schmooze University, a collection of discussion lists, run on a co-operative basis, for learners of English as a foreign language. This initiative grew up as a development of threaded e-mail discussion groups called MOOs, originally developed for role playing games on the internet. MOOs are still used independently to support language learning. The University of Hull, which developed the Merlin virtual learning environment, has also created a number of language learning courses within its framework.

The future of language learning?

We have seen from the evolution of use, described in this chapter, that the development of technology to support learning and teaching has become increasingly more sophisticated as technologies have advanced. There is every indication that the pace of change will continue. Future growth areas include automatic translation, voice recognition and speech generation which will be incorporated into programs to provide learners with feedback. Another area of interest is the development of intelligent language learning agents, which operate alongside the learner as they interact with the technology, monitoring progress, analysing needs and identifying the most appropriate next steps in the learning process.

In addition, there will be changes in the way we interact with technology as we see the advent of ubiquitous computing. This development has already been presaged by the rapid transfers which have been made from fixed line to mobile telephony, the embedding of web browsers into mobile phones and industrial and commercial applications of computers which 'converse' with their base stations, sending and receiving information to ensure they work effectively 24 hours of each day. Ubiquitous computing is the change which can make a reality of the slogans which promise that learning opportunities can be made available 'Just in Time' or 'Just for You'. We can only imagine the possibilities for the language learner of personalised learning resources at this point in time.

References

Newby H, 'Higher Education in the twenty-first century: some possible futures' in *New Reporter*, 16, 14 (University of Southampton, 1999)

Marchesse T, 'Not so distant competitors: how new providers are remaking the postsecondary marketplace' in *American Association for Higher Education* (August 1998)

Negroponte N, *Being digital* (New York: Knopf, 1995)

Papert S, *Mindstorms children, computers and powerful ideas* (Brighton: Harvester studies in cognitive science 14, 1980)

Warschauer M, 'Computer-mediated collaborative learning: theory and practice' in *Modern Language Journal*, 81 3: 470–481 (1997)

PART 4

ASSESSING PROGRESS

Assessment exemplifies some of the tensions at work in the language learning process. Should its function primarily be to test, or is there an implicit developmental role? Should control lie solely in the hands of the assessors, in other words the tutors, or is there a part that learners can play in their own assessment? To what extent can assessment break new ground against a background of directives on standards, pre-determined learning outcomes and tight specifications? Is any kind of eclecticism out of place in an education system that calls for more and more standardisation in the name of transparency, clarity and fairness? How can learners benefit from assessment practices and how can their tutors best help them to do so?

This section investigates assessment primarily from the learner's perspective within the different contexts of adult language learning and emphasises the notion of error as an integral part of the language learning process. Chapter 1 analyses the nature of errors and mistakes and demonstrates how an awareness of this distinction can help tutors understand and deal with learners' difficulties and advise on the development of appropriate strategies to promote greater accuracy. Chapter 2 looks at shifting attitudes to the assessment process and addresses its underlying purposes and principles. It invites us to examine the many roles that assessment can have from diagnostic to motivational, and to look more closely at why, what and how we assess. Chapter 3 concentrates on the importance of feedback throughout the learning process and highlights its developmental role, particularly for reducing anxiety and encouraging the learner to take a more active role in evaluating personal performance and progress. Chapter 4 emphasises the growing need for accountability and transparency in assessment, and explores the tension in adult education between liberalism and vocationalism which has its expression in blanket assessment practice and the requirement for all students to follow accredited courses, whatever their personal motivation. This final chapter ends with an overview of the situation in higher education with regard to academic review and benchmarking.

13

Understanding errors and mistakes

BOB POWELL

This chapter clarifies the nature of mistakes and errors in the learning process and charts how error-making has been treated through different approaches to language teaching. Some of the reasons for making mistakes and errors are considered and the impact on learners' attitudes to error-making is discussed. The chapter concludes with suggestions for developing self-correction strategies and the recommendation that these should form an essential part of training for improved language learning.

Learners' attitudes to mistakes

I was never any good at languages at school. I kept on making mistakes, getting things wrong. I always got low marks in the tests and eventually I dropped French. I knew I was no good. I think you have to have a special gift to learn a foreign language (Julian, Managing Director, aged 49).

The sentiments expressed in this interview response are shared by many adults returning to foreign language learning later in life after having abandoned hope at an early age. The prejudices formed as a result of any unsuccessful or unpleasant experience at school can last a lifetime. In the case of foreign language learning, the damage done through holding such negative attitudes is, fortunately, reparable, but it can take a while before good language learning habits are developed. Sometimes, the necessity to learn a language for specific reasons – the instrumental motivation – in Julian's case the opportunity to sell his product in the Italian market, forces acceptance that earlier ideas about one's personal language learning potential were flawed. In other cases, the pleasure and sense of personal fulfilment – one form of intrinsic motivation – that is gained through attending an evening leisure class where communicative language teaching approaches predominate, will prove to the new language learner that he or she has a hitherto undiscovered capability to understand and speak a foreign language. In distance learning, helpful telephone conversations with one's tutor or encouraging written comments on an assignment can have a similar, lasting effect.

139

The main problem for the business man Julian, and for many others like him, is the lasting impression that in school language lessons it was so difficult to be correct, to get things right. Total accuracy was uppermost in the teacher's mind and anything less from the pupils was unacceptable. The main form of communication between teacher and learner following completion of a written task would have highlighted weaknesses and faults: underlinings, crossings-out – in red ink, of course, marks and symbols over the text. A sense of failure was experienced so frequently by the pupil that any initial enthusiasm for a language was crushed.

Whatever the context for learning, language tutors have to display great tact and sensitivity when dealing with learners' needs and create a secure and pleasant atmosphere for learning. It is a difficult task both because the learners may be embarrassed and frustrated by their perceived inadequacy and also because, more damaging, they may have developed unhelpful or unproductive learning styles and strategies during previous study.

Understanding mistakes and errors

'*Nobody made a greater mistake than he who did nothing because he could only do little.*' (Attributed to Edmund Burke)

Many people use the words *error* and *mistake* interchangeably but possibly incorrectly in certain contexts. The Collins dictionary defines an error as '*a mistake in accuracy as in action or speech*' and a mistake '*as an error or blunder in action, opinion or judgement*', thereby giving the two words a degree of synonymity. Yet we know that, in terms of usage, even in everyday discourse, there are differences in meaning. An error can bear notions of a moral or legal dimension, in the sense that one *commits* an error like one commits a crime, suggesting that the perpetrator has engaged in forethought. One does not, on the other hand, commit a mistake. A mistake is more usually the result of imperfect or incomplete knowledge, generally an excusable aberration. We all make mistakes; we can all get things wrong. Fortunately, the consequences of most of our mistakes in life are minor. If we make a mistake, it is to be hoped that we recognise where we went wrong and, thereafter, avoid situations in which similar problems might arise. In other words, we learn from our mistakes and perhaps mend the error of our ways.

In the study of language and applied linguistics, however, the words **error** and **mistake** can take on different meanings; many pages of academic journals and text-books have been devoted to analysing and discussing the nature of errors and mistakes, their causes, their diagnosis and their treatment. In reality, the English language lacks the vocabulary now needed to define the subtle differences identified in discussions about errors and mistakes in language learning and use. Which of the two words is used is largely dependent on context rather than meaning. One commits an error, engages in error correction or sees a text that is error-free, but one makes and learns from one's mistakes. Neither really imply any intent of any kind.

For the tutor keen to understand learners' difficulties, the problems have been compounded by the fact that new writers to the field of error analysis seem duty bound to re-interpret past theories and to put their own gloss on the terminology used before creating their own taxonomy of error types. It is interesting to note that the favoured term has, in fact, become '*error analysis*' with **error** being the predominant word used; discussion of '*mistake-analysis, mistake-types, mistake-matching*' are singularly lacking in the literature.

One of the first people to raise awareness of the importance of error-making in the language learning process and to tackle the problems of definition was Corder (1967). He considered that errors, naturally enough, are due to inadequate knowledge, while mistakes occur when the learner, unintentionally, fails to perform at a level consistent with his or her potential performance. In other words, mistakes may invariably be corrected if the learner has time to put things right. Of course, that pre-supposes that the learner has the skill, or even the willingness, to correct these mistakes. Self-correction is only possible if the learner has developed what we may define, albeit unscientifically, as an **inner ear** for the language, or in the case of written language, a **beady eye** as the text is re-read. Spoken language, of course, because of its spontaneous nature, offers many opportunities for mistake or error-making in terms of pronunciation, intonation, syntax, for example. In fact, spontaneous speech is rarely mistake-free. Written language on the other hand, unless the activity is time-controlled or geared towards instant production, generally allows the author time to reflect, check, redraft, re-order, so theoretically at least there should be fewer mistakes and errors! Self-correction is only possible, too, if the conditions for discourse – written or spoken – are sympathetic. There is nothing more disconcerting to a language learner than when the person being addressed constantly interrupts while one is composing sentences or searching for the right word. Similarly, to receive back from a tutor a marked written assignment covered with corrections and negative comment can also be disheartening and dampen enthusiasm.

However, leaving language to develop by itself without drawing attention to errors and enabling the learner to understand what is wrong and how to put things right, is a rather hit and miss affair. Acquiring a new language in a community where that language is spoken – often advocated by non-specialists as the 'natural' way, the best way to learn a language – does not automatically result in error or mistake-free language. Some errors and mistakes may arise from misunderstandings over the precise meanings of words or idiomatic expressions but these are generally corrected over time. It is obvious, however, that many people who have learnt a language by immersion in the target language society and culture, retain errors that they have manifestly **not** been able to eradicate by self-correction. Sometimes these are phonological errors, poor accents which can lead to confusion or even amusement among native speakers of the language. More serious, perhaps, are incorrect use of gender, verb endings or tense which **ought** to have been eliminated through exposure and subsequent self-correction. Frequently, these types of errors become fossilised, irretrievably embedded as habits and virtually impossible to correct since they are no longer even noticed by the speaker.

Arguments about the best way to acquire a foreign language continue to preoccupy applied linguists. In the literature, a set of bipolar constructs is sometimes presented to highlight the differences between so-called traditional approaches and contemporary theories. Table 1, adapted from McArthur, offers an amalgam of different descriptors. The origins of these lists of features date from 1983; hence the reference to '*radical*' in the title of the right column. Many of these characteristics hardly seem radical now. However, it is undeniable that in some higher and adult education contexts even today, the underlying philosophy and prevailing attitudes to language and assessment processes still tend to the conservative end of the spectrum.

Table 1

The conservative position	The radical position
Explicit grammar	Implicit grammar
Deductive classroom work	Inductive classroom work
Drills and structures without context	Materials organised in both linguistic and situational contexts
A prescriptive view of grammar	A descriptive view of grammar
An analytical approach to language	A holistic and synthetic approach to language
A bias towards the graphic (reading and writing)	A bias towards the phonic medium (listening and speaking)
Formal language teaching styles	Informal teaching styles
An insistence on the value of translation	An insistence on the value of immersion
Emphasis on a *standard* form of language	Emphasis on varied use of language

(Adapted and abridged from McArthur, 1983)

With the advent of communicative approaches, writers of teaching materials and, hence, tutors have been more concerned with enabling learners to use the language for real purposes, rather than concentrate on the way the target language is organised and structured. Task-based learning, as certain ways of organising teaching are now defined, focuses on using language to achieve objectives beyond those merely concentrating on the manipulation of linguistic form. This way of organising learning can bring into play implicit language learning processes which, it has been found, can stretch the learner and improve fluency **and** accuracy (Swain, 1995; Foster and Skehan, 1999).

A tutor's ideas about accuracy, correctness and acceptability of language form are inextricably bound up with his or her method and style of teaching. Therefore, with so many different ways of approaching language teaching and a sometimes bewildering range of available tools for the task, including new technologies, we need to focus on (1) how tutors should react and respond to learners' mistakes and errors and (2) how learners can become more aware of the mistakes they make during the learning process and develop strategies for self-correction. Before these issues are tackled, the range of potential mistakes and errors a language learner might make and the terminology used to describe them need to be studied a little further. The main reason for taking time to distinguish between different manifestations of linguistic *deviance* is to provide a framework for developing tutors' sensitivity to mistakes and errors during the teaching and learning process.

Types of mistakes and errors and their causes

Identifying receptive difficulties: aural discrimination, coping with fast delivery ...

C'est ma faute
C'est ma faute
C'est ma très grande faute d'orthographe
Voilà comment j'écris
Giraffe

(Prévert, *Histoires*)[1]

The productive skills of language learning, speaking and writing are those which lend themselves to error-making and, therefore, analysis of error types. That is not to say that learners do not get things wrong during listening and reading activities – far from it – but problems with these so-called receptive skills are likely to be the result of a more limited range of difficulties for the learner, for example, poor sound discrimination, inability to keep up with the speed of the discourse on the one hand, or limited vocabulary or misinterpretation on the other. Usually, evidence for the breakdown in comprehension will be manifested in the incoherence or illogicality of the spoken or written response, so it is here that linguists have focused their attention in order to make more sense of learners' errors and categorise error types.

First-order and second-order mistakes

The vast majority of the accessible literature concentrates on the learning of English as a foreign language, but there are features in error-making that may be applied to any language. James (1998) provides a comprehensive review of the recent literature on error and ends with (and who dare disagree with his claim?):

> ... *the clearest and most practical classification of [linguistic] deviance..:*
>
> *Slips, or alternatively, lapses of the tongue or pen, or even fingers on a keyboard, can quickly be detected and self-corrected by their author unaided.*
>
> *Mistakes can only be corrected by their agent if their deviance is pointed out to him or her. If a simple indication that there is some deviance is a sufficient prompt for self-correction, then we have a first-order mistake.*
>
> *If additional information is needed, in the form of the exact location and some hint as to the nature of the deviance, then we have a second-order mistake.*
>
> *Errors cannot be self-corrected until further relevant (to that error) input (implicit or explicit) has been provided and converted into intake by the learner. In other words, errors require further relevant learning to take place before they can be self-corrected.*

Solecisms are breaches of the rules of correctness as laid down by purists and usually taught in schools... (James, 1998).

James' division of mistakes into two categories '*first-order*' and '*second-order*', is an extremely useful distinction since it implicitly suggests strategies for tutors observing language students in action or marking language tasks. If a simple comment, quizzical expression or question mark from the tutor is sufficient to trigger a learner's self-correction, the mistake is probably of the first-order; if the learner needs more prompting before identifying and correcting himself or herself, it is more likely a case of a second-order mistake.

Identifying productive difficulties: spoken and written discourse

Mistakes and errors arise from and affect many features of language. Language is, after all, manifested in different ways: the spoken word and written text. There are clearly several other media of communication, song, gestures, signs, symbols, codes, to name but a few. But in learning a foreign language it is spoken and written discourse that predominate. The opportunities for making mistakes and errors seem endless! A few of these are considered in the following paragraphs.

Grammar errors may result from **poor or incomplete knowledge** or from **mis-application of the rules** or **over-generalisation of the rules** governing the language; they may affect the structure of individual words (morphology) or longer manifestations of language (syntax). For example, in French, given the preponderance of regular –*er* verbs in the language, a learner may produce a regular form for what is, in reality, an irregular verb.

Poor modelling

Inevitably, as a learner goes through the processes of being exposed to and absorbing the new language in the classroom or through the learning materials, there will be occasions when, even at the practice stage of spoken language production, mistakes are made. The most frequent cause of these mistakes is **poor modelling**, that is the adoption by the learner of an inaccurate or completely false perception of the target language at a given moment. This could, of course, be put down to poor teaching where the tutor's knowledge of the language is flawed, e.g. inauthentic pronunciation, or when a learner's poor attempt at production is never corrected but allowed to persist until it becomes a faulty model. It may also be the result of weak aural discrimination skills during, for example, question and answer work or independent video viewing or listening activities. It is a regrettable fact of growing older that one's hearing becomes less sharp, less able to distinguish between similar sounding words. It can become embarrassing for the learner if the tutor insists on numerous repetitions in order to correct poor pronunciation when, genuinely, the sounds cannot be heard distinctly. However, where the language being learnt is Romance or Germanic, switching between English and target language sounds (vowels, consonants or combinations) can help attune the ear to the differences. A simple but effective example of this contrastive language exercise in French-English could be work on what are known as voiced and unvoiced plosive consonants such as p, b, t and d. Alternating between *thé* and *tea* can serve to emphasise the distinctive sounds of the two words.

More important, possibly, are examples of poor modelling based on the written word. Often, this will be the result of early incorrect or careless copy-writing. How else can tutors explain the frequency of incorrect spellings such as *beacoup, plusiers* and *recontrer*? The fact that these lapses are difficult to eradicate demonstrates, perhaps, the importance of helping learners develop strategies for detecting their own mistakes an early stage.

Interference

The phenomenon of interference – whereby a meaning, form or pattern from the mother tongue influences the meaning, form or pattern produced in the target language – is also responsible for many mistakes and particularly errors during more creative stages of language production. These may range from individual lexical items such as saying or writing in French *responsible* instead of *responsable*, to structural or clausal errors or infelicities. In English, the possessive adjective, which is invariable, changes only according to the person who possesses – his or her house – whereas in many other languages, it is the gender of the possessed object which determines the form: e.g. in French, his or her house = *sa maison*. Having to learn, recall and apply gender rules are perennial problems for English mother tongue speakers learning other European languages. A couple of syntactical examples will illustrate the point. A regular occurrence is neglecting to apply the subject – verb inversion in an indirect question, e.g. Can you tell me where the station is? In Italian, for example, inversion is the norm: *Mi può dire dove si trova la stazione?* In German, preoccupation with the conventional conceptual word-order for sentence construction (time + manner + place) may lead a learner to forget to situate the verb at the end of a subordinate clause. While this may not impede communication, it is an imperfect form of the language and should be eliminated if a high level of competence is sought.

In acquiring language, learners will inevitably make mistakes; making mistakes and errors is an inevitable, indeed, valuable part of the language learning process since it enables learners to test hypotheses about the rules governing the language being studied and to extend their developing knowledge. It is therefore not appropriate to treat all incorrect language output in the same way. Tutors need to set each manifestation of **deviance** in the context of the course and the learning objectives. For example, if communicating the message is the main goal of a task, tutors should adopt a tolerant attitude to incorrect adjectival endings in German whereas inappropriate use of tenses can matter a great deal, particularly if they impede comprehension.

Error and approaches to language teaching: tutor reaction and appropriate action

Learning is what happens when you take the risk of not being competent.
(Claxton, 1984)

Discussions on linguistic error have predominantly been concerned with language use in the context of first-language acquisition or second-language learning, i.e. learning a language in a community where that language is spoken or where there are frequent opportunities to hear, read and listen to it. Hammerly (1991), however, is primarily concerned with what goes on in classrooms. The starting point for his controversial book was an evaluation of the language immersion programmes in Canada and the United States. He heavily criticises what he calls the '*communicative acquisitionist naturalistic megatheory of language instruction*' which characterised those immersion programmes. In his view, the encouragement of '*loosely directed and largely unsupervised peer interaction*' and the reluctance of teachers who espouse a communicative/interactive approach to intervene when errors occur and to explain and correct them, are major flaws in their method. The concentration on developing fluency must not, Hammerly believes, be at the expense of accuracy in linguistic output. Examples of school pupils' basic errors, produced after years of immersion teaching, led him to conclude that a systematic approach to error identification and correction are essential. In a pragmatic approach to error, he identifies four causes for learner error in the classroom:

(i)   the teacher or the materials have not presented the point clearly enough;
(ii) there hasn't yet been enough practice of the point, mechanical or meaningful;
(iii) the students have not made the effort necessary to master it, even though they have had adequate opportunity to do so;
(iv) the students have ventured into linguistically 'still-to-be-charted' territory.

(Hammerly, 1991)

It should come as no surprise that Hammerly favours an approach to teaching which emphasises carefully structured presentation of language and ample, controlled and rigorous practice before production. When an error occurs after a point has been taught, understood and practised, the **blame** for the error is placed squarely on the student. Such an error Hammerly calls a '*distortion*'. He terms '*fault*' an error which is made under the conditions of (iv) above, i.e. when students are straying into unknown areas of the target language. Such occurrences are, he believes, best avoided. He even explicitly criticises teachers for allowing such situations to arise during instruction by defining these occurrences as '*mismanagement faults*'. This criticism is harsh and inappropriate and he has been taken to task for his censorious views (James, 1998). Few tutors, in the reality of classroom processes, would adopt such a rigid stance as Hammerley's regarding error avoidance. They are more likely to agree with the common sense wisdom of many of the current handbooks for language teachers which promote, rather, the idea of creativity and experimentation with language, especially at the '*communication*' or '*performance*' stage, for example:

Errors are seen as formative, part of the process of exploring language independently, coping with the unpredictable and discovering new information. (Cajkler and Addelman, 1997)

Some, however, go further in their promotion of creativity and spontaneity in the language classroom. Even those methods of language teaching which emphasise *'controlled presentation, plenty of practice opportunities followed by production are now considered 'out of favour"* (Foster and Skehan, 1999). Presenting learners with language in carefully defined chunks, controlled for length and assumed grammatical complexity ignore, it is claimed, the potential of the learner to create language and meaning without having necessarily been exposed to or having been taught all the component parts.

While classroom-based learning may lend itself to an approach in which exposure to language and language output are controllable, at least to some degree, and opportunities for exploring language may be facilitated by the tutor, the same cannot be said for distance-learning courses. It is extremely difficult to ensure such a clear framework for independent language learning. Firstly, there is no opportunity for the instant error-prompting and self-correction which goes on all the time during classroom interaction. Secondly, although the writers of the course materials may have a perfectly sensible rationale for the sequence of events and they may have an extremely logical approach to exercise or task design, there is no guarantee that learners either share their conception of the product, the course materials, or slavishly follow the instructions and advice carefully prepared for them. The result is a potentially risk-full scenario for language learning. But does that matter? Some would argue that learning will be more productive if learners, rather than teachers, have control over the way they approach their activities. Self-instruction does have the advantage of enabling learners with different aptitudes to learn at their own pace and use those strategies which best match their learning styles (Dickinson, 1987).

The skill of self-correction and how to develop it: helping learners to become more aware of their mistakes

Studies of **good language learners** have helped identify a range of learning styles and strategies which appear to favour more rapid or more thorough acquisition of the target language. One of the earliest and still the most frequently cited research investigations into good language learners was conducted by Naiman, Fröhlich, Stern and Todesco (1978). They discovered that among the impressive range of skills **good language learners** demonstrate is a constant: the ability to self-correct. This skill appears to be a general attribute for people who are defined as *'skilled performers'*:

Skilled performers quickly detect and throw out errors. This may be viewed as the speeding up of the checking (feedback) process, and it is the case that the expert performers need to run fewer checks on their actions than novices. (Reed, cited in Johnson, 1996)

Not everyone will end up a skilled performer as far as foreign languages are concerned, but there are strategies which can be acquired which should become automatic in the production of language, especially where the output is intended for assessment. These strategies should be identified by the tutor and learner together and opportunities provided for practice before the real assessment tasks are required. Dickinson (1992) provides a helpful guide to tutors who wish to develop a methodology for supporting learner training and increasing the efficiency and motivation of language learners. In distance learning, the teaching materials should prompt the learner to go through the monitoring, checking, correcting and re-drafting stages so that they become almost automatic processes, part of the learning cycle itself.

Checking one's work for accuracy, style and meaning

Graham (1997) brings together a range of language learning strategies produced by other writers and adds her own categories and interpretation based on research in schools among students aged 16 to 17. This impressive, combined taxonomy includes specific self-correction and prompted correction processes. What follows here draws heavily on Graham's work, but has been adapted to stress the importance of self-correction strategies prior to submission of assignments. These ideas are designed to show tutors how they can support learners during class contact times, individual, face to face or distance tutorials. It is important, especially at more advanced stages of learning, to scrutinise not only language **form,** but also **style** and **content.** As regards the last item, there are many general considerations, such as relevance, demonstration of understanding, presentation of ideas, knowledge, supporting argument and counter-argument, with examples, logical sequencing and so on.

---

1. Evaluation on completion

Checking one's work immediately the task is finished from the point of view of grammatical accuracy

---

This entails activities such as cross checking subject-verb concordance, genders, agreement of adjectives, correct use of cases, appropriate positioning of verbs and adverbs, spelling of words, omissions which significantly affect meaning, such as accidental omission of negative forms. In oral production, checking pronunciation and intonation in recordings of draft presentations, listening back to oneself with particular grammatical features in mind e.g. adjectival endings which change the sounds of words, can help eliminate unnecessary mistakes.

---

2. Delayed evaluation

Checking one's work after a period of time has elapsed.

It is not easy for a learner to detect his or her mistakes, but one of the values of leaving work and studying it again later is that it appears to trigger new thoughts. It is rather like coming back to a crossword clue that has been frustrating you for hours and solving it in a flash. Reading aloud, as if to the examiner or marker, can also aid error detection. **Readaloud** techniques are better than **thinkaloud** techniques because more of the senses are involved and the combined eye/ear signal can sometimes be more effective for some learners than the visual alone.

---

3. Evaluation of meaning and relevance

Checking one's work when the task is finished from the point of view of the meaning conveyed and the full execution of tasks required.

Concentrating on the checking of individual components of language is necessary, but it is also essential for learners to reflect on the whole of their production. Usually this refers uniquely to written work, but it is sometimes possible for distance learners, where they are obliged to produce recordings of oral presentations and they are allowed to rehearse their answers, to take an overview of spoken performance, too. Here, the overall form and style of the work should be considered closely. Learners should be encouraged to ask themselves questions such as:

- Does the piece of work make sense if read aloud or listened to carefully?
- Has a good range of vocabulary and structure been demonstrated?
- Is the register appropriate for the task?
- Is there sufficient variety in the construction of sentences and paragraphs?
- Have connectors been used appropriately?
- In essay writing, is there an identifiable introduction, coherent organisation, argument/counter-argument and interesting conclusion?
- Have all sources of quotations and illustrations been properly referenced?
- In oral presentation, do the ideas flow spontaneously and naturally?
- Have all elements of the task been completed?
- Have all angles of the question been considered?
- Have all the various criteria for assessment been fully addressed?

---

4. Strategy evaluation

Assessing strategies used once the work is completed, so that they can be transferred to other tasks.

Before taking a critical look at what has gone wrong, for example in a completed distance-learning assignment, learners can benefit from concentrating on **positive** self-evaluation, identifying what they have got **right**, before attending to the mistakes and errors. Then can come a moment of reflection which addresses questions such as the following:

- What were the stages involved in preparing the piece of work?
- How could these stages, e.g. planning, organising, prioritising, drafting, be improved?

- How long did the task take overall?
- What could have been done better/differently?

To benefit fully from all the self-correction strategies identified above, learners should also take time to evaluate their effectiveness. By doing so, they will come to recognise which give them most benefit, i.e. which aspects of their production need most support.

Looking positively at error in language learning

This chapter has concentrated on mistakes and errors. Assessment in language teaching has, for many years, been obsessed with identifying things that go wrong in the language learning process or during production. As McDonough usefully reminds us:

> *Success in classroom tasks is less salient and less well defined than error and failure, and therefore a more private and less publicly remarkable phenomenon in today's classroom culture.* (McDonough, 1995)

However, there has been a major shift in emphasis over the past two decades. It is now recognised that error-making is integral to the process of language learning. It is now widely accepted that not all errors should be treated in the same way since they represent different phases of the learning process. The focus in assessment schemes in the past tended towards measuring how efficient learners were in manipulating language patterns, irrespective of the context in which these patterns occurred; it was the correctness of language rather than the appropriacy or authenticity of language that predominated in mark-schemes. In chapter 15, the focus will be on supporting the learner, monitoring and giving credit for performance against agreed criteria. Before that, however, it is important to review a range of purposes of assessment and to come to terms with some of the terminology used to describe various testing procedures.

References

Cajkler W and R Addelman, *The practice of language teaching* (Fulton, 1997)

Claxton G, *Live and learn* (Harper and Row, 1984)

Corder S P, 'The significance of learners' errors' in *International Review of Applied Linguistics*, 5, 4: 161–70 (1967)

Dickinson L, *Self-instruction in language learning* (Cambridge University Press, 1987)

Dickinson L, *Learner training for language learning* (Dublin: Authentik Language Learning Resources, 1992)

Foster P and P Skehan, 'The influence of source of planning and focus on task-based performance' in *Language Teaching Research*, 3, 3: 214–245 (1999)

Graham S, *Effective language learning* (Multilingual Matters, 1997)

Hammerley H, *Fluency and accuracy* (Multilingual Matters, 1991)

James C, *Errors in language learning and use* (Longman, 1998)

Johnson K, *Language teaching and skill learning* (Blackwell, 1996)

McArthur T, *A foundation course for language teachers* (Cambridge University Press, 1983)

McDonough S H, *Strategy and skill in learning a foreign language* (Edward Arnold, 1995)

Naiman, N, M Fröhlich, H H Stern and A Todesco, *The good language learner* (Ontario Institute for Studies in Education, 1978)

Swain M, 'Three functions of output in second language learning' in Cook G and B Seidlehofer (eds), *Principle and practice in applied linguistics* (Oxford University Press, 1995)

Notes

1   Prévert parodies the religious plea for forgiveness in the Latin Mass – *mea culpa, mea culpa, mea maxima culpa* – thereby bestowing a moral significance on what is essentially a trivial spelling error.

14

Principles and theoretical approaches in assessment

MARILYN HUNT

Information on student achievement is crucial to teaching and learning.
(Weir, 1993: 167)

Contexts for language learning may range from leisure and business classes to diplomas and degree programmes, whilst modes of learning may vary from the more traditional classroom setting to self-access or distance learning methods. Nevertheless, irrespective of the context or mode of learning, assessment forms an integral part of the learning process. This chapter outlines how the shift in emphasis has changed with regard to the purposes and principles of assessment. It also investigates some key terminology and concepts in assessment.

Purposes of assessment: developing learners and tutors

Many adult learners understandably view assessment with some apprehension: for them it represents tests or examinations, certificates and marks or grades. Tests are seen as some kind of hurdle, as something negative and threatening, which interrupts and interferes with their learning rather than helping their progress. Adult learners who have painful memories of this kind of assessment from their schooldays are often discouraged from joining a class or enrolling on a distance-learning course if they suspect that they might be putting themselves into a similarly stressful situation. Traditionally, then, assessment has had a judgmental role:

- to pass or fail a student;
- to grade or rank a student;
- to identify what students have failed to learn;
- to compare the performance of students;
- to discriminate between students on the same test;
- to provide a measure of attainment which will enable a student to proceed to the next class or level – if successful.

Just as attitudes to error-making have changed from a rather negative emphasis on what is wrong in language production to an understanding that error-making is integral to the process of language learning, so too have attitudes to assessment evolved over the past two decades. Assessment is no longer a procedure which only occurs at the end of the course to judge pass or failure; it is now recognised as an important element of effective teaching and learning, informing both the tutor and the learner of what has been achieved and supporting the teaching and learning process by providing feedback for the next step in the learning. One of its prime purposes is developmental – to improve learning, and as such *'something not to be feared, but to be appreciated for its intrinsic interest and for what can be learned from it'* (Rivers et al. 1998).

Assessment needs to arise naturally out of the teaching context, rather than be introduced only as a bolt-on activity at the end of a large block of work or at the end of the course. It should therefore be regular, positive and primarily concerned with providing guidance and feedback to the learner, both during the course and at the end of the course. Above all, assessment should give learners direct input to help them develop their learning. Rawson speaks of the *'inextricable linkage between assessment and learning'* and *'the significant influence of assessment upon students' approaches to learning'*. He goes on to say that:

> *The more active involvement of the learner in the assessment process, while not without potential pitfalls, is the key to encouraging learning to learn.* (Rawson, 1999)

This shift to a more learner centred approach is especially valuable with adults, and more so when they are involved in distance learning. Assessment is now recognised to be valuable in a number of additional ways:

- to diagnose learners' strengths and weaknesses, what they know, understand and can do;
- to provide positive feedback about what has been achieved, and remedy shortcomings;
- to reward and sustain a sense of motivation and interest;
- to involve the learner in evaluation and the setting of new targets.

The purpose of assessment is, of course, not limited to the learner. Tutors evaluate continuously during a taught session what and how their students are learning (see Chapter 17 on self-evaluation). They are alert to learner needs, adjusting their planning and modifying their teaching strategies accordingly. Assessment therefore also gives feedback to the tutor and provides evidence about:

- whether specified learning objectives have been achieved;
- particular needs of groups or individuals and how to adjust strategies to meet those needs;
- planning for progression: the next step in the teaching and learning process;
- the effectiveness of teaching and learning methods and materials;
- the strengths and shortcomings of the course and what modifications might be needed.

Sharing objectives and evaluating progress

Careful planning of a course should therefore be based on clear learning objectives, taking account of both linguistic performance and socio-cultural knowledge, with possibilities for assessment activities built in at regular intervals. Planning assessment opportunities will involve decisions about:

- what exactly is being assessed (vocabulary items, grammatical structures, communicative competence, cultural content);
- when assessment should take place;
- why assessment is being carried out (measuring outcomes against objectives, planning ahead, diagnosing strengths and weaknesses);
- how the assessment will be conducted (individually / in pairs / whole class, discrete skill or multi-skill, informally by observation or formally);
- by whom the assessment will be conducted (by tutor alone, by peers, by a combination of both).

Tutors need to learn to make valid and accurate judgements about learners' progress in terms of any formal certification being sought as well as in relation to lesson and unit-of-work objectives. An important factor in checking progress rests with the learners themselves. If objectives are shared, learners can take some responsibility for monitoring their own progress. In the context of autonomous language learning, which is relevant to adult learners generally, but especially so to those involved in distance learning where tutor input is less direct, Dam and Legenhausen (1999) argue that evaluation has a retrospective and prospective function, in which the learning experiences of the past are reflected upon and transformed into future action. They view the basic questions in this process – asked by learners as well as by the tutor – are:

- *What are we doing?*
- *Why are we doing it?*
- *How are we doing it and with what result?*
- *What can it be used for?*
- *What next?*

Assessment terminology and approaches to assessment

Assessment is a very broad concept which covers a wide range of approaches and methods, from the very informal, e.g. watching and listening to students as they work in the classroom, to the highly formal, e.g. a set piece examination. When determining a policy on assessment, it is important to consider carefully:

- assessment criteria clearly linked to teaching and learning objectives;
- a mixture of both formative and summative assessment activities covering all four skills across different contexts and topic areas and including a range of different task types;

- the use of effective multi-skill language activities for assessment;
- the language to be used for instructions and feedback on assessment tasks – target language or English;
- methods to be used for marking and grading learners' work and giving feedback.

It is important to become familiar with some of the terminology connected with assessment. The definitions of some key terms used in this section are outlined in Table 1 and the remainder of the chapter explores some of these concepts in more detail.

Table 1: **Definitions of key assessment terminology**

Pre-course testing	
Diagnostic testing	aimed at identifying strengths and weaknesses and defining pointers for future work so that appropriate remedial action may be taken.
Aptitude testing	evaluation of a person's suitability or potential for foreign language study, generally by means of assessing skills and performance in a range of language tasks in another language in the same family or an artificial language.
Placement testing	is intended to provide information to place learners in a teaching programme at a level most appropriate to their abilities.
During-course or end-of-course assessment	
Formative (continuous) assessment	an ongoing process of gathering information on the processes of learning, the extent of learning, and on strengths and weaknesses, which provides learners and tutors with information for future planning to meet an individual's needs; takes place during the course of teaching and is essentially used to feed back into the teaching/learning process.
Summative (terminal) assessment	assessment which takes place at the end of a course of study or part of it and which measures learners' performance over that course or part of it; it provides information about how much learners have progressed and how effective a course has been.
Self-assessment	judgements made by the learner about his/ her own proficiency or achievement.
Peer-assessment	judgements made by one's peer(s) about one's own proficiency or achievement.
Proficiency assessment	measures what the learner can do, irrespective of any syllabus or course, in relation to the application of the subject in the real world.
Achievement assessment	measures what the learner can do on the basis of a syllabus, assessing the achievement of specific objectives, of what has been taught. Achievement tests may test progress or final achievement. Their purpose is to establish how successful individual students, groups of students or the course itself have been in achieving objectives.

Post-course moderation	
Norm-referenced assessment	assessment which measures all learners against each other and can place learners in rank order in relation to their peers. Marks are sometimes altered up or down if too many candidates based, for example, on a quota or competition system, succeed or fail, irrespective of the difficulty of the test or the ability of the candidates. Norm-referenced moderation may also be used if an exam has been found to be too hard or too easy.
Criterion-referenced	assessment which is judged according to the fulfilment of a description of a task, or a set of agreed criteria. If everyone fulfils the criteria, then everyone passes.

Testing as a diagnostic tool

Some tests are used to diagnose learners' strengths and weaknesses and determine what further teaching is necessary. Hughes (1989) states that tests may be created to demonstrate ability at the level of broad language skills (that is, whether a learner is particularly weak in speaking as opposed to reading) and even to build up profiles of a learner's performance in writing or speaking. However, it is much more difficult to obtain a detailed analysis of a learner's command of grammatical structures. His view is that because comprehensive diagnostic tests would be vast and impractical to administer in a routine fashion, very few tests are constructed for purely diagnostic purposes, and those that are do not provide very detailed information. Others take the view that such tests can, nevertheless, act as a useful guide to entry level. For adult learners returning to language learning after a long gap, a self-assessment test can be helpful. Some adult education providers routinely use diagnostic tests, which range from a brief interview to a more systematic testing of both receptive and productive language skills. Other institutions provide an optional test. Students unsure of their level can thus make their choice of course on a more secure, if not foolproof basis.

Norm-referenced versus criterion-referenced testing

The terms norm-referenced and criterion-referenced refer in the main to the way in which a particular form of assessment is evaluated. The results of a reading test could be judged in two ways. In a norm-referenced test, the mark would be interpreted in relation to the average score of the group taking the test. An individual's performance is therefore related to that of other candidates rather than giving any information about what the candidate is capable of doing in the language.

In a criterion-referenced test, however, there is no comparison of the individual's performance with that of others, but there is considerable information about expected learning outcomes and what the learner can do in the language. One example of an assessment scheme based entirely on criterion-referencing is the National Language Standards (Languages Lead Body, 1996). These provide a detailed framework for vocational language training and assessment. They focus on the active use of foreign language in the workplace, rather than the traditional approach emphasising structures and grammar. The criteria clearly outline level descriptors and specified tasks relating to each of the four skills. To support generalised assessment criteria, there are often more detailed performance criteria. An extract from the **Performance criteria** for Speaking at Level 3 is provided below:

Element 3S1.2 Ask for and provide instructions and information relating to varied work tasks by speaking

Performance criteria

3S1.1.1 commonly used familiar expressions are selected, combined and recombined accurately to request and provide instructions and information.

3S1.1.2 expressions are varied to maintain the attention of listeners.

3S1.1.3 behaviour, language and register are modified to communicate in ways appropriate to the context and the relationship of the speaker to others.

Languages Lead Body (1996)

There are also **Range statements** covering:

- types of information exchanged: numerical data; work-related instructions, requests, facts, assessments;
- speech delivery: standard social and work registers; common sentence structures and commonly used expressions;
- mode: face-to-face; telephone and recorded speech;
- contexts: one-to-one; in familiar groups;

and notes on **Performance evidence**, e.g. instructions and information exchanged during interactions with others, and **Knowledge evidence** including **Understanding of language, Context** and **Evaluation of language performance.** Finally, there is **Assessment guidance** and examples of what, typically, individuals should be able to do when they have achieved the standards at a particular level. The whole process is thus clearly communicated to both assessor and assessed.

Grade or level descriptors are also used extensively in the assessment of Open University courses and other examination schemes where large numbers of candidates are involved, for example public examinations at various stages of schooling. Once all the candidates' results have been gathered, norm-referencing may still take place, however, to ensure consistency in standards over the years. In other words, norm-referencing is used to check that criteria have not altered too drastically from one year to the next, and that the test or exam has been set at the right level.

The purpose of criterion-referenced tests is to determine whether learners can perform a task or set of tasks satisfactorily. In principle, a 100% pass rate is therefore possible and standards do not change with different groups of candidates. Learners are encouraged to measure their progress in relation to meaningful criteria rather than against other learners, and are motivated to achieve the standards set. In some cases tests are carried out only when the learner feels ready, in other words when success is likely. This again reduces the risk of test anxiety which may detrimentally affect performance.

Formative and summative assessment

Formative and summative refer not to the way assessment is evaluated, but to its function. In other words, a test designed to be used summatively, i.e. at the end of the course, could be used formatively to help both tutor and learners prepare for a final test or examination. William and Black (1996) refer to the *'assessment cycle'* which applies to both formative and summative assessment, where evidence of performance or achievement is elicited, interpreted and acted upon. The importance of formative assessment is precisely to help inform or train the learner to move forward and improve on their performance in any given skill. Formative assessment has been defined as *'that process of appraising, judging or evaluating students' work or performance and using this to shape and improve their competence'* (Tunstall and Gipps, 1996).

Foreign language learning is primarily skills-based in the early stages, and these skills will be unlikely to develop positively unless there is some kind of formative assessment providing feedback to the learner on precise ways to improve levels of performance. While formative assessment is closely allied to developing learning strategies which lead to more independent learning, summative assessments give evidence of attainment at the end of a course or part of a course and contribute to the overall grade in whatever formal qualification is being sought. For learners involved in Open University courses, for example, assignments are submitted at regular intervals. Some tutor marked assignments (TMAs), for example, may be formative (marks are awarded but they do not count towards the overall grade) or summative (marks awarded do count); they all however provide feedback. Examinations, on the other hand, do not generally provide explicit feedback beyond the judgmental result of pass/fail or degree of pass/fail.

Self-assessment

When teachers share with their students the process of assessment – giving up control, sharing power and leading students to take on the authority to assess themselves – the professional judgement of both is enhanced. Assessment becomes not something done to students. It becomes an activity done with students. (Brew, 1999)

As early as 1981, Heron was advocating a move from the traditionally authoritarian mode of assessment in higher education – unilateral intellectual authority, where staff decide what students shall learn, design the programme of learning, determine criteria for assessment and make the assessment of the student – to give the student greater power.

The initiation of students needs to be more reciprocal and consultative, with students not simply learning their subjects but also participating in decisions about how they learn them and in the assessment of their learning. (Heron, 1981)

Learners in the past, whether in HE or other learning contexts, have frequently worked to hidden and undisclosed criteria, with final assessment being the sole judge of their performance. The learner has now become much more of a partner in the teaching and learning process and the involvement of learners in assessment is equally important. It is therefore crucial to make objectives and assessment criteria transparent, especially in relation to distance learning. Peer- and self-assessment can also be of practical use to tutors, *'alleviating the assessment burden on the teacher'* (Dickinson, 1987), providing supplementary evidence and acting as an effective complement to tests and tutor assessment.

Heron argues that self-assessment presents the importance of process assessment as well as content assessment:

Assessing how I learn and how I provide evidence of what I have learned is really more fundamental than assessing what I have learned. (...) Procedural competence is more basic than product competence, since the former is a precondition of providing many good products, while the latter is one off – each good product is strictly a witness only to itself. (Heron, 1981)

To benefit most from their foreign language study, as has been stressed in chapter 13, learners should always be engaged in self-checking activities, routinely testing themselves on vocabulary or carefully scrutinising their assignments before submitting them to the assessment of others. In open learning materials, in-text questions encourage students to think about and check their learning. Boud (1995) claims that these are examples of ways in which students have traditionally tested their academic discipline knowledge and skills: what they know and what they can do. Although this kind of self-assessment is ad hoc and appears peripheral to formal assessment procedures, it is or should be a commonplace part of learning.

It is easy to question the validity and reliability of self-evaluation when it is used more formally as part of the summative assessment process. Is it possible for a learner to be realistic in self-evaluation or is an 'outside' person really indispensable? In their research into the comparison of learners' self-evaluations and external assessments, Dam and Legenhausen discovered that teacher ratings were no more valid than the self-evaluations of autonomous learners (Dam and Legenhausen, 1999). Accuracy in self-assessment can be increased by relating the assessment to clear descriptors defining standards of proficiency, by giving a specific task and by training the learners. End-of-unit profiles and 'can-do' checklists have become an important part of language learning pre-16, in order to allow learners to evaluate themselves and set targets. Such profiles can be equally effective for adult learners.

Self-assessment also helps learners of foreign languages to develop the ability to identify their own weaknesses and difficulties, and to concentrate on specific linguistic details. Learning to see how elements of language fit in with each other and manipulating new language items or new structures in a familiar context are important steps in the process of foreign language learning. For instance, in some cases The Open University provides student-marked assignments (SMAs) to assess grammatical and semantic knowledge of material covered up to a certain point in the course. The SMAs have answer sections that give detailed feedback and enable students to assess themselves and to analyse the origin of their mistakes and errors. Solutions and model answer sections perform the same function in course books. Self-assessment is therefore not only about monitoring progress, but also about extending knowledge and competence by setting further targets.

Certain computer software can also be useful in helping learners to concentrate on specific weaknesses at their own pace. In this way, directed self-study can assist in remedying the weaknesses assessment has highlighted. Boud advocates that students need to experience a process which they accept as valid. He states that the elements of such a process are likely to involve:

- *a clear rationale: what are the purposes of this particular activity?*
- *explicit procedures: students need to know what is expected of them;*
- *reassurance: of a safe environment in which they can be honest about their own performance without the fear that they will expose information which can be used against them;*
- *confidence: that other students will do likewise, and that cheating or collusion will be detected and discouraged.* (Boud, 1995)

Peer-assessment

Peer-assessment involves students making judgements about, or commenting upon each other's work. It is a term used to refer to both peer marking and peer feedback. One way of implementing peer-assessment in class-based learning involves arranging groups of three with alternating roles: A+B to carry out the task, while C completes an assessment sheet, noting if key vocabulary and structures are being used and commenting on the perceived pronunciation, fluency and independence of each speaker, or relating the performance to the assessment criteria for the particular task. After the role-play has been completed, learners can discuss the outcomes. Assessment therefore offers learners an opportunity for real communication. Peer-assessment is, of course, not normally likely to be as thorough as tutor assessment, but discussion and reflection on their own performance, even in the mother tongue, can assist learners in clarifying concepts and identifying communicative and learning strategies. It may also increase their confidence.

Despite these advantages, peer-assessment is not always popular with students, largely because it involves additional processes and potential hazards which are not always evident in self-assessment processes. Brew reminds us that to assess is to have power over a person:

... sharing the assessment with students may be, to some degree, in order to share the power of the teacher. It may be introduced with an intention to encourage students to take responsibility for their learning.... [but] care has to be exercised in the way that peer assessment is introduced. (Brew, 1999)

Beaton (1990) also warns that students are often harder than teachers on their peers in monitoring exercises, but that this can be turned to good use by the teacher sensitively pooling and then dealing in a general way with the errors noticed by the students in their partners. Changing partners fairly frequently avoids the difficulty of students becoming accustomed to and accepting partners' errors identified through role-play activities.

Profiling from self-assessment

Self-assessment can help to build up a profile of what each individual learner has achieved. Ainslie and Lamping (1995) describe a profile as a systematic recording of progress and achievement which is a way of:

- *helping learners to see where they are going in relation to the specific objectives of the course;*
- *building up a picture of learners' strengths and weaknesses;*
- *identifying areas where further work is necessary;*
- *developing the learners' ability to evaluate their own progress;*
- *helping learners to take control of their own learning.*

A profile may include the learning objectives for a given topic. Many course books start or conclude a unit presenting such a list which could be used as the basis for the profile; learners are motivated by seeing what it is they have to achieve and can feel a sense of achievement when they are able to tick items off, having achieved the learning outcomes implicit in the learning objectives. Below is an example from one of the *Faites le bilan* sections in the course books for The Open University, Level 1 French course L120 *Ouverture* (1995):

Faites le bilan
When you have finished this section of the book, you should be able to:
Use *de moins en moins* and *de plus en plus* to express change (Activités 3, 4 and 6).
Use the negation *ne ... plus* to express change (Activités 6, 7 and 8).
Use adverbs of time with the appropriate verb tenses (present, perfect, imperfect) to express change (Activités 2, 5 and 8).
Understand telephone numbers in spoken French (Activité 10).
Use *pas vraiment, c'est dommage, malheureusement* and *je suis déçu(e)* to express disappointment (Activités 14 and 15).

(The Open University, 1994)

Not all learners find reward in the mechanistic process of ticking off items on a checklist. In this case, learners should be encouraged to develop more imaginative ways of representing their linguistic achievement, perhaps in pictorial or diagrammatic form. Here is one example of a learner-controlled profile in which each circle represents a test and students shade in the relevant space for each skill as and when test results are provided.

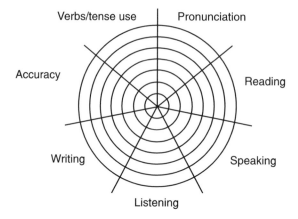

Figure 4: Learner-controlled profile

This spider's web can be used in a variety of ways: to diagnose strengths and weaknesses, to assess progress, to identify where more practice is needed. It can be divided up in whatever way an individual student finds useful. For example, shading a skill band could indicate that an activity has been undertaken or a test passed, and a mark could be included if that was found to be helpful. Completed spider's webs from whole groups of students could also help tutors (and in the long run course writers) to assess learners' needs by offering a visual representation of the overall situation.

Portfolio assessment

The benefits of portfolio assessment have been demonstrated in a number of universities' institution-wide language programmes. On submission, the portfolio should contain not only the completed language tasks, but also an initial needs analysis, evidence of remedial activities undertaken, lists of materials used for study, and a self-evaluation statement. The portfolio is assessed according to criteria which include reference to planning and reflection, independence, organisation and presentation, as well as content.

Language portfolios in the *Languages for business* context are a type of profile where the learner compiles evidence of competence in language for a national vocational qualification in the form of real-life documents. The portfolio of evidence demonstrates competence as measured against the National Language Standards. Rather than a profile from self-assessment, the evidence is accumulated when the tutor, who is also assessor, advises that the learner has competently performed an assessment. Although this is teacher assessed, the point of assessment is negotiated with the learner.

The European Language Portfolio

The aim of the proposed European Language Portfolio is to promote European democratic citizenship and mobility in Europe by providing an instrument to record all language knowledge and experiences and thereby give value to lifelong language learning. A portfolio consists of three parts, which can be updated as the owner's language learning progresses:

- a passport section to contain a record of formal and informal qualifications obtained, in an internationally transparent manner;
- a language biography to report personal contact with foreign languages and cultures through background, work and travel;
- a dossier to include evidence of the owner's linguistic competence.

Information about achievement will be presented according to the levels of the Common European Framework of Reference in order to provide efficient comparison of language qualifications. Versions of the portfolio have been piloted since 1998 in a range of educational contexts, and issues of its introduction on a wider scale are being investigated. Certainly, the prestige of a European instrument to record language knowledge and skills will be helpful in encouraging lifelong language learning.

Conclusion

This chapter demonstrates how the shift of emphasis has changed in assessment in a number of ways. Whereas in the past the teacher, tutor or lecturer tended to have sole discretion in assessment, acting as an authority in determining the framework of assessment, and often marking on a negative basis, the learner is now generally offered a greater role in assessment. Criteria for assessment make it clearer what the learner is to achieve and, in many instances, the emphasis is on what the learner can do, rather than on what he or she is failing to achieve. A variety of approaches in assessment, formal and informal, formative and summative, self- and peer-assessment can help learners to develop their learning skills. The next chapter offers more detailed advice on how tutors can monitor performance thereby enabling learners to make the most of their language study.

References

Ainslie S and A Lamping, *Assessing adult learners* (CILT, 1995)

Beaton R, 'The many sorts of error' in Page B (ed), *What do you mean ... it's wrong?* (CILT, 1990)

Boud D, *Enhancing learning through self-assessment* (Kogan Page, 1995)

Brew A, 'Towards autonomous assessment: using self-assessment and peer-assessment' in Brown S and A Glasner (eds), *Assessment matters in Higher Education*: 159–171 (SRHE and Open University Press, 1999)

Council of Europe, *Modern languages: learning, teaching, assessment. A common European framework of reference* (Strasbourg: 1996)

Dam L and L Legenhausen, 'Language acquisition in an autonomous learning environment: learners' self-evaluations and external assessments compared' in Cotterall S and D Crabbe (eds), *Learner autonomy in language learning: defining the field and effecting change:* 89–98 (Germany: Peter Lang, Europäischer Verlag der Wissenschaften, 1999)

Dickinson L, *Self-instruction in language learning* (Cambridge University Press, 1987)

Heron J, 'Assessment revisited' in Boud D (ed), *Developing student autonomy in learning:* 55–68 (Kogan Page, 1981)

Hughes A, *Testing for language teachers* (Cambridge University Press, 1989)

Languages Lead Body, *The revised National Language Standards* (DfEE, 1996)

Open University, *Ouverture: Cadences Livre 4:* 18 (1994)

Rawson M, 'Learning to learn: purely a skill?' in *The New Academic,* 8, 3 (1999)

Rivers W, K Mitchell Dell'Orto and V Dell'Orto, *Teaching German: a practical guide* (Lincolnwood, Illinois: National Textbook Company, 1988)

Tunstall P and C Gipps, 'Teacher feedback to young children in formative assessment: a typology' in *British Education Research Journal,* 22, 4: 389–404 (1996)

Weir C, *Understanding and developing language tests* (Prentice Hall International, 1993)

William D and P Black, 'Meanings and consequences: a basis for distinguishing formative and summative functions of assessment?' in *British Education Research Journal,* 22, 5: 537–548 (1996)

15

Checking on progress: developing approaches to giving formal and informal feedback

MARILYN HUNT

In all assessment, it is important to measure what we value, or we may only value what we measure. (Parr, 1997)

This chapter considers how to support language learning through assessment and feedback. Feedback is an important part of tutor-learner interaction in foreign language learning. What is important for tutors and learners to register together is evidence of what has been achieved and what needs to be worked on in order to improve achievement. The chapter concludes with a reminder of how important feedback is in sustaining motivation and developing learning.

Encouraging positive attitudes to being assessed

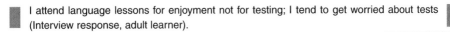

I attend language lessons for enjoyment not for testing; I tend to get worried about tests (Interview response, adult learner).

Adults embarking on learning a language may not have studied for a while, and may consequently need help with study skills, learning strategies, setting goals, and time management. Tutors may need to help learners with confidence-building strategies which encourage learners to realise that the emphasis, at least initially, is on communication rather than demanding error-free production. Equally, some adult learners may well feel resistance to being tested and it therefore becomes essential to explain fully the value of assessment, and outline clearly any assessment procedures. Even those enrolling on a distance-learning study programme in order to gain a certificate or diploma, in the certain knowledge that their work will be assessed, become excessively concerned about their ability to perform adequately, and this can detract from their overall level of achievement.

Daines et al (1992) point out that whatever type of assessment procedure is used, tutors need to be sensitive to people's feelings and reactions. Adult students may well lack confidence in themselves as learners, and too public a demonstration of achievement and especially failure, will not be welcomed, even within the safe confines of the

165

classroom group. Students on distance learning courses may be over-cautious in their production of written tasks or recorded assignments for fear of showing themselves to be less competent than they perceive the standard of the course to be. All learners will be reassured if they realise that they are not being tested against each other, but against sets of agreed criteria.

Tutors and the learning materials should help the learner by clarifying the weightings of the various assessed tasks, explaining the difference between a progress check and final examination and, particularly in the early stages, by emphasising that learners will only be tested on what the course has covered. A positive attitude towards assessment from the start of the course can boost confidence and enable learners to feel more in control of their learning.

Ongoing assessment

Ongoing assessment during a course is a useful feedback mechanism in the teaching and learning process. Every contribution, every learning activity or task, every course assignment, every lesson is assessed or evaluated in some way, although generally much more informally than a test. Daines et al (1992) argue that tutors constantly make intuitive judgements about the effects of the teaching, and identify whether learners have grasped the ideas or whether further practice is required. Yet whilst forming these overall judgements, the tutor will also be aware that a particular student is not coping too well and that another seems to have made more rapid progress. This **aggregate** feedback needs to be supplemented by a specific assessment of every individual. Tutors need to know to what extent each member of the group has met their learning objectives, so that they can offer the right help or guidance at a personal level (Daines et al, 1992).

Learning objectives or learning outcomes are important for focusing formally on those parts of the course that will be assessed. Transparency in clear course objectives benefits both tutors and learners – learners know what is expected of them and tutors know what they are evaluating. Being without such detailed knowledge is the equivalent of setting out on a journey unaware of the destination and route. Planned assessment linked to planned objectives may avoid the danger of **teaching to the test.** On the other hand, there are also concomitant risks: the tutor may hesitate to take the learner outside the parameters of the course or learners may be reluctant to do anything that does not count for assessment purposes.

Assessment activities should be chosen very carefully, have a specific focus or purpose which is clear to the learner and be designed to fit smoothly into the lesson (or identified part of the course in the case of distance learning) and should allow learners a clear sense of satisfaction. Formative assessment with feedback should be a routine part of learning, whether in the classroom or at a distance, and should use methods that are familiar to students. It is important to choose tasks which will assess appropriate learning goals for the students, whilst enabling them to perform at their highest level of ability. Hughes (1989) indicates that preparation for a test or assessed assignment can dominate teaching and learning activities, and that areas which are not tested are likely to become ignored. He argues that testing could, and should, have a beneficial backwash effect on teaching and learning:

For example, if you want to encourage oral ability, then test oral ability. This is very obvious, a straightforward matter of content validity, yet it is surprising how often it is not done. There is a tendency to test what it is easiest to test rather than what it is most important to test. (Hughes, 1989)

Bachman and Palmer underline two fundamental principles with regard to language testing: the need for a correspondence between language test performance and language use, and a clear and explicit definition of the qualities of test usefulness. They describe these qualities as reliability, construct validity, authenticity, interactiveness, impact, and practicality, and consider them vital for quality control throughout the process of designing, developing, and using a particular language test (Bachman and Palmer, 1996).

Assessment may relate to discrete skills where students are given a variety of tasks in each of the four skills, and listening, speaking, reading and writing are assessed separately. In other cases, assessment may require learners to adopt an integrated skills approach to completing a particular activity involving, for example, a variety of listening or reading texts and/or visual prompts such as photographs, diagrams or graphs, video extracts or computer software, to which students are required to respond orally or in written form. In task-based assessment, students are given much greater freedom over the resources and tools they need in order to accomplish a set task, and assessment is then generally applied to the product or outcome of their endeavours.

Testing skills: the importance of context

Awareness of the need to match assessment criteria more logically to the nature of the task and the outcome required has transformed the teaching and learning of languages. Whilst writing traditionally was used as the prime medium for measuring linguistic performance, it is far more usual to find a range of skills being tested with appropriate emphasis on speaking and listening. If the desired aim is for learners to communicate effectively in a variety of practical situations, learners should be tested on these skills. Weir highlights how there has been a growing interest in the importance of context, in defining performance conditions, and a growth of interest in what he refers to as the 'real-life' school of testing. He characterises the features of such testing as:

... focus on meaning, contextualisation, activity has an acceptable purpose (reasonable suspension of disbelief), realistic discourse processing, use of genuine stimulus material, authentic operations on texts, unpredictable outcomes, interaction based, performance under real psychological conditions, e.g. time pressure and in assessment of performance on a task, judgements made on achievement of communicative purposes. (Weir, 1993)

Evaluating performance – the ability to communicate

The aim is to improve the match between teaching, testing and target situation behaviour. (Weir, 1993)

Nowadays most popular language textbooks purport to develop communicative competence. Similarly, most language programmes for adults promote a communicative approach to teaching and learning. Tests to determine learners' ability to communicate are therefore generally based on authentic tasks and situations using authentic language and calling upon psycholinguistic and sociolinguistic features of language performance. In such contextualised communicative tasks the learner achieves practical outcomes through language use, rather than merely demonstrating a grasp of linguistic elements or principles, though these are, of course, important in supporting effective performance.

When assessing communicative competence the criteria need to distinguish the relative importance of **linguistic accuracy** and **getting the message across,** i.e. if effective communication has taken place, is total accuracy required in the production of the language, and should credit be given for comprehension? In addition to accuracy, assessment criteria may also include fluency, appropriateness, range and quality of language. Together, these enable the tester or examiner to gain an overall picture of performance, rather than concentrating solely on one or two features.

Assessing skills

Speaking skills in the classroom

Ainslie (1992) questions whether true authenticity can be created in testing communicative situations, but some tasks completed for National Vocational Qualifications (NVQ) are now conducted in the candidate's real working situation or simulated in a tutorial. Ainslie also points out the inevitable gap between linguistic competence (what the student knows) and linguistic performance (what the student is able to produce), both because of the stressful nature of an oral test, and also because the test can only sample performance. Nevertheless, competence is judged frequently through assessing performance evidence, which is often criterion-referenced, so that performance may regularly be matched against an agreed standard.

Assessment of speaking tasks can readily be incorporated into normal lessons, employing the usual teaching materials and activities. These should be designed specifically to stimulate interactive communication, preferably including elements of unpredictability. One-to-one speaking tests conducted by the tutor can take up considerable class time, leaving other learners perhaps working without support. It is therefore helpful to devise a system of assessing learners through observation and **eavesdropping** of pairs performing a role-play, interview, or discussion of a topic, or assessing a mini-talk or presentation to the group. If learners are conducting a survey, the tutor could be one of the compulsory five people to be interviewed. A real life information-gap activity in which learners seek and provide information, for example in arranging a meeting after discussing alternative opportunities and prior commitments, or exchanging information about leisure facilities, provides a natural opportunity to communicate.

The advantages of ongoing assessment of this kind, while learners are working at the activities, are clear:

- learners will feel less pressurised because, rather than a 'test', the activity forms part of a normal lesson;
- learners work in pairs or small groups in a relaxed atmosphere;
- the tutor can listen, observe and evaluate learners' competence;
- the activity is task-based and uses authentic language;
- the task can be multi-skill, so that learners note down elements of what they hear as part of the task, providing additional evidence of competence to back up tutor observation.

Speaking skills at a distance: preparation and practice

For distance learners, assessing speaking may be more problematic and there are fewer possibilities for different types of assessed tasks. Recorded oral presentations for coursework assessment are standard at The Open University's Department of Languages, and these can provide excellent opportunities for individual feedback on pronunciation and intonation. Nevertheless, they cannot test interactive skills, a key feature of spoken communication, and lack of spontaneity can be a recurrent problem. On the other hand, the summative OU end-of-course oral assessment in the form of group tasks has proved to be a very satisfactory test of both presentation and interactive skills. In order to give of their best, distance learners need to be well supported in their preparation for these kinds of tasks through tutorials and dayschools wherever possible. The week-long summer school is also an ideal opportunity to develop good interactive speaking skills. Increasingly, technological developments are creating many more opportunities for helping students practise their skills and prepare for assessment. On-line facilities for interaction and reflection with tutors and other language learners are becoming common. One example is the Lexica project at The OU, which has been piloted with French students at different levels. It is a text-based asynchronous conferencing system including a dedicated vocabulary learning software package, complemented by tutorial and peer-group discussion via an on-line forum. Other pilots in French and German have used the Lyceum software developed at The OU's Knowledge Media Institute for synchronous exchanges. Lyceum allows tutors to run seminars in real time and students to interact in pairs or small groups. It is also an ideal medium for sharing ideas and solving problems in textual and graphical modes as well as via voice.

Written skills

In assessing written tasks there are a number of issues to consider relating to accuracy versus spontaneity. Whilst communication of the message remains the most important objective, other factors relating to quality, fluency, range and appropriateness of the language are equally important. The degree of accuracy required may depend on the purpose of the written task: accuracy of form, style and language are clearly vital where a business letter is the designated assignment, whereas accuracy may be less crucial in, for example, a note-taking task.

Page (1990) argues that grammar does have a communicative value, but not necessarily in the transmission of the objective message. Rather, it transmits an image of the speaker:

> *In foreign language learning the image projected by the learner to the native speaker can be a powerful motivator, particularly among adult learners. They are frequently the ones who want to get it **right** because they don't want to appear foolish.* (Page, 1990)

Written assignments need to reflect appropriately work covered in the unit or module, allowing learners to provide evidence of their achievement in a number of areas, for example, The OU's tutor-marked assignments (TMAs) which assess students on **content, structure** and **personal input** as well as on **linguistic accuracy** and **range**. This assessment strategy allows students of different abilities to demonstrate clearly their areas of strength as well as weakness, and enables them to identify areas they need to focus on in order to improve.

Reading and listening skills

Assessing reading and listening should also involve authentic language in **real** situations. Assessing listening can also be informal: how learners respond to instructions in the target language or how they interpret language in pair work as well as whole class activities. More formal testing might involve listening for specific items of vocabulary or listening for gist. It is important to create a balance between general comprehension and **overloading** of memory. Assessing reading can range from comprehension of items of vocabulary in signs, notices, and snippets to longer items in letters, books, for wider meaning or for guessing meaning from context.

Tutors today have access to a wide range of activities and tend increasingly to use the target language in testing language skills. Test types may include multiple choice, gap filling, and matching language to symbols or images, note-taking, answering comprehension questions, sequencing and re-assembling texts and summaries. Whatever type is chosen some basic principles remain for test design:

- test only what has been taught;
- test types should match learning activities and tasks;

- the need for instructions to be clear and, if in the target language, to be pitched at the right level;
- the importance of unequivocal diagrams or illustrations used to cue responses;
- the need for the balance between **closed** and **open** activities.

Assessing cultural competence

Early definitions of communicative competence (Hymes, 1972) concentrated on analysing linguistic features of a person's ability to interact with speakers of the target language and the use of certain strategies to get the message across and sustain meaningful dialogue. Socio-linguistic aspects tended to be restricted to notions of appropriacy of language use or attitude towards target language speakers, their culture and society. Over the years, however, interest in how people interpret different cultures and communicate between cultures has been growing and has led to a much clearer understanding of what one leading writer in the field has coined '*intercultural communicative competence*' (Byram, 1997).

Today, few would argue with the assertion:

> ... *cultural competence is a key component of language learning, especially at advanced level, interacting with motivation and learning strategies, and representing potentially either an obstacle to or an enrichment of the language learning experience.* (Coleman, 1996)

The Prévert poem in chapter 13 (p143) is a good example, since full understanding of it depends on cultural knowledge, but it can also be understood as it is.

Assessment of linguistic performance is generally, but naively, assumed to encompass some measurement of a person's cultural competence. In reality, however, cultural competence per se is rarely assessed overtly. It is relatively easy to assess cultural knowledge in the guise of factual information that can be accumulated about socio-cultural phenomena of the target language community. Testing or examining the interpretation and evaluation of cultural manifestations is a far more complex activity. It is possible to devise assessment criteria which refer to the degree of accuracy or inaccuracy of the data presented and the learner's personal reactions. For example, from the descriptor of the top band of the assessment grid:

- provides an accurate and full account, with excellent development of ideas and opinions on the theme, including personal response, where appropriate;

to the lowest band of the same grid:

- gives an inaccurate and inadequate account, with poorly developed ideas and/or no opinions expressed.

Byram extracts from his global definition of '*intercultural communicative competence*' four dimensions which, he argues, may be assessed, preferably not as discrete elements in some form of summative assessment scheme, but rather as part of a process-based, performance assessment *'in which knowledge and abilities are evaluated as they are used and evident in activities which might be an application of what has been learnt'* (Byram, 1997).

He defines the dimensions as:

- **knowledge** (*savoirs*): of social groups and their products and practices in one's own and one's interlocutor's country, and of the general processes of societal and individual interaction;

- **skills of discovery and interaction** (*savoir apprendre/faire*): ability to acquire new knowledge of a culture and cultural practices, and the ability to operate knowledge, attitudes and skills under the constraints of real-time communication and interaction;

- **skills of interpreting and relating** (*savoir comprendre*): ability to interpret a document or event from another culture, to explain it and relate it to documents or events from one's own;

- **attitudes** (*savoir être*): curiosity and openness, readiness to suspend disbelief about other cultures and belief about one's own;

- **critical cultural awareness** (*savoir s'engager*): an ability to evaluate, critically and on the basis of explicit criteria, perspectives, practices and products in one's own and other cultures and countries.

It is certainly difficult to devise criteria for what in many cases are private effects on learners of engaging with new cultures through their language learning experiences. However, Byram has led the way in producing an initial framework and some examples of modes of assessment to be applied to these undoubtedly influential affective factors on language learning.

Giving constructive feedback

Too often assessment tasks are set in a context which is artificial and unfamiliar to students and the tasks are fragmented. They are marked by staff on measuring scales which have vague and poorly understood divisions. Marks are frequently reported to students with inadequate commentary to explain what they signify. (Boud, 1995)

Feedback of progress and performance is vital for every learner no matter what the mode of learning. Whether feedback is given to a whole class (perhaps picking up on common errors and practising the correct version as a group), face-to-face to an individual or, as is often the case for distance learners, in a written form or recorded on tape, by telephone or e-mail, this feedback should be sympathetic to the learners' needs and offer support and encouragement. The information gained from assessment should be communicated constructively to learners in order to give useful advice, to encourage them to reflect upon and evaluate their work and achievement.

Formative assessment concentrates on an **individual's progress**. Daines et al (1992) recommend striking a balance between honesty and objectivity on the one hand and a recognition of an individual's potential level of achievement and his/her sensibilities on the other. They are concerned that too much criticism, even when intended to be constructive, may be difficult for adults to cope with. Certainly, learners need an honest appraisal from the tutor, but if there are doubts about progress these need to be expressed in an encouraging way and remedial help offered at the same time.

An integral part of tutor assessment is the marking of and error correction of learners' oral language production or written work. When tutors interpret the **evidence,** that is the learner performance in any of the skills, they are determining gaps in learning, and to qualify as feedback, the information given must be useful in closing the gap between the actual and the desired levels of performance. The tutor needs to be clear what constitutes mistakes in the strictest meaning of the term (see chapter 13) or unacceptable deviations from the expected norm and feed back to the learner some element of prescription about what must be done to remedy mistakes or improve performance. A couple of examples of constructive feedback on written assignments are given below:

> *A very good start, but lacked clarity as you went on. Make sure you structure your work with an introduction, development of ideas and a conclusion. Some good ideas but they tended to get lost. Good range of vocabulary and structure. Check your noun-adjective agreements.*
>
> *You have clearly worked very hard to improve XX and made a lot of progress. Could I suggest that you have another look at section XX on XX pXX and try Activity XX again. Compare your answer with your previous attempt.*

All this implies that tutors should themselves become more aware of learning strategies if they are to recommend more independent learning. OU students, for example, submit recorded speaking assignments and the tutor may record comments after the speaking test regarding organisation and structure of content, quality of language, and pronunciation and fluency. Here are some sample comments:

> *You clearly understood the subject matter well, but should have included some more concrete details from the reading material to illustrate your points. Good development of ideas. On the language side, there was some lack of clarity caused by faulty intonation. It sounded in parts as if you were reading a prepared text, which at times made the rhythm sound artificial. Have a listen to the examples I have recorded for you at the end of your tape.*

> *Excellent work! To improve your pronunciation of XX however, I would suggest that you have another go at Activity XX pXX*

Using criteria for marking and to encourage language development

It is now common for learners to have their own copies of the assessment criteria and/or the mark scheme. If the criteria are detailed enough, this too will give learners clear guidelines about what learning needs to take place next, where effort should be concentrated and where specific improvements can be made to reach a higher level of performance. Learners need to be clear about what constitutes good performance in each element of the course. Models of what is expected at a given standard that can be imitated and adapted can help learners to know exactly what is required at a particular level or stage.

It is easy to view listening and reading tasks as **testing** comprehension where the answer is simply right or wrong. However, all skills in foreign language learning are progressive and developmental, and feedback on listening and reading comprehension needs to help the learner acquire further learning or coping strategies. For example, transcripts can be used to emphasise aspects of aural discrimination. Learners also need to become sensitive to interpreting what they hear. It is not much help simply to be told the right answer.

An effective marking system should be consistently implemented, be understood by the learners and be positive and encouraging about their work. An impression mark or comment is not particularly helpful, and returning assignments covered in red ink, grades or mysterious symbols without explanations can prove demotivating for learners. Feedback on written work should therefore:

- include a clear identification of good points and of those which require more work on the part of the learner (for example, '*good use of past tenses, excellent range of expressions of time*', etc);

- identify mistakes and errors either through a familiar code system of marks and symbols familiar to the learner or by means of written notes, preferably with examples.

Electronic feedback

Nowadays feedback is not necessarily of a personal nature. More language specific software and interactive CD-ROMs are available where instant, automatic feedback is provided for the learner. In this case tutors need to check the appropriateness of such feedback and help learners interpret it. In addition, e-mail is increasingly used as a tool for communication on assessment. It is particularly helpful in the context of supporting learners in environments where there is no frequent contact with a tutor. Makin (1994) outlined the advantages of e-mail for the language learning advisory service in personalising messages, providing immediacy of advice, re-invigorating flagging enthusiasm and breaking the sense of isolation that can develop when working independently.

Effective self-assessment

In order for feedback to work effectively, tutors need to help learners to develop a real awareness of the assessment process, including how to monitor learning and ways to act on feedback. The *Common European Framework for Modern Languages* stresses the importance of this:

> *Feedback only works if the recipient is in a position (a) to notice, i.e. is attentive, motivated and familiar with the form in which the information is coming, (b) to receive, i.e. is not swamped with information, has a way of recording, organising and personalising it; (c) to interpret, i.e. has sufficient pre-knowledge and awareness to understand the point at issue, and not to take counter-productive action and (d) to integrate the information, i.e. has the time, orientation and relevant resources to reflect on, integrate and so remember the new information* (Common European Framework for Modern Languages, 1996).

The previous chapters examined self-correction and self-assessment in some detail. If self-assessment is to be successful, feedback on learners' ability to carry this out is also essential. Brew (1999) emphasises that the ability to self-assess effectively does not happen on its own. Students need systematic practice in judging their own work and getting feedback on their ability to do so.

To sum up, effective feedback should have all of the following characteristics:

- ongoing – given throughout the learner's development;
- positive – informs the learner of what has been achieved;
- appropriate to the level/ standard/ stage at which the learner is operating;
- specific – relates to particular targets so that learners know where they are performing well and where further development needs to take place;
- constructive – if the learner is not doing something well, any barriers to progress should be identified and suggestions made about how to improve performance.

Feedback needs to be an interactive process that motivates and encourages learners to take responsibility for their own learning, to evaluate their own progress and to be able to progress to higher levels.

References

Ainslie S, 'Testing language performance' in Arthur L and S Hurd (eds), *The adult language learner: a guide to good teaching practice* (CILT, 1992)

Bachman L and A Palmer, *Language testing in practice* (OUP, 1996)

Boud D, *Enhancing learning through self assessment* (Kogan Page, 1995)

Brew A, 'Towards autonomous assessment: using self-assessment and peer-assessment' in Brown S and A Glasner (eds), *Assessment matters in Higher Education*: 159–171 (SRHE and Open University Press, 1999)

Byram M, *Teaching and assessing intercultural communicative competence* (Multilingual Matters, 1997)

Coleman J A, *Studying languages: a survey of British and European students* (CILT, 1996)

Council of Europe, *Modern languages: learning, teaching, assessment. A common European framework of reference* (Strasbourg: 1996)

Daines J, C Daines and B Graham, *Adult learning, adult teaching* (Publications Unit, Department of Adult Education, Nottingham University, 1992)

Hughes A, *Testing for language teachers* (Cambridge University Press, 1989)

Hymes D, 'On communicative competence' in Pride J B and J Holmes (eds), *Sociolinguistics* (Penguin, 1972)

Makin L, 'Language advising by e-mail' in Esch E (ed), *Self-access and the adult language learner* (CILT, 1994)

Page B, 'Why do I have to get it right anyway' in Page B (ed), *What do you mean ... it's wrong?* (CILT, 1990)

Parr H, *Assessment and planning in the MFL department* (CILT, 1997)

Weir C, *Understanding and developing language tests* (Prentice Hall International, 1993)

16

Assessment procedures and quality issues

BOB POWELL

In general, there is a growing homogeneity, based on regulated systems of outcome-based assessment, between higher, further and adult education, and the compulsory sector. (Swann and Arthurs, 1999)

This chapter will consider assessment in the broader perspective, from an institutional and national perspective. All sectors of education have undergone major reforms in recent years. Most notable in the context of adult education, whether provided through traditional continuing education, lifelong learning or higher education programmes, has been the introduction of accreditation, that is the provision of some formal qualification at the end of a course of study. This implies that learners are assessed and the results of their performance are recorded and made public. In many cases, the introduction of accreditation has been a prerequisite for the allocation and distribution of local or national funding to support the delivery of programmes. There has been much adverse reaction to the advent of what appear to be government imposed controls on the content and delivery of leisure learning.

On the positive side, what has emerged in all sectors is an acknowledged need for greater transparency and accountability in assessment schemes. As well as being required, and better prepared, to describe how learners are assessed, tutors also have to be able to demonstrate the effectiveness of their teaching methods and assessment schemes, not only to the learners themselves but to external agencies charged with evaluating the quality of the learning experience.

This chapter will present the background to these developments, consider issues in the continuing debate about standards, teaching quality assessment, subject review, benchmarking, credit transfer, and thus highlight some current and possible future challenges facing language teachers.

Transparency and accountability in assessment

The world of education is renowned for its jargon, and educationists quickly latch on to new terms which reflect the prevailing preoccupations of a particular era. In

177

discussions on assessment and evaluation, the words **transparency** and **accountability** are now frequently employed. However, as always when certain short-hand expressions gain familiarity and inevitably become overused, the full breadth of their meaning may be lost, as indeed may the implications of the processes which they represent.

In many ways these words express two viewpoints on the increasing importance of communication in education. Transparency in assessment may be defined as the provision of clear sets of information about the assessment process and the right of access to these for the learners being assessed. The information will be in terms of:

- defined syllabus content – the subject-matter to be assessed in terms of language (vocabulary, grammar), topics or themes;
- quantity, timing and status of coursework, continuous assessment or independent work, and expectations of time involvement outside class or face-to-face tutor contact;
- entitlement to explicit feedback, frequency of meetings and details about mark scheme for continuous assessment;
- consequences of late delivery of assignments, failure to produce or absence;
- test or examination length, format, mark scheme;
- provision of specimen papers, model answers and the range of test-types likely to be employed;
- publication of overall grading system, to enable comparisons to be made by the learner with other assessment or examination schemes;
- weighting (credit-value) of the course being studied in terms of the provider's other qualifications;
- details of opportunities for credit-transfer, i.e. the value of the qualification sought set against those of other institutions' programmes;
- opportunities to review, after results are published, not only marked coursework assignments but also marked examination scripts, including examiners' marks/comments;
- procedures for appeal against grades/results.

The information given to learners is also required by those bodies charged with the responsibility of inspecting the quality of education in an institution – hence the concept of accountability. In addition to the above details, however, the institution must ensure, among other things, that there is consistency and fairness across programmes (e.g. courses in different languages or different syllabuses/courses in the same language which carry the same status) and that the examination conventions used to determine final results are explicit and applied uniformly across the range of subjects.

There can be no doubt that greater transparency and accountability in assessment are desirable. Learners will no longer tolerate a situation in which the system by which they are judged is shrouded in mystery, and where tutors are evasive or seem insecure about the methods they use to assess them. Learners are now defined as **stakeholders** in the education process. They need to be able to trust their tutors, so it is incumbent on the latter to familiarise themselves with the fine detail of the assessment procedures within which they are operating, lest they be judged to be ill-prepared or worse, unfair, or even incompetent.

Accrediting language learning

Assessment is concerned with measuring performance and formalising judgements about performance. Assessment without communication between tutor and learner is of little value. As has been seen in the previous chapters, it is essential in language learning that assessment not only provides a reliable and fair measure of learners' level of competence or attainment, but also that it is used in a way which will motivate, help identify both strengths and weaknesses and provide the essential feedback information for future strategies for learning to be developed by both tutor and learner.

Accreditation is the formal, public acknowledgement of performance. It is associated both with the official recognition of programmes or syllabuses and the awarding of certificates to people following them. Accreditation similarly provides a means of communication:

a) between the awarding institution and learners: learners are thus able to identify their level of achievement against published criteria or grades;

b) between learners and those who require information about their level of proficiency: current or future employers, further or higher education institutions, other examination or awarding bodies, for example.

Adult education in Britain for much of the last fifty years has not included formal accreditation. The tradition was one of liberal education: the pursuit of knowledge per se was perceived as a healthy leisure activity. The subjects studied reflected personal interests and a desire to keep the brain active. The social dimension of learning, in evening classes, for example, were almost as important – some might argue more important – than developing competence or acquiring new skills. Where some form of test or examination was offered at the end of a course of language study for non-academic purposes, it was generally presented as an option or even, possibly, as a special arrangement for those who wished to obtain recognisable proof of their participation in study.

However, through the eighties and nineties, government policy vis-à-vis education shifted generally towards promoting subjects deemed to be contributing to the economic welfare of the nation. Vocationalism was preferred over liberalism. When policies were transformed into practice (through the White Paper of June 1991 *Education and training for the twenty-first century* and the 1992 Further and Higher Education Act), stricter control of funding mechanisms through local authorities and institutions was introduced. In the majority of cases, this has involved the requirement to introduce accreditation and to pay greater attention to financial factors. The National Open College Network (NOCN) continues to play a major role in the accreditation of foreign language courses. Founded in 1983, the NOCN consists of approximately 900 organisations, including consortia of colleges, guidance and career services, voluntary and community agencies. The Open College Networks operate accreditation within the National Credit Framework, that is they award credits for learning achievements within agreed definitions of levels and credits which are recognised by the National Council for Vocational Qualifications (NCVQ). Nevertheless, the introduction of more or less blanket accreditation has led to a regrettable narrowing of the range of subjects on offer and, even for those subjects that are approved as having intrinsic vocational value, class sizes have to be viable. Languages have been affected in so far as learners now have to prove their ability to make progress by taking tests or examinations, and it has become more difficult for programme providers to sustain small classes in minority interest languages.

These developments then have not been without their critics. At the time of the introduction of accreditation into post-compulsory education programmes, serious concerns were expressed about the new direction adult education was taking, for example by the National Institute for Adult Continuing Education (NIACE) in its survey report on learning and leisure:

> *It will be a step backwards if the current need to assess and measure economic benefit imposes artificial definitions of what is educationally, socially and culturally valuable, even if it is more difficult to define these qualities.* (Sargant, 1991)

There were also more specific doubts expressed about the potentially undesirable consequences of accreditation. It has long been argued that exposure to assessment may be an obstacle to creativity and independence (Rogers, 1983). More recently, with increasing pressure from all quarters to provide defined levels of educational attainment across all sectors of education, these arguments have been resurrected and redefined in the promotion of a more problem-based approach to assessment:

> *Focusing on learning for assessment leads to assessment-driven teaching and a trivialisation of programme content. Significant features of understanding, for example, cannot be readily specified. With assessment-driven teaching, that which cannot be readily specified tends to be neglected.* (Swann and Arthurs, 1999)

Others view the introduction of formal assessment leading to accreditation, however supportive and flexible, as inevitably altering the respective roles of teachers and learners (Ecclestone, 1993). The imposition of mandatory accreditation was criticised as being short-sighted, inflexible and liable to hinder the development of a mass, accessible, higher education system (Taylor, 1993).

Some research into learners' attitudes towards accreditation in the continuing education department of a Scottish university has reinforced this critical viewpoint: learners feared it would have a negative effect on their own learning or on the ethos of language learning as they had experienced it. Yet, positive reactions were also expressed, focusing on better motivation and improved feedback on the learning experience (Cooke et al, 1996). The importance of transferability of qualifications was also mentioned, especially by learners in business classes.

It is true that not all learners, particularly the large and growing proportion of retired students, need certificates as a positive motivating influence or proof of achievement. Nevertheless, accreditation can be used as a mechanism to:

- encourage teachers to be more conscious of learning objectives and outcomes;
- extend and enhance the value and status of language learning;
- improve the quality of learning by formalising good assessment and feedback practice.

The introduction of accreditation may also lead to greater accountability and more extensive planning on the part of the providers, with staff and student development programmes becoming accepted as an essential element of delivery.

Assessing teaching and learning in higher education

The last decade of the twentieth century also saw many changes in the higher education system of the UK. The creation of several new universities, by the granting of university status to the polytechnics, brought far-reaching developments in terms of monitoring and assessment procedures. The polytechnics, without the authority to award their own qualifications, had grown accustomed to submitting their plans, their course proposals and their assessment schemes, to external agencies such as the Council for National Academic Awards (CNAA). They were also accustomed to scrutiny by inspectors and visitors from other professional organisations or validating bodies.

The older universities, however, operated a much less bureaucratic system of external review, relying almost uniquely on the long-established system of external examiners. External examiners or assessors are essentially respected academics from other institutions, specialists in the subject knowledge being taught, who check a sample of work by students on a given degree programme, give advice on borderline cases and provide judgements on the overall standards of the results. Many external assessors are invited also to comment on syllabus and course design, as is the case in The Open University, for example. These peer evaluations are based almost uniquely on the experience and personal wisdom of the examiner, without reference to any particular sets of criteria other than those defined by the department being visited.

With successive governments calling for greater accountability in higher education, and with the coming together of higher education institutions into a unitary system, it was inevitable that standards of teaching and learning would be more rigorously evaluated and the results of inspections made public. Initially, there was a relatively loose system of inspection involving a department's claim for excellence and selective visits. From 1995, however, teaching quality assessment (TQA) in higher education was firmly based on an externally directed system of scrutiny, a revised scheme involving universal visiting and a core set of aspects of provision. Specialist departments in the institutions were obliged to compile documentation about their courses and their working practices – the *Self-assessment* – before presenting themselves for external review. The form, length and contents of the self-assessment report were heavily influenced by the external, nationally applied assessment criteria. Following receipt of the self-assessment report by the Higher Education Funding Council, a team of subject assessors was sent to the department, spending three days scrutinising the work and, to all intents and purposes, measuring the accuracy and validity of the claims contained in the self-assessment report. Judgements were made under six aspects of provision:

- Curriculum design, content and organisation
- Teaching, learning and assessment
- Student progression and achievement
- Student support and guidance
- Learning resources
- Quality assurance and enhancement

A four-point scale was applied to each component and the resulting public report identified marks corresponding to grade criteria within each cell and a total out of twenty-four. These details are important because they demonstrate a philosophy of assessment in which it is accepted that evidence from diverse sources made by several people interpreting various phenomenon over a period of time can result in a public judgement on the quality of education, as measured against the provider's own sets of aims and objectives.

In a way, it was remarkable that such a system – essentially an accreditation procedure for universities – was able to be implemented. After all, failure in one aspect of provision would automatically lead to re-inspection and a second failure would result in withdrawal of government funds. What emerged, however, out of the quality assessments of the nineties, especially as far as languages are concerned, were clearer perceptions of what constitutes **good practice** in teaching, learning and assessment. As regards assessment, it became clear during scrutiny of language departments in 1995–96, that certain developments were being given special emphasis by assessors and specific criticisms were being repeated almost ad nauseam. The subject overview report on French, for example, had this to say about the assessment processes:

> *...in just over 20 per cent of cases the range of assessment methods was considered too narrow to test the stated learning outcomes. Innovative assessment processes include the production of portfolios of independent work, dossiers of achievement of various kinds, and group projects, sometimes involving the imaginative use of technology. There is a need for staff to give more thought to assessment criteria. In some 30 per cent of institutions, criteria were judged to be unclear or inconsistently applied... . (HEFCE, 1996)*

Criticisms about the narrowness of assessment methods and the lack of appropriate criteria have probably been justifiable given the changes in teaching methods that have swept through the profession over recent years. These have sometimes been adopted through a genuine desire for change and the recognition that language learning is much more than understanding and applying grammar rules. Occasionally, though, the real reason for change has been the increase in student numbers and the wider range of ability and aptitude to be catered for among the student population. Many more opportunities for independent learning, including distance-learning and the use of new technologies outside classroom-based instruction, have also been introduced and assessment schemes need to take account of these 'alternative' forms of language acquisition.

Towards benchmarking

There is now, however, an even greater drive, largely from government quality assurance agencies, for the elaboration of defined levels of attainment, or **learning outcomes** as they tend now to be called, in all subjects, including languages, and that will inevitably – some might use the word inexorably – lead to tighter control on assessment schemes and during formal review or approval (accreditation) of courses. This impetus coincides with a new system of quality assessment in which **teaching quality assessment (TQA)**, in practice both expensive and excessively time-consuming, is replaced by **academic review**. The basic difference is that, whereas TQA began from an institutional self-assessment, academic review will start with subject by subject benchmark statements. So what are benchmarks? And how are they likely to affect the teaching, the learning – and most important the assessment of language study? Benchmarks have been defined by the Quality Assurance Agency (QAA) as *'broad statements which represent general expectations about standards'* (QAA, 1999). Benchmarking is:

> ... about the conceptual framework that gives a discipline its coherence and identity; about the intellectual capability and understanding that should be developed through the study of that discipline... . (op. cit. 4)

It may be that the introduction of benchmarks is initially planned for higher education, but their use is likely to spread into other sectors and impact upon adult language learning generally.

As one significant conclusion to his report on comparative research into the proficiency, background, attitudes and motivations of students of foreign languages in the United Kingdom and Europe, Coleman had no hesitation in making the following recommendation:

> Universities should clearly state proficiency levels in all course documentation, defining linguistic objectives, level descriptors and assessment criteria [...] Agreed national or international standards should be adopted. (Coleman, 1996)

It was Coleman's belief, and he did not mince his words, that *'employers, students, parents, and universities themselves are being short-changed, and language teachers are falling short of normal professional standards'* (op. cit: 58) in their unwillingness *'to define the linguistic objectives of their courses in any but the vaguest terms'* (op. cit: 58). His main lament was the lack of benchmarks against which to measure progress.

In many ways Coleman anticipated the drive for benchmarking which gathered pace during the late nineties. The report of the National Committee of Inquiry into Higher Education (1997), better known as the Dearing report, proposed a form of quality assessment in higher education which was based on partnership, with academics setting, monitoring and maintaining national subject standards in conjunction with the QAA, which was created in the same year. The proposed new scheme envisages the creation of benchmark standards for all subjects and that these will be used in the new subject review cycle which will run from 2000 to 2006. It is proposed that the benchmark statements will identify not only the subject-specific *'learning outcomes'* but also *'generic intellectual attributes that are likely to be possessed by graduates generally'* (QAA, 1999).

At the time of writing, benchmark standards have been published for 22 subjects and the second phase involving 21 more subject groups, including languages, started work in May 2000. There is considerable speculation in the profession about what the final version of the language benchmarks will look like. There is, of course, the risk that the approved model for all subsequent benchmarks will have been determined by the preparatory work of the other subject groups. However, there is scope to be really creative in a discipline such as foreign language learning provided that the working group reflects adequately the differing traditions and cultures of the discipline, takes into account the considerable range of methodologies employed, the differing priorities regarding syllabus content (language, literature, socio-political themes, socio-cultural topics, etc) which are represented across the institutions and, finally, the diversity of assessment schemes that are employed.

Conclusion

There can be no doubt that, irrespective of the mode of delivery or location of lifelong language learning – whether in traditional adult education classes, in distance learning mode, in further or higher education settings – the current emphasis on standards and benchmarks, on programme specifications and learning outcomes, will have a profound impact on the way languages are assessed and programmes are accredited. It is only to be hoped that in the pressure to define and differentiate proficiency levels, and to specify how these may link to a national qualifications framework, the teaching profession and those responsible for programme delivery do not fall into the trap of reducing the results of language learning to mere statements of grammatical or lexical knowledge arranged in some form of graduated scale of difficulty. Such an over-simplification would run counter to our growing awareness of the language learning process. It would also undermine, if not negate entirely, so much of the constructive endeavour that language tutors and course designers have shown in recent years in their efforts to ensure that learners approach assessment with a positive attitude, confident that being assessed and receiving feedback are natural, indeed essential features of the language learning process.

References

Coleman J A, *Studying languages: a survey of British and European students* (CILT, 1996)

Cooke A, K Mackle and M Spöring, 'Sleeping at the back: student attitudes to accreditation' in *Scottish journal of adult and continuing education*, 3, 25–42 (1996)

Ecclestone K 'Accreditation in Adult Learning' in *Adults Learning*, 4, 7 (1993)

HEFCE, Subject overview report, 'Quality assessment of French' in *Higher Education Funding Council*, 21–22 (1996)

QAA, 'Higher Quality' in *Quality Assurance Agency*, 5, (1999)

Rogers C R, 'Towards a theory of creativity' in Rothersburg A and C R Hausman (eds) *The creativity question* (Durham University Press, 1983)

Sargant N, *Learning and 'leisure': a study of adult participation in learning and its policy implications* (NIACE, 1991)

Swann J and J Arthurs, 'Empowering lecturers: a problem-based approach to improve assessment practices' in *Higher Education Review*, 31, 2, 50–74 (1999)

Taylor R, 'Accreditation and the future of university continuing education' in *Adults learning*, 4, 10 (1993)

PART 5

THE PROFESSIONAL CONTEXT

The extent and rate of change in society today means that all of us have to become lifelong learners if we are to survive professionally. Language tutors are no exception. They see that their work is constantly evolving as a result of changes in society, government policies, technological and research developments. Learners, employers and governments have become 'consumers' who expect value for money. Changes in government policies as well as in learners' lifestyles and working patterns have affected the nature of programmes offered, how they are delivered and accredited. Quality assurance and accountability have become paramount. Research into the nature of language and technological developments such as the Internet is harnessed in many ways to support language learning and change the teaching environment. All tutors will be aware that the languages they teach are also constantly evolving.

Initial training can only provide a foundation for continuing development throughout one's teaching career. Being a professional today means taking responsibility for one's own continuing development. To remain employable, language tutors need to review and regularly update their skills, practice, knowledge, linguistic and technological expertise. What possibilities are open to them? Chapter 17 explores how tutors can reflect on their own practice in order to identify and implement changes, and how this can be achieved individually or with the help of colleagues. It then examines ways of maintaining and enhancing one's subject knowledge and expertise. Chapter 18 investigates modes of accreditation for language tutors, including competence-based accreditation and the use of portfolios. The final chapter looks ahead to the future and examines the effects of increasing globalisation, the challenge of the new technologies and the possibilities for collaboration across the European Union.

17

Continuing professional development

Linda Murphy

For many people, the phrase **continuing professional development** (CPD) conjures up an immediate vision of training courses. However, there are other ways of reviewing and enhancing practice and keeping up to date with the ever changing world of language teaching. This chapter explores two possibilities. Firstly, how individual tutors can reflect on their own practice in order to identify and implement changes. Secondly, how this can be achieved by working with colleagues, observing and being observed by others. The process of reflection may point to specific development needs and the chapter goes on to consider a variety of approaches to maintaining subject knowledge and enhancing language teaching skills. Finally, tutor-led classroom research is considered as a further means of developing practice.

The reflective practitioner

Schön (1983) argues that the traditional separation of theory and practice did not account for or enhance the development of professional expertise. The traditional view is that professionals mastered a body of theoretical knowledge which could then be applied in practice. Schön points out that the application of theories and principles may be fine where situations are straightforward and predictable, but very often this is not the case. Professionals have to weigh up situations, form rapid judgements and take action accordingly. In doing so, they often draw on spontaneous, intuitive knowledge derived from experience. Schön contends that professionals can bring together both experience and theoretical knowledge through reflection on practice. He proposes the development of **reflective practitioners** rather than **technical experts** who would consciously, systematically and rigorously scrutinise their actions and the attitudes and assumptions underlying their judgements in order to learn from them and develop new understandings.

The role of reflection in professional development

Apart from a realisation of the limitations of **theory,** the importance attached to becoming a reflective practitioner lies in the recognition of the role which reflection can play in effective learning. Kolb (1984) describes this in a model which has been widely used in professional development programmes to encourage reflective practice (see also chapter 1). In this model, experience is seen as central to learning. The model sets out a cycle of activity (shown in Figure 1) to explain how experience is transformed through reflection in order to create new knowledge. Kolb maintains that working through each part of the cycle provides a framework for the conscious, systematic, rigorous reflection needed in order to develop as a reflective practitioner.

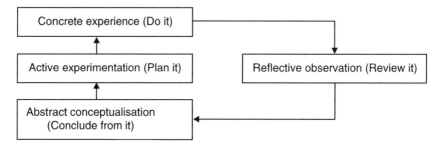

Figure 1: The Kolb learning cycle (adapted)

Boud et al (1985) elaborates on what might be involved in **reflective observation.** They suggest two main activities: firstly, **returning to the experience,** secondly, **re-evaluating the experience**. They are of the opinion that the original experience is often given too little attention in the rush to decide what action might be needed next. They emphasise the need to recognise and accept feelings generated by the experience. Positive feelings need to be built on, obstructive feelings need to be overcome and removed. As accurate a picture of the experience as possible has to be established, before attempting to re-evaluate it. Re-evaluation may involve consultation with others, perhaps further reading about teaching and learning or a review of any relevant theoretical knowledge in order to understand why the experience happened as it did and what it might mean. The outcome of this analysis is a new perspective on the experience, a commitment to a change in behaviour and a readiness for action. Figure 2 shows how might this apply to the experience of a language tutor.

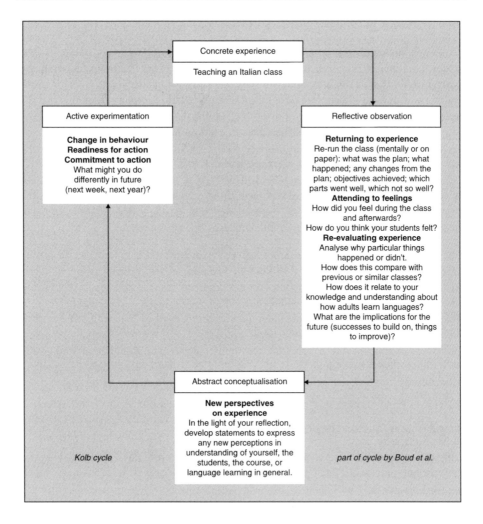

Figure 2: Reflecting on a language class
(Adapted from SOL Staff Development File, Section 1.5.3, The Open University, 1996)

Despite widespread use in professional development activities, many find the notion of reflection difficult. They are not sure how it differs from the way most tutors think about their teaching from day to day. As Lewis and Dowling (1992) state:

> *On a daily basis each of us, to one degree or another, looks back on how things went and reviews actions taken. We puzzle over nuances that have made today's presentation better than a previous one, marvel how well we did 'on our feet' or realise with hindsight what else we might have done to resolve a situation.*

Reflection means thinking about our own thinking, about what we've done, how we did it and why, with a view to gaining understanding and insights to use in the future.

For the reflective practitioner, this means a conscious, systematic and rigorous process.

Why such an emphasis on the conscious, systematic and rigorous nature of the process? Schön (1983) points to the way in which practitioners can bring their existing experience and knowledge to bear without consciously considering it, what he terms **knowing-in-action.** This derives from the knowledge, beliefs and assumptions that the practitioner brings to any situation or problem and can draw on spontaneously. There is a danger that such **tacit practices** become unthinking and routine; they may be based on stereotypes, inaccurate understandings or outdated models. Through the process of conscious reflection on experience, tutors can examine their practices, underlying assumptions and values and identify why, in some cases, tacit practices may no longer be adequate to deal with new situations. As Boud et al (1985) stress: *'It is only when we bring our ideas to consciousness that we can evaluate them and begin to make choices about what we will and will not do.'*

Two different kinds of thinking are involved in reflection. The first can be called **reflexiveness.** The purpose of this kind of thinking is to become aware of one's existing knowledge, skills, attitudes and assumptions about language teaching and how these have influenced actions taken. In other words, what was the rationale for a certain activity? Why were those materials chosen or used in that way? The second kind of thinking can be termed **critical analysis**. Here, assumptions, judgements, application of models and theories are questioned. Does that rationale still hold good? Have things always been done this way, even though students' needs have changed? Is this really the only way to practise this grammar point or is there a better way?

Barriers to reflection on practice

Criticism has been levelled at the models of the learning cycle described here because they do not give sufficient attention to the potential barriers to reflection which practitioners might face. There is often too little time between one session and the next; there are too many competing demands on one's time in the form of family and other work commitments; past experience may give rise to the expectation and belief that performance is assessed by others. Convery (1998) suggests that individual reflection or self-evaluation often tends to focus on immediate problems and solutions rather than on questioning underlying values and assumptions. In other words, it may be possible to engage reflexiveness but critical analysis may prove to be far more problematic. To question these underlying values and assumptions may be too difficult for an individual, as it is too much like questioning one's self-image. The distinction made by Argyris and Schön (1974) between **espoused theory** and what they termed **theory in use** highlights this tension. In contrast to declared principles, the latter is based on undeclared perspectives. A study by Murray and Macdonald (1997) showed that methods described by tutors did not really match up with their stated beliefs about their role. Convery feels that tutors are often too close to the action to question their motivation and argues that collaboration with a trusted colleague is crucial in order to achieve both the reflexiveness and critical analysis which reflection on practice requires.

How can busy language tutors develop the habit of conscious, systematic and rigorous reflection? The following section examines three possible methods for use by individuals or in collaboration with colleagues: self-evaluation, evaluation via feedback from learners and peer observation.

Self-evaluation

The starting point for individual reflection and development for most tutors is some form of self-evaluation exercise (see also chapter 14). There are many models available, including forms to fill in and checklists of questions to consider. They may be provided by the institution, suggested in practice guides and handbooks or devised by individual tutors. Another approach is to keep what may be called a reflective diary or log, a place to record ideas, questions and insights gained from thinking about a teaching session or a course. Minton (1991) explains the sort of format which a reflective diary could take and how it can be used. It can be argued that it is not really necessary to fill in a form, write a description or keep a diary in order to carry out a self-evaluation. However, writing thoughts down ensures that the process of reflection is indeed conscious and that all appropriate aspects are covered.

Figure 3 gives an example of a simple post-lesson questionnaire. It follows the Kolb learning cycle in that questions 1–7 encourage the tutor to review the experience, questions 8–10 encourage the tutor to draw conclusions and formulate new perspectives, and the remaining questions encourage a commitment to change and future action.

Course: **Date:**   **No. of students present:**

Aim:

1. Planned learning objectives/outcomes:
2. Planned activities, timing and mode (e.g. whole group, small group, pairwork):
3. How was the room arranged?
4. Were there any changes to the plans? Reasons?
5. What went well? Why?
6. What didn't go well/didn't work? Why?
7. Which learning objectives/outcomes were achieved? How was that checked?
8. Did students have enough opportunities to interact with each other?
9. Did the materials work? Too easy? Too complex?
10. What could be done differently next time?
11. Are changes needed to the content for next time?
12. What needs to be kept in mind for the next session?
13. Anything else to note?

Figure 3: A sample self-evaluation form
(Adapted from SOL Staff Development File, The Open University, 1996)

Figure 4 is an example of a more detailed checklist of good practice which enables a detailed review of teaching experience in an individual session or over a period of time. The questions encourage tutors to identify aspects of their teaching to work on in future.

1 Do I respect the learners as adults and meet them on equal terms?

Do I create a friendly informal and welcoming atmosphere treating each learner as an individual and using their name?

Do I make it apparent that I have time for people, especially before and after a session for those who may want to discuss something privately?

2 Am I clear about the aims and objectives for the session and have my planning and preparation taken full account of them?

Do the learners know what they are trying to achieve at any given point ... are their needs being met?

Who sets the standards they are expected to reach? When I do, is it clear to them at what level they have to achieve?

3 Do I show a sufficient willingness to negotiate as well as consult with the group, especially about content?

Do I know my material sufficiently well and have I thought out the order and structure of what I propose to do?

Do I present material step by step ... relate new content, ideas, grammar and vocabulary to what they know already using appropriate examples?

Do I use the target language all the time as far a possible?

Do I ensure that learners have genuine reasons to communicate with each other in the target language in every session?

4 Do people feel confident and at ease within the group ... how do I know? ... what have I done to promote it?

Do I enable and encourage them to draw on and contribute their experience and expertise, valuing what they offer, sensitively dealing with errors or misapprehensions?

Does everyone get the opportunity to participate according to their level and ability? How do I bring this about?

5 Do I use a range of teaching and learning methods ... and have changes of activities during the session?

Do learners have the opportunity to work with a variety of other people during the session?

Do I use audio visual material and other learning resources including examples of authentic language when and where they will help people's learning?

Do I make a task quite clear to learners, then sensitively monitor what they are doing?

6	Am I fair in allocating my time and attention to individuals and groups?
	Can I diagnose and assess learners' difficulties and, once knowing what they are, can I help individuals in a sympathetic and constructive way?
	Do I give specific practical suggestions about ways in which individuals can improve their accuracy, intonation, listening skills etc?
	Do I identify learners' strengths and encourage them to build on them?
7	Do I encourage learners to be aware of their own strengths and weaknesses and to set themselves learning targets?
	Do I monitor learner's progress and encourage them to do the same?
8	Do I give the group an opportunity to say what they think about the session and the course ... do I listen?
	Am I clear about what has been achieved during a session and the extent to which the session's learning objectives have been attained?
	Do I ensure that the group and individuals leave with a sense of having accomplished something, a desire to learn more and a clear idea of what they will work on before the next session?
9	Do I show my enthusiasm for the language I teach, the people who speak it and the learners?
	Do I remember that it is the learners' progress and achievement which is all important?
10	Do I enjoy what I do and do I do it well? If not, what am I going to do about it?

Figure 4: Self-evaluation checklist
(Adapted from *Adult Learning, Adult Teaching:* Daines, Daines and Graham, 1993)

The examples in Figures 3 and 4 are designed for face-to-face teaching, but could be adapted to telephone, correspondence or on-line teaching modes. Tutors working by telephone or on-line with individuals or group conferences might consider how they ensure that the learners are at ease with the technology or how they make opportunities for getting to know each other. Tutors on distance learning programmes might consider the time it takes them to return scripts and audio-cassettes to students and the coherence and tone of their written and oral feedback.

Self-evaluation may be concerned with working relationships with learners, with teaching a particular session or a whole course. It may have a wide focus, taking in all or most aspects of teaching, or it could have a narrower focus, concentrating on one particular aspect, such as setting up group and pairwork, giving instructions or modelling pronunciation and intonation. The focus depends on the experience and circumstances of individual tutors. Richards and Lockhart (1994) give examples of forms to assist in reviewing teaching from a number of perspectives, such as the way in which it is structured or the interaction that takes place. The use of forms and checklists has its dangers. If used too rigidly, this may become a mechanical exercise, a style of reflection (Boud and Walker, 1998) that is applied unthinkingly and therefore does not develop practice.

At this point, many tutors may be wondering how they will find the time to carry out detailed self-evaluation within their teaching timetable and other commitments. An individual may decide to reflect in this way on a regular basis but perhaps once a week, once a month, or at the end of a term or semester. For some, it may even be possible to reflect after each session. Better to set realistic goals for real reflection than to rush or do it mechanically. In order to engage in critical analysis, some more probing questions may be necessary. Figure 5 gives an example of the sort of examination that may be carried out perhaps in the context of a longer-term review of one's practice.

Aspect of teaching : (e.g. developing listening skills with advanced students)

My approach is _____

I use these methods because _____

Alternatives might be _____

The advantages and disadvantages of each are _____

Over the next course I will _____

Because _____

Figure 5: Engaging in critical analysis

Seeking feedback from learners to aid reflection on practice

When trying to build up an accurate picture of one's practice, it is important to consider it from the learner's perspective. There are a number of ways in which feedback can be sought from learners. A general discussion might be held to elicit their views on particular activities and materials. Similar discussion might be held in small groups, with each group invited to contribute a few points to a plenary session. Learners can be asked to note a few comments on post-its or on pieces of paper which are then displayed, grouped by theme and discussed. Perhaps the most common way of eliciting feedback from learners is via a questionnaire. The advantage of a questionnaire is that learners are more likely to be open and honest in their responses than when they are questioned directly, particularly in front of others. Individual, anonymous completion can ensure that everyone's view is heard. Questionnaires may elicit views on specific activities, a single session, a series of sessions or a whole course. When designing a questionnaire, it is important to think through exactly what information is required from learners so that appropriate questions can be asked in a way that will not be too time-consuming to answer. Questions must be clear and unambiguous, but avoid leading learners to give particular replies or to assume there is a right answer. Language tutors also have to weigh up the advantages and disadvantages of using a questionnaire in the target language. It is always a good idea to pilot a questionnaire, perhaps with a colleague, in order to ensure that it will achieve the type of feedback intended. Bell (1987) summarises a range of question types that may be used and considers how to avoid the pitfalls in question wording.

Working with others to reflect on practice: peer observation

Interest in peer observation has grown considerably in recent years. Cosh (1998) identified a number of uses of peer observation of teaching, from accountability and assessment to staff development. Practice varies considerably between institutions, from those where peer observation is a requirement to those where it is not formally encouraged at all. In a growing number of institutions, mutually arranged peer observation is encouraged as a valuable form of staff development. Observation by a colleague can help to provide the objectivity and clarity which self-evaluation or learner feedback may not be able to achieve, and can assist in producing that accurate picture of the experience which Boud et al emphasise as such an important starting point for further analysis. Martin and Double (1998) describe a model consisting of four stages: (1) identifying a partner, (2) mutual briefing, (3) observation, (4) feedback and review. This model has been extensively piloted and refined by the FDTL project Developing Excellence in Language Teaching through the Observation of Peers (DEVELOP)[1] which has produced a video pack giving detailed guidance for each stage in the process, based on application of Kolb's experiential learning cycle. Although developed in higher education, the model is transferable to any other language teaching situation.

Identifying a partner, mutual briefing and observation

Where peer observation is by mutual arrangement, whether formally supported by the institution or carried out informally by tutors themselves, the first step is to find a colleague who is also interested in reflecting on practice and would appreciate support in doing so. In many circumstances this may be easier said than done. Part-time language tutors and those involved in distance teaching often work in isolation and rarely meet their colleagues. It is possible to get to know other language tutors via Netword[2] groups or ALL[3] branches as well as via institution staff groups. Such groups might be persuaded to focus one of their meetings on self-evaluation and obtaining feedback with a view to facilitating peer observations between members. The key to success is mutual respect and trust between observer and observed, who take both roles in turn.

Partners set up a meeting where they give each other background information about their groups and agree when they will observe each other. Each tutor should be ready to suggest those aspects of practice which she or he would like the other to observe. For example, a tutor might ask the colleague to observe how instructions are given or the learners' response to a new type of activity. Alternatively, the tutor might request a more general observation of the session and how far the planned learning outcomes are achieved. Practical matters should be considered too, such as how the room will be arranged and where the observer should sit so as to avoid causing too much disruption. Part of the preparation also involves agreement on how observers are to record what they see and hear. For example, whether there will be descriptions of behaviour and activities or whether certain types of responses or actions are to be counted. Martin and Double (1998) suggest that a narrative approach is most appropriate, where the observer writes a brief description of the activity at fixed intervals or full descriptions of significant points, such as the introduction or a complex explanation. The purpose of these notes is to capture the essence of what happened and give an accurate basis for subsequent reflection.

Even the most careful observer is bound to have some impact on the situation. It is important that she or he be involved but not participate in the session. Learners should be briefed about the purpose of the visit, the observer's status and role. No matter how experienced and confident the tutor, being observed by others is often a stressful experience, even if the observer is a trusted colleague and the observation is to assist reflection on practice. Observers need to be alert to the way their own background and teaching style may influence their perception of what happens. The observer's role is to reflect back to the tutor, not to act as expert and make judgements about what happens.

Feedback and review

This should take place as soon as possible after the observation, in comfortable surroundings free of disturbance or distractions. It may be useful to start with a reminder of the purpose of the observation and the areas which the observed tutor wants to focus on. The tutor may then comment on how things happened from her or his perspective before listening to the observer's account. In subsequent discussion, it is important that the observer is a good listener and does not try to impose an interpretation of events. It is preferable to ask open questions that may help the observed tutor to reach an understanding and learn from the experience. The authors of DEVELOP (1999) explore appropriate styles of questioning and techniques for this stage.

The activities described so far correspond to the **concrete experience** and **reflective observation** stages in the Kolb cycle. At the end of the feedback meeting, or subsequently, it is time to sum up the new perspectives which have been gained, the '*abstract conceptualisation*' stage. What has been learnt from the experience? For example, a tutor might conclude that some confusion among learners is due to giving the instructions too fast and not explaining the purpose of activities. The scene is then set for '*active experimentation*' and commitment to action to slow down and explain more clearly in the next session. The results might be monitored via a later peer observation.

The cycle of peer observation can be repeated and the benefits increase the more times one moves through each stage. However, circumstances may limit opportunities for repetition and even a single experience can be very valuable. Pairs of part-time Open

University tutors from a wide geographical area, many of whom also teach in adult and further education and/or other universities, took part in a single round of mutual observation and confirmed this view:

> This [peer observation] has given me the confidence to perhaps be a little more daring and experimental in future (...), (...) has probably done more for my professional development than any other [activity](...).

Potential problems in peer observation

Despite the positive outcomes noted above, there are a number of potential problems. Concern is sometimes expressed that tutors who select their own partners may be tempted to engage simply in mutual back-patting and gain nothing from the experience. This seems a rather pessimistic view and is contradicted by comments from one tutor who participated in a peer observation partnership:

> One of the points I think it is very important to make (...) is that you must trust and feel very comfortable with the person with whom you are doing the observation (...). On the other hand, you don't want a relationship that is so cosy you won't make any constructive criticism.

The ability of individuals to handle negative comments may be another concern. This problem is minimised if there is clear agreement about the purpose and focus of the observation. Observers should concentrate on giving an accurate picture of what happened, rather than offering opinions, and always invite the observed tutor to comment first. However, there may well be aspects which the observed tutor was unhappy with or which did not go as planned. In these cases, as Martin and Double (1998) suggest *'the observer should be prepared to offer a particular perspective and to engage in speculation on how things might be improved'*. However, they point out that there is always likely to be more than one suitable alternative solution and that each should be explored so that the tutor can make a conscious choice about future action. An open approach to peer observation can really encourage tutors to experiment. As one tutor remarked:

> It is possible to select an ambitious objective and see how far one can achieve it, which method may work best in enabling students to work towards it (...). We had the confidence to try out activities and discuss them freely afterwards.

Enhancing subject knowledge and language teaching skills

One of the outcomes of reflection on practice may be a realisation of the need to enhance one's subject knowledge or update linguistic skills. Subject knowledge for a language tutor can be divided into three main areas:

- knowledge of language teaching and learning;

- knowledge of the culture and preoccupations of the peoples who speak the target language;

- knowledge of the language, its structures, vocabulary, registers, etc along with the ability to understand and communicate readily in the language.

In what ways can this knowledge and these skills be developed and extended? Formal means of professional development are available via training courses. These may be offered by institutions or professional associations. As well as the intended content, courses can provide a valuable opportunity to get to know other tutors and to build up networks that might be useful for collaborative learning activities, such as peer observation. Armitage et al (1998) suggest a number of other ways in which tutors can work together to enhance their professional development:

- developing and planning jointly-run courses;

- developing new resources together, particularly course materials, perhaps by recording dialogues or interviews or pooling authentic materials and producing ideas for using them in classes;

- conducting trials with one another's course materials; team teaching with one another's groups or setting up tasks for learners which involve them making contact with another tutor or group, perhaps via e-mail groups or telephone surveys.

Some of these suggestions may be more difficult to arrange than others, depending on the circumstances in which teaching takes place. In some cases the support of the institution is necessary, in others the mutual assistance of colleagues is required. For example, part-time language tutors at an Adult Education Centre met to pool visuals gathered from a variety of sources, classify them and discuss their use, as suggested by McAlpin (1980). Other groups have met to review language course books or record extension materials for each other. For part-time teachers who work in isolation, once again Netword or ALL branches may provide a forum for such cooperation.

Some tutors may have experienced micro-teaching on training courses, where they teach an aspect of their subject to the rest of the group for a short period, say ten minutes, followed by a feedback session. This activity can also be set up by groups of interested language tutors for mutual benefit. Many tutors have found it very beneficial to experience learning an unfamiliar language. For example, a French tutor might try learning Cantonese or a Gujarati teacher might try learning German. This could be set up as a one-off staff development session where a tutor teaches a short lesson in an unfamiliar language, followed by discussion of the experience. Alternatively, a tutor might register for a full course. The insights gained from experiencing the needs and feelings of a learner can be enormous.

A variety of sources offer materials for individual study or group discussion. Professional associations publish journals which enable tutors to keep up to date with the debates on developments in methodology, accreditation or materials. Journals also provide summaries of research findings, references to other books or journals, as well as reviews of new materials. Increasingly, material is available via the Internet at the web-sites of professional associations, examination bodies, government departments, etc. The Centre for Information on Language Teaching and Research (CILT) maintains a network of 14 Comenius Centres in England, and the National Comenius Centre in Wales. These centres, along with Scottish CILT, aim to provide practical assistance to all language teaching professionals whichever sector they work in. Tutors working in higher education also have the support of the Languages, Linguistics and Area Studies Subject Centre.[4]

Maintaining and enhancing knowledge of the language and culture

When living and working in an environment where one's main contact with the target language is via one's teaching, it is easy for tutors, wherever they work, to become out of date and to lose fluency. This can apply just as much to native speakers of the target language. Similarly, tutors can lose touch with the current state of historical, artistic, political, economic, environmental and social frameworks within which the target language is spoken. They need to keep up to date through accessing information from a variety of sources. In addition to books, magazines and newspapers, many of which are available on-line, there is also Satellite TV and a range of Internet websites. Professional associations and centres are also likely to be a source of relevant information, contacts, publications and courses. At local level, tutors can meet together to pool information and arrange discussions and debates on current issues or explore trends in language use, new expressions and changing registers. On-line dictionaries and grammars are another useful source of up-to-date and accurate expressions which can be accessed by any tutor with Internet facilities.

Regular active use of the target language and, where possible, regular trips to the country where the language is spoken are the best ways to maintain one's own language skills. With the obvious exception of those who are teaching minority community languages, many tutors find that this only occurs in the teaching context. This can be very limiting if the learners' level is low, or if the tutor is working at a distance and has limited contact with the learners. The opportunity to accompany group or exchange trips may be very limited in the post-compulsory sector. Many tutors work in isolation and do not meet colleagues or native speaker assistants. Family holidays are not necessarily the ideal way to brush up linguistic skills, except perhaps in the case of native speakers returning home, and many tutors are not in a position to take courses abroad or spend periods away as paying guests or even with friends in the countries where the target language is spoken. Other solutions often have to be found.

Writing in the context of Japanese teaching in Australia, Marriott (1994) identified a number of informal methods '*which teachers can use to plan or create actual situations of interaction for themselves, thereby maintaining their communicative language ability*'. These included using the print and electronic media and other public networks, creating Japanese-speaking networks between educational institutions, making contact with Japanese people living in the community and establishing an institutional link with a similar institution in Japan via letters, fax or e-mail. In discussion, one group of part-time adult, further and higher education language tutors agreed that passive skills are relatively easy to maintain because of the accessibility of books, newspapers, magazines, radio, video, film and satellite TV. However, they felt that maintaining active speaking skills presented more of a problem. Some suggestions included setting up **tandem** links with adult native speakers in the neighbourhood or abroad, as mentioned by Marriott (1994), agreeing to hold tutor meetings in the target language as far as possible, and setting up self-help groups where tutors could meet regularly to discuss and debate in the target language. Local native speakers could be invited to join the group. Advanced courses are another possibility. Refresher courses may be available abroad, but participation often depends on availability of funding which may be difficult to access. Part-time tutors may have less call on institutional staff development budgets to support attendance, but this is an avenue to explore. Some tutors may need reassurance that expressing a need for linguistic up-dating of this sort is not an admission of weakness or incompetence on their part.

The tutor as researcher

This chapter began with a reference to Schön's criticism of the separation of theory and practice. Research has been viewed by many tutors as something carried out by specialists, which often has little practical relevance to the problems encountered daily in teaching. However, the last 20 years have seen the rise of a movement which brings research and practice firmly together in the tutor as researcher. As this term suggests, research into practice is carried out by practitioners themselves in what Kemmis (1993) defines as a form of self-reflective enquiry *'to improve the rationality and justice of their own social or educational practices, their understanding of these practices and of the situations in which practices are carried out'*. Advocates of tutor research see it as a means to reflective self-development but also maintain that the tutor is the one who is best placed to study what happens in a teaching/learning situation and to contribute relevant new insights into practice. Critics such as Hammersley (1993) suggest that tutors are too close to what they are doing to be objective; they may not recognise their own intentions or see the wider context; they may be limited by their own experience or by their relationships with learners. Kemmis (1993) rejects the idea that lack of objectivity undermines the contribution which tutor research can make, but stresses that tutors need to be self-critical, challenging their assumptions and habits and trying to make explicit the rationale for the decisions which they make in carrying out their research. Regular, systematic reflection on practice is also a pre-requisite of practitioner research. Richards and Lockhart (1994) show how issues arising from a tutor's reflection on her or his practice can form the basis for classroom investigations. Wallace (1998) suggests teacher research as a valuable tool to facilitate structured reflection on practice and as an effective method for improving professional action. He gives advice on how the questions which tutors often ask themselves about practical issues, such as group management, appropriate materials or teaching oral skills, may be developed into a small scale research project, either by an individual or collaboratively.

Although it may not be possible to generalise from the sort of small-scale studies which tutors can carry out with their own groups, their value lies in this contribution to professional development and the way in which they can illuminate particular issues. In language teaching there is still, for example, much to be learned about how adults actually learn a language, what they do when they learn, what they understand by 'learning' and how their learning can be enhanced. McDonough (1995), assessing research carried out on language learning strategies and skills development, quotes Hosenfeld (1976): '*Too often our focus has been on what students **should be doing**; we must begin by asking what our students **are doing**.*' McDonough notes that tutor research is likely to reveal more about '*students' perceptions, strategies, and component skills of learning and communication*'. If similar studies can be carried out by a number of tutors, this can increase generalisability. McDonough suggests that such research carried out collaboratively could be fed back into decisions about methods, materials and programmes and could influence these with an authoritative relevance not found in other kinds of language teaching and research.

All tutors can contribute to our knowledge about adult language learning and teaching. There are numerous journals on language learning and teaching which provide an avenue for publication. Tutors who carry out research in this way really have a duty to make their findings public even if they embark on the research primarily as a means of self-development.

Reflection on practice can be carried out alone, with learners or with colleagues. It can produce new understanding and knowledge or pinpoint personal subject teaching or linguistic needs. It can be pursued in the interests of collaborative development and research. Reflection on practice is a vital component in continuing professional development and lifelong learning for language tutors.

References

Argyris C and D A Schön, *Theory in practice: increasing professional effectiveness* (Jossey-Bass, 1974)

Armitage A, R Bryant, R Dunhill, M Hammersley, D Hayes, A Hudson and S Lawes, *Teaching and training in post-compulsory education* (Open University Press, 1999)

Beigy A and J Woodin, *Developing tandem observation* (Leeds Metropolitan University, 1999)

Bell J, *Doing your research project* (Open University Press, 1987)

Boud D, R Keogh and D Walker, 'Reflection: Turning Experience into Learning' in Edwards R, A Hanson, and P Raggatt (eds), *Boundaries of adult learning* (Routledge, 1996)

Boud D and D Walker, 'Promoting reflection in professional courses: the challenge of context' in *Studies in Higher Education*, 22, 2 (1998)

Convery A, 'A teacher's response to 'reflection-in-action'' in *Cambridge Journal of Education*, 28, 2: 197–205 (1998)

Cosh J, 'Peer observation: a reflective model' in *English Language Teaching Journal*, 53, 1: 22–27 (1999)

Daines J, Daines C and B Graham, *Adult learning; adult teaching* (University of Nottingham Department of Adult Education, 1993)

Developing Excellence in Language Teaching through the Observation of Peers (DEVELOP): www.lmu.ac.uk/cls/fdtl/develop

Hammersley M, 'On the teacher as researcher' in Hammersley M (ed), *Educational research: current issues* (Chapman, 1993)

Hosenfeld C, 'Learning about learning, discovering our students' strategies' in *Foreign Language Annals*, 9, 2: 117–129 (1976) in McDonough S H, *Strategy and skill in learning a foreign language* (Edward Arnold, 1995)

Kemmis S, 'Action Research' in Hammersley M (ed), *Educational Research: current issues*, 1: 177–190 (Chapman, 1993)

Kolb D, *Experiential Learning: turning experience into learning* (Prentice Hall, 1984)

Languages Fund for the Development of Teaching and Learning (FDTL): http://fdtl.ac.uk

Lewis L and L A Dowling, Editorial in *Adult Learning* 3, 2: 7 (1992)

Marriott H, 'Keeping the rust at bay: how to maintain and develop your language skills' in *Babel*, 29, 2 (1994)

Martin G and J Double, 'Developing Higher Education teaching skills through peer observation and collaborative reflection' in *Innovations in Education and Training International*, 35, 2: 161–170 (1998)

McAlpin J, *The Magazine Picture Library* (George Allen and Unwin, 1980)

McDonough S H, *Strategy and skill in learning a foreign language* (Edward Arnold, 1995)

Minton D, *Teaching skills in Further and Adult Education* (City and Guilds/Macmillan, 1991)

Murray K and R Macdonald, 'The disjunction between lecturers' conceptions of teaching and their claimed educational practice' in *Higher Education*, 33: 331–349 (1997)

Richards J C and C Lockhart C, *Reflective teaching in second language classrooms* (Cambridge University Press, 1994)

Schön D A, *The reflective practitioner* (Temple Smith, 1983)

Subject Centre for Languages, Linguistics and Area Studies: www.lang.ltsn.ac.uk

The Open University, SOL Staff Development File (Milton Keynes 1996)

Wallace M J, *Action research for language teachers* (Cambridge University Press, 1998)

Notes

1 DEVELOP is a collaborative project between Leeds Metropolitan University and the University of Sheffield funded by HEFCE, 1999.

2 Netword groups are groups of language tutors of adults in A/F/HE supported by the Centre for Information on Language Teaching and Research (CILT).

3 Association for Language Learning ALL-languages.org.uk.

4 The Subject Centre for Languages, Linguistics and Area Studies was set up by the funding bodies for higher education in England, Wales, Scotland and Northern Ireland as part of a network of 24 subject centres covering all academic subjects in a National Learning and Teaching Support Network. www.lang.ltsn.ac.uk/

18

Accreditation and recognition of skills, knowledge and experience

LINDA MURPHY

The previous chapter examined ways in which tutors can develop their practice, enhance and update teaching and linguistic skills. This chapter looks at ways in which they can gain recognition for this development. First of all, it considers why such recognition is necessary. It then goes on to examine the changes that have taken place in accreditation with the introduction of competence-based approaches and the increasing use of portfolios and professional development plans. These offer language tutors in any context an opportunity to enhance both their skills and their employment prospects in a rapidly changing environment where employers seek to assure quality and require evidence of willingness to continue learning and updating.

Subject and professional accreditation for language tutors

Subject and professional qualifications are increasingly required in all sectors of post-compulsory education as part of the process of quality assurance. The Dearing Report, *Higher Education in the Learning Society* (1997), recommended training and qualifications for all teachers in higher education. As a result, the Institute for Learning and Teaching in Higher Education[1] has been established as the professional body and main source of professional recognition for teachers in higher education. In further education, the Further Education National Training Organisation (FENTO) has recommended a three-level professional qualification for teachers in further education with a similar professional body. A study carried out by FENTO[2] indicated widespread support among part-time tutors for a teaching qualification to be a requirement to teach in a college (TES, 25 August 2000). Under the Learning and Skills Act (2000) an Adult Learning Inspectorate (ALI) is being created with responsibility for post-19 education and training, including adult and further education. According to the Act, inspectors will evaluate the quality and effectiveness of teaching, courses, guidance and management.

In a competitive market, where institutions are also judged by how well they retain the students they recruit, tutors are expected to demonstrate the skills, knowledge and experience necessary to deliver programmes of the highest possible standard.

205

Institutions are also looking for evidence that tutors' skills and knowledge are up to date. The OFSTED report (1998) on a survey of modern foreign language learning by adults noted the need for language teachers to have recent, specialist updating and training. The types of accreditation and qualifications available to language tutors can be summarised as:

- generic teaching or language teaching qualifications, the latter being more appropriate (OFSTED 1998) as they cover specialist language teaching skills;
- initial qualifications or recognition at more advanced levels, including accreditation of experience gained through periods of practice or in-service training;
- qualifications in the target language.

Rather than describing individual qualifications, this chapter considers the main styles of accreditation available: **traditional** accreditation, based on completion of course work and examinations, and **competence-based** accreditation, where evidence is put together by an individual to demonstrate that she or he has the appropriate level of knowledge and skills for the award of credit. The latter may or may not involve attendance at a course.

Traditional accreditation

The traditional forms of accreditation, i.e. qualifications, are probably familiar to most language tutors who will have experienced them at least during their schooling, if not subsequently. Traditional qualifications test knowledge and understanding gained through course attendance, usually under examination conditions. Entry is often restricted according to previous courses attended, age or existing qualifications. Attendance at around 80% of course sessions is expected. Satisfactory completion depends on producing course work to a required standard and passing the examination. The success criteria may or may not be clear to candidates. Failure in one part may mean failure overall, though a modular format is increasingly being adopted. The results are either a pass, perhaps with a particular grade, or a fail. A pass may be separated from a fail by a few marks. Candidates are usually assessed and graded against other candidates (norm-referenced assessment). The assessment opportunities are limited by the examination timetable and candidates have little or no say in how they are assessed (see also chapter 14).

Competence-based accreditation

Competence based accreditation is not concerned with giving people credit for what they know at a given point in time after a pre-determined period of study, but for demonstrating that they can perform certain functions to a given specification. They can present evidence to this end in a variety of forms: practical demonstration, written documentation, visuals or artefacts. At the same time they are required to demonstrate that appropriate knowledge, understanding, values and ethical principles underpin their performance and present any evidence. Assessment can take place in a variety of settings including the workplace. Candidates can choose the evidence they wish to present to demonstrate their competence. They decide when they are ready to submit their evidence for assessment. They are either judged competent or not yet competent. If the latter, they can continue to produce evidence. Candidates are assessed against known criteria (criterion-referenced assessment) and if they meet the criteria, they are judged competent no matter how many others meet the criteria.

In the UK, competence-based accreditation has its origins in the establishment of the National Council for Vocational Qualifications (NCVQ) in 1986 and the development of National or Scottish Vocational Qualifications. The factors which lay behind these developments can be summarised as:

- concern to improve the country's economic competitiveness by increasing participation in post-school education and training and by establishing coherent national standards of vocational education and training;
- concern about the academic/vocational divide which gave higher status to academic study than to vocational training;
- an increasing preoccupation with public accountability;
- concerns about the dominance of theory over practice.

Employer-led groups for different occupational sectors, now known as national training organisations, have identified the standards to which employees in those sectors can be expected to work. The standards are identified using an approach called functional analysis which breaks down a particular occupational role into its separate functions and sub-functions. **Performance criteria** are defined for each function against which an individual's competence can be judged by examining **performance evidence.** The circumstances in which the person has to perform the functions are also important, and **range statements** set out the specific conditions in which competence must be demonstrated. Finally, for each function, the knowledge and understanding to be demonstrated are also specified, the **knowledge evidence.**[3] (Chapter 14 explained how this system operates in the National Language Standards when assessing student performance.)

Language tutors working in adult or further education may be familiar with this approach from the City and Guilds 7306 *Further and Adult Education Teachers Certificate* (NVQ) which uses the Standards developed by the former Training and Development Lead Body (TDLB). The scheme for this certificate can be contrasted with that for the 7307 *Further and Adult Education Teachers Certificate* (Stages 1 and 2) which follows a more traditional approach involving the completion of course work. An example of one of the broad functions of a teacher or trainer, defined in the Training and Development Standards, is to '*create a climate conducive to learning*' (City and Guilds 7306, Unit C21, 1995). In order to do this, one of the sub-functions is to '*establish rapport with learners*'. To be judged competent against the performance criteria for this sub-function, the tutor must show that:

- learners are made to feel welcome and are given appropriate time and attention;

- the manner of interaction demonstrates a non-judgemental acceptance of the learner;
- responses to learners are based on both their verbal and non-verbal communication;
- learners are actively listened to;
- learners are encouraged to feel comfortable to express concerns, make comments or ask questions at their own pace;
- learners are encouraged to express their personal beliefs, wishes and views, except where these may adversely affect the rights of others;
- the manner, level and pace of communication with the learners is appropriate to their abilities, personal beliefs and preferences;
- constraints on communication with learners are identified and minimised.

The **range statements** for this Unit indicate the types of communication and the constraints on communication which the tutor must be able to handle:

- types of communication: verbal; non-verbal: facial expressions, body language;
- constraints on communication: environmental, social, cultural.

The **performance evidence** required may be provided by tutors through their actual interaction with learners, observed by an assessor, or by records of that interaction prepared by the tutor which give examples and a rationale for the styles of interaction chosen and explain how this promoted the establishment of rapport.

The **knowledge evidence** which tutors must provide is as follows:

- factors that affect the establishment of rapport;
- how to put learners at ease;
- ways of creating an atmosphere that is conducive to establishing rapport;
- methods of eliciting personal views;
- how to interpret non-verbal communication;
- techniques of active listening;
- how to gauge the appropriateness of language and non-verbal communication for learners;
- issues of equality of opportunity and non-discriminatory practice.

This detailed specification leaves tutors in no doubt as to what they have to do and how their work will be assessed.

The impact of competence-based accreditation

The influence of this approach has been far-reaching and continues to grow. As noted above, qualifications for teachers in adult and further education have already been re-designed to bring them within the competence-based framework. Hyland (1994) points out that, having already become a major part of the further education and workplace training scene, NVQs, and the philosophy that underpins them, have moved downwards into schools (in the form of GNVQs) and upwards into higher education.

Here the influence is seen in an increasing emphasis on the specification of learning outcomes, strengthened by Dearing's recommendations (1997). This approach has been adopted for the training for teachers in higher education mentioned earlier. Higher education tutors wishing to gain accreditation and membership of the ILT must present a portfolio of evidence showing that they have satisfied criteria in five areas of professional activity. At the same time they need to demonstrate their commitment to a set of professional values by showing that these underpin their evidence. The portfolio may be achieved via one of three routes: successful completion of an institution-based programme accredited by the ILT, or via direct or institutional accreditation of prior learning (APL)[4].

This is an example of the way in which other forms of professional accreditation have been developed, based on the achievement of learning outcomes rather than employer determined occupational competences. In this respect, the programmes accredited by Open College Networks (OCNs) are perhaps most widely known. The *Modern Language Tutors' Consolidation Course,* developed by Buckinghamshire Adult and Continuing Education and accredited by Chiltern Region OCN, is a good example. (See also chapter 16, for student accreditation by OCNs.)

Criticisms of competence-based accreditation for tutors

The competence-based approach represents a major change and, as such, has been the subject of heated debate, particularly when applied to accreditation for teachers and other professionals. There are a number of major criticisms of competence-based accreditation for tutors. Many feel the definition of competence is too narrow and too mechanistic, inappropriate to the range of skills, exercise of judgement and complex mix of knowledge, attitudes, ethics, assumptions, values and beliefs that are involved in teaching. The emphasis on the **product,** i.e. the competence to be demonstrated, is seen to be at serious odds with the development of reflective practitioners focusing on process. It is also suggested that this approach fails to take account of the collaborative aspects of the work of teachers in the post-compulsory sector. The language of the standards is felt to be over-complex and obscure. Hyland (1994) argues that the NVQ approach is not primarily concerned with learning, but with collecting evidence to satisfy competence criteria.

Advocates see competence-based accreditation as part of a continuum based on the use of learning outcomes which has a far longer history than NVQs. Intended learning outcomes have been specified for courses leading to traditional forms of accreditation for many years, though usually in very broad terms and not linked directly to assessment as they are in competence-based accreditation. Garland (1994) feels that a learner-centred approach is promoted by the clear statement of anticipated learning outcomes to be achieved or competence to be demonstrated. Individual tutors know exactly what they are aiming to achieve. They can identify their strengths and weaknesses and channel their efforts accordingly; there is no need to re-learn existing knowledge and skills. Programmes can be tailored to individual tutors' needs as defined by themselves in personal learning or development plans.

The process of reflection involved in selecting evidence even for closely prescribed occupational standards can lead to a substantial review and evaluation of practice in the light of theory and experience, an opportunity for *reflection-on-action* as advocated by Schön (1983). A key function in the Training and Development Standards is competence in evaluation and the ability to use the results effectively, both to adjust one's teaching and to identify and plan for further personal professional development. Part-time language tutors, who already had substantial experience in adult, further and higher education, noted the effect which participation in a competence-based accreditation scheme had on their practice. It had forced them to revisit their rationale and re-evaluate their approach.

> I now think more about preparing and teaching classes. (...) With languages there is a danger that one does activities which students enjoy because it gets them talking. But that's not really enough (...) I think it has focused me and made me more rigorous. (OU, 1999)

Continuing reflection on professional practice is one of the underpinning professional values which tutors in higher education must demonstrate when seeking accreditation and membership of the ILT.

The use of portfolios in continuing professional development

Whatever the concerns about the constraints of occupational competence, there is increasing emphasis on the use of portfolios of evidence, whether to demonstrate competence in specific teaching functions for accreditation or to demonstrate the outcome of continuing professional development. There is considerable variation in the degree to which the competence or learning outcomes are prescribed. At one end of the spectrum are the NVQ competences described above; at the other, tutors, rather than an institution or professional body, are responsible for deciding the nature and extent of the professional development outcomes which they want to demonstrate. Underwood (1995) describes how this works in a course run by Anglia Polytechnic University. Tutors first produce a professional autobiography which forms a framework for long-term review. They then identify evidence of changes in their practice which demonstrate learning. Individuals may claim to have become better teachers or curriculum developers, for example. The next stage is to refine these statements into specific outcomes for which they set out to provide appropriate evidence. Underwood makes it clear that tutors must critically evaluate their own learning and development experience in the light of relevant theory. The extent and significance of the experience determines the amount of credit that can be claimed.

The use of portfolios for continuing professional development has been widely recognised and adopted, not simply for accreditation purposes. Bond (1993) lists a number of other uses for professional development portfolios, for example:

- evidence of competence to practise;
- for job interviews or to demonstrate readiness to take on more responsibility;
- to increase one's self confidence/self esteem;

- to audit one's personal skills and competence;
- as a basis for staff appraisal or peer review.

With so many uses and so much interest in portfolios and their role in many accreditation options, it appears that language tutors would be well advised seriously to consider constructing and maintaining their own if they have not already done so. But what is the best way to go about it and what is involved?

Building a portfolio

A professional development portfolio is a record of an individual tutor's learning and achievements. It may include examples of session plans, materials, feedback from learners, self-evaluation records or reflective diaries or logs. These are the **evidence.** In any one item of evidence, it should be possible to see the knowledge, theory and values on which it is based. For example, in order to show one's ability to provide feedback and assessment of students' learning, evidence might include examples of marked assignments and the accompanying written feedback, sample recordings of verbal feedback on tape-recorded oral presentations, or a note of the feedback given verbally in class and how it was delivered. The feedback may demonstrate understanding of theory in the areas of error-correction and student learning, for example by making use of a code to encourage learners to self-correct. Some separate notes may be necessary to explain the theoretical rationale or to make explicit **underlying values,** such as equal opportunities, concern for student development and scholarship. For example, it may be necessary to explain how verbal feedback is handled in groups to ensure confidentiality, motivation or that absent students are not disadvantaged.

The structure of the portfolio needs to be clear and accessible both to the owner and to any potential assessor or reviewer. The format and content of the portfolio will obviously depend on the purpose for which it is being constructed, the personal style and preferences of the individual concerned. Where a portfolio is to be presented for accreditation, it will probably be organised around the outcomes or competences which it is to demonstrate. A contents page and simple referencing system make it easier to find relevant items. An up-to-date CV or **professional autobiography** provides a useful starting point for an audit of existing skills/competence and consideration of future learning goals. The portfolio should not only demonstrate skills, knowledge and experience gained, but also indicate future development needs and how they may be met.

The first stage is to begin assembling items of evidence. This is an on-going process. Any activities involving reflection on practice can provide useful portfolio evidence, for example self-evaluation or peer observation. The temptation to tidy up material should be resisted. Original plans or teaching materials should be included. However, evaluation may have indicated that the teaching materials needed revision to make them more comprehensible. For example, the level and volume of new vocabulary may have been too high and for the next time the material was simplified or a glossary or pre-teaching exercise added. The inclusion of both the original and the revised material would be a very appropriate way to show reflection, evaluation and learning from experience.

While assembling evidence, it is advisable to allocate it immediately to a particular category depending on the purpose of the portfolio. It may be evidence of a specific competence, such as the design of teaching sessions, or evidence which shows progress towards an identified professional development goal, such as increasing one's repertoire of techniques for teaching pronunciation. A note can be made on anything that may be used as evidence for more than one outcome or competence. At intervals, it is necessary to review and analyse the evidence collected, and to begin selecting what to include in the portfolio. It is easy to assemble far more than is needed. As one tutor commented: *'I was enthusiastic and collected much irrelevant material'*. It is better to **sift** regularly rather than wait until a mountain of evidence has been accumulated.

Evidence can be sifted by posing certain questions. If the portfolio is for accreditation, do individual pieces of evidence really indicate the values, theoretical knowledge and assumptions that provided the rationale for choices made? Would some brief annotation on the evidence itself help to make this explicit? Or is a longer explanation necessary? Are there examples from the range of situations required, such as working with individuals or larger groups, or demonstrating the required number of different teaching methods? Are further pieces of evidence needed? Are there some outcomes or competences for which no evidence has been produced as yet? If the portfolio is to demonstrate continuing professional development, do the pieces of evidence clearly show change and development? What skills or knowledge have been acquired or how have attitudes changed and how does the evidence show this? Have professional development goals been met and how can this be demonstrated? What new goals have been identified? How might they be achieved?

Some pieces of evidence will inevitably be discarded as more appropriate evidence is found. A portfolio can be said to be a process as well as a product, since it involves constant review, refinement and updating. At some point, the evidence will be complete, achievement of all the competences, learning outcomes or personal professional development goals will appear to have been demonstrated. If it is to be presented to a third party for accreditation or some other purpose, it is time to look again at the structure, label and cross-reference items of evidence as appropriate and draw up a contents list. At this final stage, it is useful to ask a colleague to read it through, as it can be difficult to stand back from the work and the students one knows so well, and take an objective view.

Personal professional development plans

Personal professional development plans are an important part of any portfolio which seeks to demonstrate reflective practice and continuing professional development, but they are a useful tool for any tutor. It is a good idea to get into the habit of drawing up a plan at the start of the teaching year, based on reflection on the previous year's work. Like New Year's resolutions it is easy to make a mental note of things to be achieved, but, as Boud et al (1985) emphasise, consciously making a plan means that decisions are made about the priorities, when and how they will be achieved. The plan can serve as a reminder, a yard-stick to measure how much progress has been made towards the targets or to assess whether some targets have now become unrealistic due to unforeseen circumstances. The preparation of such plans provides evidence of commitment to taking responsibility for one's own professional development. Many institutions encourage individuals to draw up such plans as part of appraisal schemes. Whether or not plans are **required,** they can be extremely valuable in that they provide a structure for longer-term planning to meet development needs and can enable tutors to identify the resources and support which they require from others in order to fulfil these needs. This can be helpful in making a case to employers for time, finance or other resources. Figure 1 gives an example of a format that might be used.

Issue	What do I want to achieve?	How will I set about it?	Target Date and Progress towards completion
1. Lack of materials for communicative practice	A bank of materials related to the course. content	Check if other tutors have the same problem. Suggest pooling ideas and materials. Agree each of us will produce two new items. Request resources for copying and cataloguing material.	Sept – March Almost completed. Materials need cataloguing.
2. Only teaching beginners level groups.	At least one more advanced group next year.	Speak to line manager.	June ?

Figure 1: Example of a Personal Professional Development Plan

The issues can be derived from subject teaching concerns. They might include aspects of group management; measuring learning and checking progress; syllabus design; adapting teaching to ensure learners with hearing or sight impairment or with dyslexia can participate fully or, indeed, any of the many concerns which confront tutors in day-to-day teaching. On the other hand they might include longer-term development goals relating to new skills, accreditation or employment opportunities.

Language tutors, like all professionals, need to ensure that they gain appropriate qualifications and accreditation for their skills, knowledge and experience as these develop. By maintaining a portfolio of evidence of their achievements and preparing personal professional development plans from year to year, tutors can demonstrate current competence to practise to the highest professional standard and gain the relevant accreditation and recognition for their achievements.

References

Bond C, 'Using portfolios for continuing professional development' in *Training and Development*, 11, 8: 9–12 (1993)

Boud D, R Keogh and D Walker, *Reflection: turning experience into learning* (Croom Helm, 1985)

Buckinghamshire County Council Adult and Continuing Education: conedav@buckscc.gov.uk. For general course information: www.adultedbucks.org.uk

City and Guilds, NVQ in *Further and Adult Education Teachers Certificate, Candidate Pack, 7306, 1995* (City and Guilds, 1998)

City and Guilds, *Further and Adult Education Teacher's Certificate, Scheme Pamphlet, 7307* (City and Guilds, 1999)

City and Guilds: www.cityandguilds.co.uk

Crequer N, 'Part-time lecturer qualifications push' in *Times Educational Supplement* (25 August 2000)

Dearing Sir R, *Higher education in the learning society* (HMSO, 1997)

Garland P, 'Using competence-based assessment positively on certificate in education programmes' in *Journal of Further and Higher Education* 18, 2: 16–22 (1994)

Harwood J, 'The knowledge incendiary' in *Times Higher Education Supplement* (28 July 2000)

Hyland T, *Competence, education and NVQs: dissenting perspectives* (Cassell, 1994)

Institute for Learning and Teaching in Higher Education: www.ilt.ac.uk

Languages National Training Organisation: www.languagesnto.org.uk

National Open College Network: www.nocn.ac.uk

National Training Organisations: www.nto-nc.org

Office for Standards in Education, *Accent on adults: a survey of modern foreign language learning by adults* (1998)

Open University in the South, *Teaching in Higher Education HH851 (APEL) Evaluation report of 1998–99 pilot* (June 1999)

Schön D A, *The reflective practitioner* (Temple Smith, 1983)

Underwood B, 'The accreditation of experiential learning for teachers: its contribution to continuing professional development and its viability as a process' in *British Journal of In-service Education*, 21, 1 (1995)

Whittaker M, ''Licence to practise' for lecturers' in *Times Educational Supplement* (12 November 1999)

Notes

1   www.ilt.ac.uk

2   *A functional analysis of the part-time lecturing staff in further education colleges in England and Wales*, FENTO, 5th Floor Centre Point, 103 New Oxford Street, London WC1A 1DD.

3   Definitions of NVQ/SVQ Levels (www.dfee.gov.uk/nvq August 2000)

4   For an initial period only, until September 2001, experienced higher education teachers are able to apply for fast-track membership of the ILT by writing a short reflective analysis of their experience supported by two referees.

19

Looking ahead – the European context and the effect of increasing globalisation

LINDA MURPHY

What does the future hold for language tutors? This chapter will explore some of the opportunities and challenges ahead, arising from the UK's position in Europe and increasing globalisation brought about by rapid advances in communication technology. The world is shrinking. The Internet has opened access to information and communications on a global scale, whether for business, educational or personal use, in a way scarcely dreamt of a decade ago. What are the likely language needs in this information age and how will they be met?

The future of language teaching and learning in the UK: the Nuffield Inquiry

In 1998, the Nuffield Foundation set up an inquiry into the UK's capability in languages. The brief was to estimate the UK's needs over the following 20 years, to examine the extent to which existing policies and practices could meet those needs and to determine what strategic planning and initiatives would be required (Moys 1998). For many years, there has been unease about the apparent lack of interest in language learning in the UK. This has been fed by a perception that language learning is difficult, or that it is an activity for the better off, more academically advantaged, and is possibly not necessary anyway as '*they all speak English*'. A survey among adults in the UK, carried out by the National Institute of Adult and Continuing Education (NIACE), seems to confirm this picture. It found that almost 6 out of 10 adults speak only the first language learned and only 5% of adults were currently learning a language (Tuckett and Cara 1999). However, the same survey also showed that 41% of respondents expressed a wish or intention to learn a language.

The final report of the Nuffield Inquiry (2000) found other encouraging signs. In addition to buoyant demand for languages among adults, examples of excellent initiatives in support of language learning and teaching were reported across the country and a number of policy strengths were identified. Nevertheless, the report concluded that '*the national capability in languages is inadequate for the demands of the 21st century*' since policy weaknesses were found to outweigh these strengths and

216

such excellent initiatives remain isolated and uncoordinated. The main area of concern was the lack of a national policy for languages encompassing all aspects of language teaching and learning. The report recommends the appointment of a languages '*supremo*' to coordinate and drive forward such a policy. Powerful arguments are made for fundamental change in the way languages are perceived and therefore taught and learned in the UK. These arguments include the impact of globalisation on the world economy together with the UK's position in Europe; the dangers of relying on English as a global language; the challenge of increased mobility both to and from the UK; changing patterns of employment and demands for a flexible workforce; changing views of what it means to '*learn*' a language and the role of language learning in promoting tolerance, respect and intercultural understanding.

The report maintains that government, public bodies, employers, language providers and the media need to get these arguments across and change attitudes so that it becomes the '*norm*' to learn at least one other language and to continue to learn languages throughout life. The ability to communicate in another language should be seen as a key skill at all levels including HE, alongside communication in English, numeracy and IT. Changing attitudes and increasing demand will require accompanying changes in programmes and funding. The report contains many recommendations aimed at achieving these changes. Key among them for language tutors are: (i) a coherent national framework of provision so that access to a full range of high quality language learning opportunities and pathways is no longer dependent on where a person lives; (ii) language study as an integral part of learning programmes in all sectors with a far wider range of languages on offer. Particular concern is expressed at the lack of opportunities or encouragement to include language study in vocational courses in further education, even in those geared to the travel and tourism industry. This is of even greater concern when the role and success of colleges in widening participation in formal education is taken into account (Tuckett, 2000). The report strongly recommends the development of a national framework to define levels of language competence and descriptors for levels of attainment to which all language qualifications should be connected. This framework should be transparent and easily intelligible to learners, providers and employers alike. It should also allow recognition of basic language skills and partial competences.

The report recognises the need to attract more people into language teaching and to provide high quality training, support and continuing professional development, especially for part-time tutors who may work in isolation and have little or no access to accredited training and development. All these recommendations point to a bright future for language tutors who are ready to accept the challenges, both here and abroad.

The European context

Language learning is an important focus for the activities of the Council of Europe and the European Union. It is vital in achieving the Council of Europe's objectives of co-operation between states, mutual respect and understanding. It is also a significant element in the European Union's objectives of freedom of movement for European citizens and economic co-operation. Both sets of objectives will continue to influence language provision in the UK and impact on the opportunities for language tutors. The Council of Europe has pursued its objectives through a series of Languages Projects, such as the *Threshold Level* descriptions of languages and the development of a *Common European Framework of Reference* (1998). The latter is a planning instrument which provides a common basis and language for describing objectives, methods and assessment in language teaching. It also defines levels and proficiency. In a world where there is such diversity of language learning opportunities and needs, it is vital to make that diversity accessible and have clear frameworks within which to construct increasingly individualised programmes. Learners and tutors need clear information about content, levels, assessment and how performance may compare, both within and across national boundaries. The *Common Framework of Reference* sets out to achieve this.

The Nuffield Inquiry recommends that the proposed *'national standards framework should be based on the Council of Europe Framework and take account where appropriate of the existing UK National (Vocational) Language Standards'* (recommendation 15.1). Language tutors will be aware of the advantages such a framework can bring. The survey of modern foreign language learning by OFSTED (1998) noted that lack of national uniformity in level descriptors was a serious problem both for learners and for employers or other providers seeking to understand the attainment level of individuals. Swanton (1998) writing on the situation in adult education comments that:

> ... *finding and choosing the most suitable language learning courses as an adult is a complex affair. There is no common standard for the descriptors of level systems which are a usual way of presenting provision.*

Many tutors will be used to dealing with learners who find themselves in a class that does not meet their needs or expectations. There may be a high dropout rate as a result. Moves to remedy this situation must be welcome.

As well as proposing that all existing language qualifications should be linked to this framework, the Nuffield Inquiry also notes the need for ways of recognising basic language skills which, *'while falling short of existing qualification requirements, are nonetheless of positive value and allow learners to get on to the ladder of success in language learning'*. They suggest that this might be within a national system of graded objectives awards, or take the form of the *European Languages Portfolio* (see chapter 14). One major aim of the portfolio is to contribute to mobility in Europe by providing a clear and easily understood record of all language learning achievement in and out of formal education throughout life which can support job applications and entry to education and training. The other major aim is to promote the concept of European citizenship by providing a record of all language knowledge and experiences including, where appropriate, the learner's mother tongue and the heritage languages of ethnic minorities. An advantage of the portfolio is that it allows people to record and value language skills acquired outside the educational system, such as fluency in a language other than English spoken in the home, and partial competences such as a working knowledge of a language acquired by adults working abroad or basic language skills developed through family connections or holidays. In future, language tutors may find their work includes assisting students to construct such portfolios and they may find it worthwhile to construct their own.

Teaching and learning programmes funded by the European Commission

The European Union aims to give all European citizens access to a broader baseline of knowledge and to build up their abilities for employment and for economic life. The Commission's White Paper, *Teaching and learning: towards the learning society* (1995), contains an objective '*to develop proficiency in three community languages*', i.e. people should be able to speak at least two community languages as well as their mother tongue. The Commission funds two major trans-national education and training programmes, Socrates and Leonardo, which support this particular objective. The first phase of these programmes ran from 1995 to 1999.

Within Socrates II (2000–2006), there are a number of Actions relevant to the post-compulsory sectors: Lingua, Grundtvig, Minerva and Erasmus. The **Lingua** Action encourages and supports linguistic diversity throughout the EU, seeks to improve the quality of language teaching and learning and promotes access to lifelong language learning opportunities. To achieve these aims, it funds projects which raise awareness of the advantages of language learning, motivate individuals to learn languages, provide them with information on the means and methods available and facilitate access to language learning. The Action also seeks to encourage the development of innovatory language learning and teaching tools, and the dissemination of best practice, with particular emphasis on functional and partial competence.

DIALANG[1] is an example of a project funded under the Socrates Lingua Action, and has been set up to look at the assessment of language proficiency. It aims to develop diagnostic tests for fifteen European languages whereby learners will be able to receive an assessment of their language skills regardless of the way they have acquired them. The test system will make use of self- and external assessment and give feedback using the Council of Europe proficiency scale, providing an analysis of the strengths and weaknesses in performance and advice on how further improvement can be achieved. It will cover all levels and include separate tests for reading, writing, listening and speaking as well as for structures and vocabulary. The aim is to use new technologies to deliver the tests and enable the testing of interactive skills. This kind of development together with an agreed set of descriptors for learning programmes will greatly assist the kind of individualised tuition and support which tutors are likely to have to deliver for an increasing number of independent learners.

The **Grundtvig** Action supports the development of lifelong learning including the development and dissemination of modules and materials, information services for adult learners, tools and methods for assessment and mobility for those working in adult education. It also includes the opportunity for *Learning Partnerships* enabling a small number of adult education groups to work together on a joint project. The **Minerva** Action on Open and Distance Learning supports the development of innovation and the exchange of ideas and experience in the use of ICT in teaching and learning.

The **Erasmus** programme is also part of Socrates. It promotes the exchange of teaching staff, students and administrators in higher education across Europe. The exchanges involve students from a wide range of disciplines. It is recognised that many students may not participate in the exchanges and therefore there is considerable emphasis on teaching exchanges and trans-national curriculum development, bringing Europe to all students with the opportunity to learn through another language.

The **Leonardo** II programme (2000–2006) supports the development of language competences in the vocational context, including language audits, training tools and dissemination projects. It also supports the development of networks to facilitate the transfer of experience and good practice in vocational training. All these programmes can offer considerable opportunities for tutors to become involved in wider European professional networks or exchanges. Reports of projects are available via the Internet, with details and addresses, encouraging contact from tutors who have comments, suggestions or seek involvement.

The globalisation of business

The designation of 2001 as the *European Year of Languages* provides an opportunity for business, education and training organisations to raise the profile of languages and maintain the interest and impetus in languages for business. Worldwide, it is worth noting that over 60% of UK exports now go to traditionally non-English speaking markets and the areas with the greatest potential for medium- to long-term trade growth are in Latin America, Eastern Europe and Asia Pacific (Hagen, 1998). UK businesses need to be able to operate in a multi-lingual, global market place. Hagen argues that global competition is now much more concerned with building and managing multi-national infrastructure for mergers, take-overs and joint ventures, than with cross-border selling or competition. This means the effects of internationalisation are felt throughout a company. Cross-cultural communication skills are no longer simply required in the export department. Increasing inward investment by foreign companies means that even home-based companies may be affected at all levels. BMW and Lyonnaise des Eaux provide good examples of this. Hagen cites a 1997 Department of Trade and Industry (DTI) *Language Study* report indicating that around 20% of companies surveyed experienced language and/or cultural barriers. This means a potentially major loss of trade. He also points out that cultural barriers increase with distance from the UK and Europe, and that available language skills decrease rapidly once languages other than French are required. There appears to be a serious mismatch between the language training readily on offer and the needs of the business world.

But what are these needs? In Hagen's view, international trade now requires:

- understanding of multi-lingual documentation;
- an ability to react quickly to problems as they arise;
- skills in scanning literature in a foreign language rather than waiting for a translation;
- cultural knowledge for localisation of product design, packaging and preparation of sales and trade literature.

In industry it is generally recognised that using the customer's language is essential in only a limited number of situations such as:

- building up rapport in social contact;
- conducting local market research;
- dealing with orders, first inquiries, complaints and bad debts or unpaid invoices;
- making telephone contact;
- conducting direct correspondence in the language.

Other linguistic needs can be met by translators or interpreters, passed on to an agent or given to the local office. Graddol (1998) notes that the trend in global service industries is to use local languages. It is recognised that English is no longer sufficient to reach global markets. Localisation is seen to give companies a strong competitive advantage. However, even where local people are employed, there is still a need for liaison and presence from the parent company from time to time. E-commerce, business via the Internet, is also developing rapidly and, contrary to the anglo-centric view, is doing so in an increasing variety of languages.

Changing patterns of language use, employment and mobility

Despite the rise of English to world language status, Graddol (1998) predicts that the future will be multi-lingual. He points out that by the middle of the 21st century, Chinese, Arabic, Spanish and Hindi/Urdu will have as many, or more, native speakers as English. The *Nuffield Inquiry Final Report* notes that English is not the exclusive property of native English speakers, and that UK English is likely to become a localised dialect of international English. The ability to speak it will only continue to confer advantage if the skills and techniques are taught to adjust the use of UK English for effective communication with non-native speakers of international English. The Inquiry concludes that a far wider range of languages should be taught and that different learning purposes, such as those listed above, should be acknowledged and catered for accordingly. The authors point out the importance of developing good comprehension skills and the circumstances in which it may be more appropriate to hold multi-lingual conversations where each party speaks her or his own language, but understands the other. They also note that there is a pool of unrecognised and under-utilised knowledge and skill among, for example, the Chinese, Arabic and Hindi/ Urdu speaking communities resident in the UK. It is acknowledged that in future the focus will be on communicating for a specific purpose in a number of languages rather than aiming for native speaker levels of competence in one or two.

Businesses may acknowledge the need for languages and recognise their value but, nevertheless, there has been a reliance on English, or a tendency to recruit native speakers who have moved to the UK. This may solve one immediate problem, but in the long-term removes employment opportunities for UK citizens in two respects: (i) those job opportunities within the UK for which some language competence is essential or an advantage; (ii) the opportunities arising from the increased ease of mobility within the EU in particular and the world in general. *The Nuffield Inquiry Final Report* argues that business should emphasise the value of languages for employment and ensure that employees with appropriate language skills are adequately rewarded. This is particularly important in view of the evidence that employers actually prefer people with language skills, *'not merely because they can communicate across borders but because language skills tend to go hand in hand with the ability to adapt and an awareness of the importance of empathising with others'* (*Nuffield Inquiry Final Report 2.1.1*).

The challenge of new technology

Technology is changing language needs and the way in which business operates, but it can also facilitate the transformation of provision and provide the flexibility required in order to meet changing needs. Technology is opening up opportunities that bring tutors into contact with learners across the world, while at the same time widening access to language learning for those who would not otherwise be able to study a language. The Nuffield Inquiry sees an important role for technology in meeting the language learning needs of the 21st century.

Satellite links and video or electronic conferencing give specialist teachers the opportunity to support dispersed groups of learners who could not otherwise be brought together in a traditional class. This can transform the opportunities available to learners in remote areas, or those who want to learn *'minority interest languages'* beyond beginner level. As Swanton (1998) points out: *'Those interested in minority languages face enormous difficulties in the pursuit of intermediate and advanced progression'*. Most tutors will be familiar with the scenario where a class is cancelled because too few students have enrolled. On-line programmes can have a limitless catchment area, and it is possible to offer far more individualised learning programmes to cater for the variety of specific language needs. For example, a number of sales staff in small firms who need Spanish for dealing with telephone inquiries may be spread across a wide area. The products and services which they deal with may be very different and generate different types of questions and responses. They may have different levels of previous learning experience. An on-line learning programme can bring them together, but can also be customised for individual needs.

There is increasing recognition that if people are to be encouraged to take up learning, whether in languages or any other subject, the learning programmes must fit into their lives and not follow a rigid pattern. The University for Industry (UfI) is encouraging a shift to more flexible home and workbased learning through its *Learndirect* centres which are located in venues such as shopping and community centres. The centres offer on-line courses in *'bite-sized chunks'*. Centre staff help people get started in using the on-line materials, but it is anticipated that once they have gained confidence many learners will no longer need to go to the centres to learn. Announcing the first network of centres in November 1999, Dearing expressed the government's aim:

> By dropping into centres and learning on-line through the Internet, people and business will realise that learning can be accessible, flexible and affordable. We aim to transform how and where people acquire new skills and qualifications and to deliver learning that fits the needs and lifestyles of individuals and employers.

Such ambitious aims to change the culture and attitudes to learning must include language learning, particularly in view of the concerns about participation and the potential mismatch between business language needs and provision. The Nuffield Inquiry suggests that the UfI and the National Grid for Learning[2] are well placed to lead the way in on-line language learning. It also points to the need for more efficient, collaborative and cost-effective use of resources to ensure that adult language learners are not denied access to new technologies when attending evening classes. In the future, therefore, many more tutors may find themselves using technology in their teaching and/or supporting distant, independent language learners via synchronous or asynchronous electronic communication rather than teaching in a classroom. However, technology alone is not the answer. It needs to be harnessed in ways that bring the most advantage to learners. It is not simply a matter of transferring class-based approaches to a new medium, but of taking the most appropriate methods for the purposes to be achieved within the constraints of specific circumstances. As Swanton (1998) points out, without appropriate and adequate levels of support, independent learning in languages can result in failure. Independent study of languages does not appear to come naturally. The judgement, expertise, skills and support of tutors will still be crucial, though the focus of their role may change.

Teaching and learning on-line: pilot projects

Many tutors may be concerned that the essence of language teaching, and the motivation for many learners, is the development of interpersonal communication and they feel that such individualised or remote tuition cannot be a substitute for face-to-face communication. After all, most learners want to be able to talk to real people in the target language. Researchers are examining ways in which interactive language skills can be developed through new technology. At The Open University, Hauck and Haezewindt (1999) have investigated ways in which Internet-based, real-time audio conferencing can promote genuine, synchronous interaction between learners. In their project, groups of learners of French or German met regularly each week via the **Fluent**[3] conferencing system and participated in role plays and other pre-arranged learning tasks requiring collaborative interaction. They were involved in problem-solving activities which were designed in such a way that they had to arrange 'meetings' between the official sessions in order to exchange ideas, negotiate solutions and prepare a joint presentation of their work. Feedback from learners was positive. They perceived noticeable improvements in spoken language and appreciated the opportunity for regular communication in the target language in a purposeful way with people they had never met before.

Lamy and Goodfellow (1999) report on the **Lexica** project through which they examined teaching strategies for the support of learners using web-based conferencing to learn a second language. Three groups of learners of French, enrolled on The OU third-stage French course *Mises au point,* were encouraged to reflect, in the target language, on their learning of French during a short course focused on vocabulary and vocabulary learning[4]. They found that the approach adopted by the tutor facilitating the conferences had an important influence on the outcomes. The volume of learner-learner interaction was far higher where the tutor gave greater emphasis to the social/affective needs of the learners. Where the tutor gave higher priority to learners' reflection on the syllabus content, there was less interaction, but subject knowledge was raised. Lamy and Goodfellow suggest that, by modelling teaching strategies for tutors and styles of participation for learners, it may be possible to achieve a balance between these equally desirable outcomes. Supporting on-line learners will certainly place different demands on tutors from those of traditional face-to-face teaching. Tutors will have to find ways of establishing rapport with and between learners they may not see and who do not meet each other. They will need to develop skills to manage video or electronic conferences so that everyone has an opportunity to participate effectively. They must develop strategies which require students to take a more active role in the learning process and consider carefully how they will approach issues such as error correction (see also chapters 13 and 14).

Resources from the Internet

In the past tutors have spent a considerable amount of time finding and preparing materials for their students to use. The Internet offers access to a vast range of resources for teachers and learners alike. Virtual language centres are being developed which will enable tutors to exchange materials and ideas across the country and beyond. **Lingua@NET** is an example which has been set up as part of the National Grid for Learning and is managed by CILT. It has now been extended as Lingua@net Europa and provides information and links to quality-assured on-line resources from Europe and further afield in a wide range of languages. This is a school-focused initiative, but plans for a National Learning Network for further education (TES, 19 November 1999) will to lead to similar developments in that sector. The proposals include a national college e-mail system whereby all staff and students would have an e-mail address, and suggest the development of a central bank of learning materials for all colleges to use. The **WELL Project**[5] (Web Enhanced Language Learning) aims to help language tutors in HE to access and exploit the array of multilingual, multimedia resources available via the Internet. The University of Hull, location of the Computers in Teaching Initiative Centre for Modern Languages (CTICML), and now the C&IT

Centre of the HE Language, Linguistics and Area Studies Subject Centre, maintains a large, categorised, and continuously up-dated, list of links to useful Internet sites for language learners and teachers[6]. Downloadable teaching toolkits and materials are becoming available at many web sites set up by education and training providers. Individual institutions are setting up their own intranet sites to enable easy exchange of materials and ideas, for example The Open University's STARWeb initiative. Language tutors can further reduce their isolation and share ideas via mailbases or e-mail discussion groups such as Lingua@NET forum.

There is an increasing number of commercial multi-media and on-line language programmes. Reviews of a large number of CALL software packages are listed alphabetically on another CTICML website[7]. As yet, these packages rarely address the needs of more advanced learners of languages or those with special purposes because they are designed for a mass market. Tutors are not able to adapt them in the way that they might do traditional text or audio-visual material. This challenge has been taken up by the **MALTED** (Multimedia Authoring for Language Tutors and Educational Development) Project based at the University of London and supported by substantial funding from the European Commission. The project aims to create a set of authoring tools and a system of access to content materials.

> *Tutors who wish to develop materials (...) will be able to download the range of tools they require to produce pedagogically sound courseware with high production values and minimal training overheads (Bangs, 1999).*

Implications for language tutors

What are the main implications for language tutors of these changing patterns of language use? Most significant is a likely increase in the number of people learning a language for work-related reasons, with language training offered to a wider range of personnel within a particular company. Tutors should expect to work more often on shorter programmes with a very specific functional focus, designed to meet needs which change over time. Depending on the role of the employee, greater importance may be attached to cultural issues such as understanding local business etiquette, the way businesses are managed, and general aspects of social behaviour, or to comprehension skills rather than to extensive, in-depth knowledge or production of the target language.

Graddol (1998) describes the key challenge as:

> *... to transform languages provision so that it supports an ever-increasing diversity of languages, allows for, and encourages, all levels of proficiency and provides a flexible basis for introducing new languages into the curriculum.*

To that one might add the flexibility to meet the changing needs and time pressures faced by learners and businesses. Technology too presents many challenges to tutors. There are new skills to be developed: from mastering the tools to managing a different kind of learning environment and producing new styles of learning activities. But the challenges also present opportunities to widen access to language learning and increase the amount of language teaching in terms of levels and languages as well as reducing tutors' isolation and improving their access to resources and professional development.

The trend towards shorter courses, focused on specific needs, can be expected to affect all sectors of post-school language learning. In higher education, fewer people are studying single or joint honours in languages, but recent years have seen strong growth in non-specialist language programmes and subjects studied 'with languages' (Pilkington, 1997). This growth in non-specialist programmes (often known as Institution-Wide Language Programmes, IWLP) perhaps reflects the stronger vocational focus that has developed in all areas of education over recent years, including higher education. Knowledge of a language is a useful complement to a degree in law, business or engineering, for example, particularly in view of the opportunities afforded by job mobility in the EU and increasing globalisation referred to above. Language is seen more as a tool to enhance employability than as a subject for study in its own right. This trend is acknowledged by the Nuffield Inquiry in its acceptance of the need to teach many more people to communicate in a number of languages, as well as the need for an increase in the number of specialist linguists to teach them.

At the same time, attempts are being made to define and accredit all the skills gained by graduates, not only their subject knowledge. Dearing (1997) recommended that higher education institutions should develop '*programme specifications*' which give the intended outcomes of programmes. These are to include not only the knowledge and understanding, subject specific and cognitive skills which students will be expected to have achieved, but also the key or transferable skills of communication, numeracy, use of IT and learning how to learn. (See also chapter 16 for information on the Quality Assurance Agency's requirements for higher education). The **Translang** project[8] has explored the nature of the transferable skills which are gained through the study of non-specialist language programmes and how these skills may be accredited. The project identified four categories of skills involved in any language learning task: subject specific skills; communicative/interpersonal skills; cognitive/research skills and self-management skills. The Nuffield Inquiry recommends that the

> ... *communication strands within the post-16 Key Skills qualification for all students should include communicating in other languages and the effective use of English when communicating with speakers of other languages* (recommendation 9.3).

Language tutors are more likely to find themselves working with students who are studying a language as an adjunct to other subjects than they do at present. They are also likely to have to give far more attention to the explicit development and accreditation of all the key skills in future, wherever they work.

This chapter has given a flavour of some of the challenges and opportunities that lie ahead for language tutors. They have the potential to offer excellent support to good language teaching and learning and to continuing professional development. Tutors as lifelong learners will want to keep abreast of change in order to contribute actively to the many innovations in language learning and teaching, both current and future. It is an exciting time for all those involved in adult learning and, in particular, adult learning of languages.

References

Bangs P, 'MALTED: Europe's largest Call project at the language centre of University College, London' in *European Language Council Information Bulletin* 5 (http://userpage.fu-berlin.de/~elc/Bulletin5/english/bangs.htm July 1999)

Council of Europe, Council for Cultural Co-operation, Education Committee, *Modern languages: learning, teaching, assessment. A common European framework of reference* (Strasbourg: 1998)

The Council of Europe, *The Modern Languages Projects* http://culture.coe.fr/lang/eng/Doc_info_text_E_brochure.htm (August 2000)

The Council of Europe, *European Language Portfolio:* http://culture.coe.fr/lang/eng/eedu2.5.html(August 2000)

Dearing Sir R, *Higher Education in the learning society* (HMSO, 1997)

ERASMUS Action: http://erasmus.ac.uk

European Commission Leonardo Programme: www.europa.eu.int/comm/education/leonardo.html

European Commission, Socrates – Erasmus Action:
http://europa.eu.int/comm/education/index_en.html

European Language Council, DIALANG – a project for the development of a new European system for diagnostic language testing: www.sprachlabor.fu-berlin.de/dialang/ (September 2000)

European Year of Languages: www.eyl2001.org.uk

Graddol D, 'Will English be enough?' in Moys A (ed), *Where are we going with languages?* (Nuffield Foundation, 1998)

Hagen S, 'What does global trade mean for UK languages?' in Moys A (ed), *Where are we going with languages?* (Nuffield Foundation, 1998)

Hauck M and B Haezewindt, 'Adding a new perspective to distance (language) learning and teaching – the tutor's perspective' in *ReCALL* 11, 2: 46–54 (1999)

Johnstone C, 'On-line race hots up' in *Times Educational Supplement* (19 November 1999)

Lamy M-N and R Goodfellow, 'Supporting language students' interactions in Web-based conferencing' in *Computer Assisted Language Learning*, 12, 5: 457–477 (1999)

Languages Fund for the Development of Teaching and Learning (FDTL): http://fdtl.ac.uk

LEONARDO Programme: http://leonardo.org.uk

Lingua@NET: www.cilt.org.uk/projects/linguanet.htm (August 2000)

Lingua@net Europa: http://linguanet-europa.org

Moys A (ed), *Where are we going with languages?* (Nuffield Foundation, 1998)

Office for Standards in Education, *Accent on adults: a survey of modern foreign language learning by adults* (1998)

Pilkington R, *Survey of non-specialist language provision in Further and Higher Education institutions in the UK* (TRANSLANG Project November 1997)

Socrates European Action Programme for Education 2000–2006: www.britishcouncil.org/cbiet/socrates/index.htm

Swanton P, 'Adults learning languages' in Moys A (ed), *Where are we going with languages?* (Nuffield Foundation, 1998)

The Nuffield Foundation, *Languages: the next generation* (The English Company (UK), 2000)

Transferable Skills Development for Non-Specialist Learners of Modern Languages (Translang): www.uclan.ac.uk/facs/class/languages/translang/tlweb.htm

Tuckett A, 'At the final Hurdle' in *Adults Learning,* 11, 10: 6 (2000)

Tuckett A, and S Cara, *Tongue-tied but trying: a NIACE survey on the languages adults speak in Great Britain* (NIACE, 1999)

University for Industry, *First learning centres open as UfI says learndirect,* Press Release (24 November 1999): www.ufiltd.co.uk

Web Enhanced Language Learning: http://well.ac.uk

Notes

1 www.sprachlabor.fu-berlin.de/dialang/ (September 2000)

2 The National Grid for Learning will involve nearly 500,000 teachers in 33,000 schools, 250,000 staff in 900 FE institutions and eventually 22,000 library staff in 4,300 public libraries used by 60% of the UK population. (Nuffield, 2000)

3 FLUENT was a synchronous audio conferencing system which allowed tutors to run seminars in real time and students to interact in pairs or groups. It has now been superceded by the Lyceum software developed at The Open University. For more information on Lyceum, see Part 4 Chapter 3.

4 The Lexica project has now been extended to include level one French learners

5 The WELL project is one of a number of projects funded by the HEFCE Languages Fund for the Development of Teaching and Learning (FDTL)

6 www.hull.ac.uk/cti/langsite.htm

7 www.hull.ac.uk/cti/resources/reviews/revlist.htm

8 Another project funded by the HEFCE Languages Fund for the Development of Teaching and Learning (FDTL),

The contributors

Dr Lore Arthur is a lecturer in the Centre for Educational Policy and Management at The Open University with responsibilities for postgraduate teaching and research in lifelong learning. She has been involved in the training of adult education language teachers over many years. Her research interests and publications include lifelong learning, comparative/intercultural adult education and adults learning languages.

Marilyn Hunt is a lecturer in Modern Languages at the University of Warwick, based at the Language Centre. She has been involved in the teaching and assessment of adults' language learning both in this setting in adult leisure classes and in the commercial world for business clients. She is jointly responsible for the PGCE Modern Languages course with particular responsibility for the Spanish element. Her personal research focuses on career change entrants to modern languages initial teacher training.

Stella Hurd is a senior lecturer in the Department of Languages and Head of French at The Open University. She started her career in adult education where she taught for many years before moving into the higher education sector in 1992. Her publications are in the area of adult learning, distance language teaching and learning methodology, learner autonomy and metacognition.

Dr John Klapper is Director for the Centre for Modern Languages, University of Birmingham. He has interests in applied linguistics, language teaching methodology, materials development and language teacher education. He has published books on Russian language, German grammar and immersion learning, and articles on various aspects of language learning and teaching.

Linda Murphy is currently working as a Staff Tutor for Languages in The Open University Faculty of Education and Language Studies. She is based in the Oxford Regional Centre of the Open University in the South. Prior to this post, she worked for many years in adult and further education, where she taught and trained tutors of modern languages and English as an Additional Language. Her current research interests focus on the language learning skills and strategies deployed by distance language learners.

229

Dr Bob Powell, after eighteen years as a teacher trainer and researcher at the University of Bath, took up the Directorship of the Language Centre at the University of Warwick in 1993. He oversees the undergraduate module programme and the University's Open Studies foreign language courses which attract over 1,000 adult learners every year and is also academic co-ordinator for the BA European Studies course which is designed specifically for mature students. His research interests include assessment and testing, and gender differences in language learning. He has published teaching materials in French and Italian.

Lesley Walker is French co-ordinator in the Modern Languages Teaching Centre at the University of Sheffield. She is involved in the promotion of autonomous learning and has played a leading role in the development of Tandem Learning. She has published articles on both face-to-face and e-mail tandem learning.

Su White is learning and teaching co-ordinator at the University of Southampton in the Faculty of Engineering and Applied Science. She is based in the Intelligence Agents and Multimedia Research Group, itself part of the Department of Electronics and Computer Science. Her particular research interest is in the impact on UK higher education of the introduction and widespread use of learning technologies.

Jane Woodin has been the Spanish Co-ordinator at the Modern Languages teaching Centre at the University of Sheffield since 1993. She is a trained teacher and has worked in secondary, further and community education. Her research interests include language teaching methodology, language teacher education and intercultural aspects of language learning. She has published in all of these fields.

Vicky Wright is the Director of the Centre for Language Study within the School of Modern Languages at the University of Southampton. She is also Academic Co-ordinator for Languages for the UK LTSN (Learning and Teaching Support Network) Subject Centre for Languages, Linguistics and Area Studies which is based at Southampton. She has co-ordinated a number of projects in the area of independent language learning and has a particular interest in the use of multimedia and new technologies.